D0080844

THE INVISIBLE MEDIUM

The Invisible Medium

Public, Commercial and Community Radio

Peter M. Lewis
and
Jerry Booth

HOWARD UNIVERSITY PRESS
Washington, D.C.
1990

BOWLING GREEN STATE
UNIVERSITY LIBRARIES

Copyright © 1990 by Peter M. Lewis and Jerry Booth

All rights reserved. No part of this book may be
reproduced or utilized in any form without permission
in writing from the publisher. Inquiries should be
addressed to Howard University Press, 2900 Van Ness
Street, N.W., Washington, D.C. 20008.

Printed in Hong Kong

Library of Congress Cataloging-in-Publication Data

Lewis, Peter M.
    The invisible medium.
    (Communications and culture)
    Includes bibliographical references (p. 230).
    1. Radio broadcasting. I. Booth, Jerry, 1945–
II. Title. III. Series: Communications and
culture (Basingstoke, England)
HE8675.L49 1989   384.54   90-4357
ISBN 0-88258-032-9
ISBN 0-88258-106-6 (pbk.)

Contents

Acknowledgements

Being an academic and writing books was always a form of moonlighting. Nowadays especially, in the age of cuts, writing and research take place at the expense of teaching, even if, as is becoming increasingly necessary, you raise the money to replace yourself. The part-timers who replace you cannot be expected to take on the administrative and pastoral part of the job, and so an extra burden falls on full-time colleagues, both teaching and non-teaching staff.

Both of us are grateful to the colleagues who have thus supported us in the writing of this book, and to the students from whom we have absented ourselves or with whom we have discussed our obsessions.

Specific thanks also to: the organisers of AMARC 1 and 2; the BBC's Written Archive Centre at Caversham; the British Council's Media and Higher Education Divisions; the Council of Europe; Goldsmiths' College – the Department of Communications, the Faculty of Arts and the College Research Committee; Charles Hamilton of the University of Maryland for comments on Chapter 7; IAMCR's Working Group on Community Radio and Television; Anne Karpf for allowing access to her files on women and radio; Len Kelly of Bampton Books, Tiverton, and Brian Schwartz of Off-Stage Bookshop, Chalk Farm, for bargains and bibliographical information; Helene Littman and Vancouver Co-op Radio; the RELAY collective and staff; Steve Kennedy, Victoria Yogman and Keith Povey for their editorial help and support.

Jerry Booth thanks Penny Willis for giving him the space to

x

write, and Josh and Lily for invading it. Peter Lewis thanks Anne
Karpf for sharing time and life in and around the writing.

PETER M. LEWIS
JERRY BOOTH

Introduction

Radio, as we approach the last decade of the century, enjoys a peculiar, not to say paradoxical position – at once present, and absent. The first of the broadcast media to be developed, it created precedents for domestic consumption and institutional exploitation that were followed by the more powerful medium of television and which lasted for most of the century. First – but now last, for nowadays, radio is marginalised in policy debates in favour of the newer media, and has been displaced by television from its former command of the domestic hearth.

Yet for that very reason, radio has been taken up by young people and carried off into their spaces and journeys where it is used, along with pre-recorded music as a symbol of difference and a soundtrack for living, enjoyed outside the confines of the home and often provided by groups transmitting outside the constraints of the law.

For other social groups, too, radio is also a vital medium – old people, especially if they live alone, those who are visually handicapped, those whose social arrangements restrict them to housebound work or must make journeys by car.

A mass medium, and yet, in the Western world now, received personally, and susceptible of personal, variant or subversive readings, not least perhaps because another simultaneous activity colours the meaning of what's heard. Yet, again, individual reception is inflected by a sense of 'imagined community'. (Whether this sense has to pre-exist the transmission or whether the latter can 'create community' is something we discuss.)

Present in all these ways, and yet displaced by the glamour of television, radio has suffered the same fate in the world we come from – academic institutions of teaching and research. Compared to film and television, radio is hardly noticed in academic literature and as a practice is mostly taught in a vocational context as a preparation for journalism. As a result, radio practice and policy lacks a language for critical reflection and analysis. Why we have the radio we do, what radio we could have if things were different – these questions are as difficult to debate as the hidden histories are to uncover or the alternative practices to publicise.

In the time we have been writing this book, radio in Britain and some of its neighbours has undergone change, at first in small unnoticed steps, more recently in rapid bounds. At either pace, history is made to play its part with appeal to public service or the free market as ideals which justify particular positions. These mobilisations of myth are as real components of public perception, professional practice and public policy as the institutions they are intended to support – even if their historical validity is questionable.

An example is the myth in Britain of shortage of frequencies. This was never true as the American radio boom of the early 1920s showed. But in Britain it cloaked the decision of the Imperial Communications Committee to hold on to spectrum space and allow only a few frequencies for public use. The 'few' frequencies that were begrudged justified monopoly, and monopoly in turn justified control by a few professionals. Although from the crucible of paternalism and 'shortage' came the gold of BBC radio, it also elevated professionalism as an end in itself and a view of 'needs' which proved mistaken time and again.

Our aim in this book is to uncover the myths and try to give equal status to alternative interpretations – of history, of current policies and of an alternative practice of radio which we refer to as 'community radio' in a shorthand that has become widely used and abused, but which we elaborate and analyse later.

We look at both sides of the Atlantic and at the position of radio in Third World countries in many of which the original, Western systems of broadcasting have been found wanting and in some of which alternatives have been developed.

The book begins with a discussion of myth and history, and a brief sketch of the three models or types that both define themselves by difference from each other and are engaged in actual struggle: the free market model, the public service model and community radio (Chapter 1).

We then turn (Chapter 2) to the pre-history of radio: the corporate and military manoevrings which turned the invention of wireless into the social institution of radio broadcasting. This chapter includes a simple explanation of frequencies and a discussion of contemporary 'spectrum management' policies, so as to lay the ground for the arguments which follow.

Chapter 3 deals with the American free market model, and Chapter 4 with the BBC's public service model.

Chapter 5 examines how under the exigencies of war the BBC popularised its address to the Forces and the Home Front and the similar adjustment made inevitable at the end of the 1960s by the BBC's failure to attend to the musical tastes of a new generation. We continue (Chapter 6) with an examination of a particular variant of the public service model – local broadcasting – because we believe that it points up the contradictions inherent in that model. This variant was the result of the yoking of two powerful myths – public service broadcasting itself and the notion of the geographical community. We show how this occurred and why it has not worked either in its purest form with the BBC or its attenuated form in commercial broadcasting.

At this point we turn our attention to the phenomenon of 'community radio', first as it developed in the USA, Canada and Australia (Chapter 7), and then in Europe (Chapter 8), where the examples of Italy and France illustrate how easily radical moves to break broadcasting monopoly and democratise public service can open the way for a flood of de-regulation, powered by the search of multinational conglomerates for new markets. Chapter 9 examines the extent to which in Third World countries Western models, both of the traditional and 'community' radio type, have been modified and sometimes rejected in the cause of economic development and revolutionary struggle.

In conclusion, Chapter 10 discusses whether there is a place for community radio within a programme which attempts to redefine public service broadcasting. An historical narrative in Appendix A gives a brief chronological summary of the development of the medium. It can be read by readers who wish to get a quick sweep of radio history, while a chronological table serves the same purpose for British local radio.

The detail of the references and a full bibliography are consistent with our project to raise the visibility of radio. Although academic studies of the medium are relatively scarce compared, as we remarked above, with those on film and television, there exists a considerable seam of material which lies generally unnoticed. Our aim in bringing some of it together here is to encourage readers to study these sources for themselves and make their own interpretations.

We hope the book will be useful in drawing attention to the importance of radio within current debates on communications policy and so we have borne in mind a wider readership besides those teaching and studying the medium in communication studies courses.

Chapter 1

Founding Myths

Socrates: I wonder if we could contrive one of those convenient stories . . . some magnificent myth that would in itself carry conviction to our whole community, including, if possible, the Guardians themselves . . . Do you think there is any way of making them believe it?
Glaucon: Not in the first generation, but you might succeed with the second and later generations.[1]

The founding myth in Plato's *Republic* was intended to justify the hierarchical and stratified social system over which the Guardians were to preside. The three approaches to broadcasting which we discuss in this book each embrace a cluster of founding myths. This is not to deny the other motivations of each system, or the social, political and economic realities which produced and continue to reproduce them. But, simply put, commercial broadcasting draws on notions of individualism and free enterprise; community radio harks back to a 'community' in which mutual help and solidarity were proof against the abrasions of the outside world; public service broadcasting has perhaps the richest myth troves of all, and the role of one in particular comes curiously close to the 'noble lie' which is at the heart of Plato's social engineering. The supposed shortage of frequencies (a myth we examine in Chapter 2) justified entrusting broadcasting to a monopoly controlled by professionals who diagnosed and interpreted the needs of listeners.

Myth, as Barthes said, 'has the task of giving an historical intention a natural justification, and making contingency appear eternal'.[2] The point about myth is that it is essentially ahistorical. In the same essay, Barthes compares it to an ideal servant whose discreet preparation of wardrobe and table renders invisible all trace of the work involved: in myth 'history evaporates . . . all that is left for one to do is to enjoy this beautiful object without wondering where it came from'.[3] A British broadcaster, who was also for a time a government minister responsible for broadcasting, once used a rather similar metaphor, comparing the way changes come about in broadcasting policy to the game of grandmother's footsteps – creeping up on us in moves too small to be noticed.[4] It was an apt metaphor for the period he was summing up, the fumbling consensus of the pre-Thatcher era – a consensus indeed which had existed since the origins of the BBC. Such policy changes are presented as extensions of founding principles. History is rewritten to accommodate the innovation and deny a break with the past. So BBC local radio was introduced as 'serving neighbourhood and nation' and the IBA's commercial version as 'public service without public expenditure'. By contrast, the challenges presented by a radical government like Mrs Thatcher's cast a shocking light on the taken-for-granted myths, forcing choices about which to jettison and which to defend.

In either case, history is mobilised and re-presented to support the new positions. In either case, radio is particularly vulnerable. In the grandmother's footsteps mode, change goes unnoticed, the implications of change are not discussed, the basic assumptions not analysed; when radical policy shifts burst upon the scene, there is no perspective against which to measure them, no discourse available to debate the issues.

Radio's marginalisation in policy debates largely focused on television and new technologies is matched by its lack of standing in academic circles. After early sociological studies of radio audiences,[5] attention moved to television and with rare exceptions[6] has stayed there. French screen theory was a dominant influence in British cultural and media studies so that again, in study of the broadcast media, it has been on television that critical attention has focused.[7] Radio drama, it is true, has attracted some academic notice,[8] based usually in the framework of literature studies, or in accounts of practice by broadcasters, often within autobiographies. These last make little connection with the kinds of issues addressed by film and television theory, although they do have historical importance.

Radio history figures the most strongly in academia. Briggs's detailed four-volume history of the BBC is an unrivalled record.[9]

Scannell and Cardiff[10] have shown that use of the same sources – the BBC's Written Archive Centre at Caversham, can be interpreted from a more critical perspective. Jean Seaton has also added to the understanding of the early period of British radio.[11] Briggs's history stops before the advent of local radio, and his abridged history of the First Fifty Years[12] has only a page or two on the subject. We comment later on the lack of a history of British local radio and on the few accounts of it that do exist (Chapter 6, note 2).

Within media studies in higher and further education, radio finds a small place in media history, while radio practice almost everywhere concentrates on radio journalism, in most cases unquestioningly reproducing the techniques and assumptions of that genre.

This academic absence of radio contributes to its vulnerability, though the main reason is the relative position of radio in economic terms compared with television. BBC network radio can call on some eminent defenders through its prestigious connections in the worlds of literature and the theatre, but they do not carry the same weight outside academic circles as do their Italian and French counterparts – if there can be a comparison: to touch on the status of the 'intellectual' in British culture may take us too far afield. Suffice it to say that, at the present time, radio piracy and its forbidden forms come nearer to setting the Thames on fire than, say, the defence of Radios 3 and 4.

Academic neglect, then, is partly responsible for the invisibility of radio, and this critical history tries to make some reparation. It is critical in the sense that it tries to make visible the work history is made to do in supporting present positions.

History does not consist in the sum total of all that happened in the past – that would indeed be some Platonic ideal. Still less is it a project, in principle infinitely perfectible, to recover bit by bit what we can of that Ideal History. History, at any particular time, is the preferred version of events – 'preferred' as in 'preferred meaning', an idea made familiar in media studies by Stuart Hall's analysis of the encoding and decoding of the television message.[13] 'Any society/culture tends, with varying degrees of closure, to impose its classification of the social, cultural and political world.' The outcome, Hall argues, is not a single or uncontested version, but a pattern which bears the imprint of the 'dominant cultural order' and which is read off differentially according to the viewer/reader's different cultural and political alignments. Although this analysis has provoked considerable debate around the conditions in which readers are free to make meaning, it provides a useful model for understanding the workings of what Raymond Williams called 'the selective tradition' in history. This tradition, according to Williams, will 'always tend to correspond to its *contemporary* system of interests and values'.[14] Williams underlined the need to see such a tradition not only as a selection but as an interpretation. Since we can never return to the historical period in question we can at least 'make the interpretation conscious, by showing historical alternatives . . . relate the interpretation to the particular contemporary values on which it rests; and by exploring the real patterns of the work, confront . . . the real nature of the choices we are making'.[15]

A history of the kind we are undertaking here has, then, a two-fold task. It must on the one hand contest the versions of history presented by the 'selective tradition' of the broadcasting organisations. In so doing we struggle against power which is, as Milan Kundera said, 'the struggle of memory against forgetting'.[16] On the other hand we put forward interpretations which implicitly lay claim to truth, or at least to be less distorted than those produced by the dominant order in conditions in which power is not equally shared. In the absence in the real world of what Habermas[17] called an 'ideal speech situation' – that is, an arena where argument takes place in conditions freed from asymmetrical relations of power – the best we can do is to assert an equal claim to validity of a version which has not hitherto been given wide circulation. It will be apparent that our position is one which is generally supportive of the critique of mainstream broadcasting implied in the practice of community radio; following Williams, this is to make our interpretation of history 'conscious'. So, in the chapters that follow, we will be looking successively at two models of radio, each attached to a certain view of the audience and each presuming a certain relationship with it – the American, free market model and the British public service model – and contrasting them with a third type, explicitly opposed to the first two, which takes a variety of forms, known as listener-supported, community, public, free or alternative radio. For the purpose of outlining the argument at this stage we will label these forms 'community radio', subsuming them all in an ideal type. Our concern is with radio, and radio was historically the first form of broadcasting to appear, but the first two models can also refer to a way of organising television in its traditional and more recent forms. Community television, too, does exist, but less widely than community radio.

The *free market model* (its first appearance in the USA is described in Chapter 3) is radio financed by advertising and sponsorship whose ultimate purpose is to make a profit. Networks may be operated by profit-seeking conglomerates at a loss, whether out of temporary expediency, or as part of a strategic plan which uses the outlet as a stepping-stone to the acquisition of other media interests, or plays off tax incentives in different sectors or countries. Murdoch's empire has been built in this way. Radio for commercial purposes must acquire and transmit programming which costs as little as possible, and maximise its profits by giving advertisers and sponsors access to as large a number of potential consumers as possible; in a specialised market, the aim is to reach as large a number as possible of a particular sort of consumer. The need to maximise audiences and to achieve economies of scale drives commercial operators towards syndication of programme material and the formation of networks. As far as programming is concerned, if there is a market for, say, plays or documentaries, investigative journalism or urban contemporary music, commercial radio will supply it. The general run of radio programming for mass audiences, however, is based on music – the repetition of a limited number of popular hits, supplemented with studio chat by presenters and guests, often responding to listeners phoning in. But it is the market which ultimately will determine the type, volume and timing of the supply of programming.

In some systems, like British commercial radio up till the late 1980s, a regulatory Authority intervenes in the market to require operators to provide particular sorts of programming, such as news or, in the words of the IBA Act, 'programmes (of) a high general standard . . . and wide range in their subject matter',[18] or to serve special tastes and interests, whether these are defined by locality or by reference to ethnic or language communities. It is also possible to identify other profit motives for the introduction of public service programming in commercial systems, such as the wish to improve corporate image, or increase client goodwill, or for tax loss purposes. In Britain, the commercial television companies first introduced schools programmes, before they were obliged to, partly because they discovered that, under regulations which forbade advertising around schools programmes but which allowed a certain proportion of advertising to total output, the revenue from the advertisements, displaced to peak-time slots, more than offset the cost of schools programmes.

Any such modification of out-and-out commercial programming constitutes, at least minimally, public service, according to the Peacock Report.[19] Public service motives, too, may very likely inspire the work of many people making programmes in a commercial system. These include the same desire as can be found among staff in public service organisations to impress peers and critics and please audiences by professional performance and product. Overall, though, it is in the nature of the commercial model to treat listeners as consumers whose main role is to hear the advertisements carried and to act on them, that is, spend money on the goods and services advertised.

Public service broadcasting (its origins in Britain are described in Chapter 4) amounted to considerably more than the Peacock Committee's minimal definition referred to above. There were four elements in Reith's original conception: a non-profit aim, universality of service, unified control and the maintenance of high standards in programming. This last principle, as we discuss later in Chapter 4, carried with it a view of the audience which assumed its members capable of being led to 'high' standards of taste and outlook by a mix of popular and serious programming. A recent summary of these principles in the Peacock Report runs:

> (i) Broadcasting is a national asset which should be used for the national good rather than for the benefit of particular interest groups.
> (ii) Responsibility for broadcasting should therefore lie in one or more broadcasting authorities appointed as 'trustees for the national interest' in broadcasting.[20]

What is not explicitly stated in these principles is the constitutional position of the BBC *vis-à-vis* the state. What is the 'national interest' and who decides it? Caroline Heller's useful monograph *Broadcasting and Accountability*[21] centres on this question. Her historical analysis shows that over the years 'broadcasters' views on the matter have . . . shifted to accommodate the changing views of government' in a process in which 'history is somewhat battered', but in which nevertheless there was a broad area of unspoken agreement to maintain and defend the existing institutions and their independence from government. Heller was writing before the arrival of a Thatcher government called this tradition into question, and, over the affair of the Cheltenham-based Government Communications Headquarters (in which the government sought to ban trade unions from a workplace where sensitive security information was handled) obtained a judicial ruling upholding the right of the government of the day to define 'the national interest'. The BBC's Licence and Agreement make it clear that the government of the day can veto or insist on the transmission of particular programmes, and appoint (through the 'Queen/King in Council') the Governors. The formal power of censorship has rarely been invoked, the British style being to achieve the same effect behind the scenes, while for the first 60 years appointments to the Board of Governors were representative of a broad political consensus. Till recently, then, the BBC has enjoyed a position of 'relative autonomy'. The Thatcher government has broken with this tradition. Its appointment of more partisan governors, and its censorship of programmes has brought British broadcasting nearer to the systems of some of its European neighbours, where the extent of open political control is often marked by new governments making wholesale changes in senior broadcasting appointments.

Breached or not, this principle is summarised by Peacock as

(iii) the broadcasting authorities should be free of government intervention in their day to day affairs and in the content of their programmes.[22]

(That said, a government may, through its economic policy, deliberately allow the operation of the market to do the work of the state in censorship and in the competitive constraints put on a public service organisation.)

As the BBC responded to commercial pressures and to the trend towards decentralisation (a story we trace in Chapters 5 and 6), further additions and modifications were made to the notion of public service. Some of these are discussed in the reports of the Pilkington (1962) and Annan (1977) Committees,[23] and a recent reckoning identified eight principles (which include some we have noted already):

1. Universality; geographic – broadcast programmes should be available to the whole population.
2. Universality of appeal – broadcast programme should cater for all tastes and interests.
3. Minorities, especially disadvantaged minorities, should receive particular provision.
4. Broadcasters should recognise their special relationship to the sense of national identity and community.
5. Broadcasting should be distanced from all vested interests, and in particular from those of the government of the day.
6. Universality of payment – one main instrument of broadcasting should be directly funded by the corpus of users.
7. Broadcasting should be structured so as to encourage competition in good programming rather than competition for numbers.
8. The public guidelines for broadcasting should be designed to liberate rather than restrict the programme makers.[24]

Public service broadcasting addresses its audience as rational citizens, rather than individual consumers motivated by self-interest. Furthermore, the citizens it addresses are those of the nation-state whose interest the organisation represents, and whose boundaries mark the limits of the intended service. At present this limitation is in contrast with the international tendencies of capital- and market-based media, but the concerns of the EEC and UNESCO about, for example, satellite broadcasting may see an extension of the boundaries of the public service citizen-audience on to a regional scale.[25]

The *community* type of radio (discussed in Chapters 7, 8 and 9) has emerged in explicit contrast to the two previous models, or rather to the practice of particular historical institutions and systems organised along the lines we have summarised. A key difference is that, while the commercial and public service models both treat listeners as objects, to be captured for advertisers or improved and informed, community radio aspires to treat its listeners as subjects and participants.

Like other forms of community media, community radio is an open or implied criticism of mainstream radio in either of its two models. It charges such radio with distortion, omission and marginalisation of the points of view of certain social groups, and within its own practice tries to offer listeners the power to control their own definitions of themselves, of what counts as news and what is enjoyable or significant about their own culture. Community is defined geographically, as well as in terms of interest, language, cultural or ethnic groupings. Many stations will serve multiple overlapping communities, and it is of the essence of this type of radio that each community or interest group participates in station policy, programme production and operation. This is achieved by a variety of democratic structures that ensure representation in the management body of both listeners and station staff, paid and unpaid. The presence of volunteers is not the result of cost-saving calculations but is an essential means of contact with the community or communities involved, ensuring that they are represented in the day-to-day running of the station. Community stations of this type are non-profit in aim, and generally attempt to diversify their sources of funding in order to avoid dependency on any one source. Public funding, listener subscription and advertisements of a limited kind and quantity constitute a major part of these sources in different countries, although one or other are objected to on ideological or pragmatic grounds in some places.[26]

At different times, for example in Italy and France and most recently perhaps in Britain, the push for free, alternative or community radio of the type described above has been overtaken by commercial radio operating under the same label – and indeed deliberately co-opting it – and similarly opposed to a state monopoly/duopoly but for different reasons.

These, then are the models or ideal types whose embodiment in actual practice we discuss in the following chapters. Each defines itself by its difference from at least one other. A public service is not commercial, and, for such a service, the acceptance of advertising as a source of revenue would have a symbolic significance. Commercial systems on the other hand define themselves in contrast to what they call 'state broadcasting', meaning thereby to focus on the method of funding (and therefore control) by grant from the public exchequer or by licence fee. Thus in Britain, the label 'Independent' Television (ITV) and 'Independent' Local Radio (ILR) connotes independence from the licence fee and hence difference from the BBC. (It was also invented to avoid the negative connotations of 'commercial'.) Community radio emphasises that it is not commercial, and does not share what it would call the prescriptive and paternalistic attitude of public service. In its sources of funding, although ideally it strives for a distinctly different public funding arrangement, it differs less from mainstream broadcasting than in its claim to share power with its listeners on a democratic basis.

These three models are more than an analytical system of differences: politically and economically they are engaged in mutual struggle. The logic of the commercial system is to swallow up new markets and extend its frontiers to compete with, even undermine the public service domain. The logic of public service is to defend national territories, industries and identities against such invasion. The logic of community radio is to defend human rights against the intrusions of both state and capital.

Since each of these models presupposes a different way of looking at the world, each comes with its own history, a history which, as we have argued, is constantly revised and updated, and mobilised in moments of stress. The current threat to public service broadcasting systems posed by free market ideology and new technologies like cable and satellite is one such moment. But there was never a time when British public service broadcasting was not under pressure. In the early days Reith had to argue for separation from the wireless industry, then justify the monopoly. Subsequently the attractions of Radio Luxembourg and Radio Normandy caused problems, while, as Cardiff and Scannell have shown,[27] throughout the inter-war period an unresolved tension built up in the BBC's treatment of the 'serious' and the 'popular' in both speech and music programming. The pressure for the Forces Programme at the start of the Second World War, and the need in the 1960s to counter the North Sea pirates with local radio and a popular national channel – all these responses drew on and adapted the ideology of public service which in turn rested on the concept of monopoly (or 'duopoly' after the arrival of ITV in 1954).

The need to defend encroachments on monopoly or justify extensions into new services have made the broadcasting organisations, and governments, practised at the kind of myth-making revisions of history which it is our aim to uncover.

Chapter 2
The Making of Radio

'Get another electrician!'
'Alas, Your Majesty, England has no Marconi.'[1]

This chapter is concerned with the 'pre-history' of broadcasting and with the determining factors which, present at the birth of broadcasting proper, have continued to influence the development of the medium. 'Wireless', as radio was first called – short for 'wireless telegraphy', had served maritime and military purposes for two decades before it was used to transmit information, education and entertainment to the public at large. Many of the decisions taken thereafter were made on pragmatic grounds, but have since become reified and their cultural consequences elevated to the level of principle: in the case of Britain that of 'public service broadcasting', in the United States the virtues of diversity and commercial competition. These principles in turn have had a considerable effect on subsequent developments in broadcasting in both countries.

The Background

The exchange, quoted above, between Queen Victoria and an official reporting Marconi's refusal to leave the royal garden – he was setting up, at the Queen's request, a temporary wireless telegraphy link between her Isle of Wight residence and The Prince of Wales's yacht at Cowes – encapsulates the position of the invention in Britain at the turn of the century.

A scientific community scattered across the advanced industrialised nations had begun to take the first steps towards the

11

practical application of Clerk Maxwell's theory of electro-magnetism.[2] Marconi's special contribution was to draw these discoveries together, produce a workable device and market it. His inventive technical skill was matched by a business flair which foresaw the commercial possibilities and ruthlessly exploited publicity and patent law to realise them. These were not qualities valued by the British ruling class. The nation dismissed by Napoleon as one of shopkeepers had by the middle of the century devised in the public schools a system of education designed deliberately to turn its back on commerce and produce 'gentlemen' to run Whitehall, the Empire and the armed forces. Engineering and science, despite the efforts of the same Queen's late husband, were in these schools held in less esteem than the classics and sport, and the ignorance and condescension implicit in the Queen's remark were unfortunately typical of those who presided over the birth and subsequent development of broadcasting in Britain.

It was quite otherwise in America. Well before Marconi's first successful demonstration of wireless telegraphy in London in 1896, Britain's position as leader of the industrial world had been overtaken by European rivals and by America. In the USA, the emergence of giant corporations, the development of mass production techniques and the growth of advertising, coupled with an ideology that honoured profit, the pioneer and 'individualism', created a peculiarly different seedbed for radio.

From Telegraph to Wireless

The early term for radio, wireless, gives an insight into the way the medium was first perceived. It was seen as an extension of the electric telegraph and the telephone, and to begin with its purposes were circumscribed by that view of it.

The first forms of telegraphy were developed by the French in the late eighteenth century. Claude Chappe invented a kind of mechanical semaphore, consisting of towers with moveable arms in line of sight. The position of the arms designated a letter or a concept. The towers were set between six and ten kilometres apart and the message were read with telescopes. The system proved its usefulness in the revolutionary wars, and by the mid-nineteenth century most European countries had adopted similar systems.[3]

By this time, the growth of railways, and the speed of trains on them, had demonstrated the need for a faster system of telegraphy which was not limited by visibility. The electric telegraph met this need. One was operating between London and Birmingham in the 1830s, others were developed in many European countries during the 1840s. The way the electric telegraph was developed on each side of the Atlantic prefigured the development of broadcasting. In the United States a grant from Congress led to the building of a telegraph line between Washington and Baltimore in 1844. To begin with this was supervised by the US Postmaster General, but it did not manage to cover its costs and was sold to private interests. From that time onwards telegraph services in the United States were operated privately. In Europe however the telegraph was generally nationalised from the beginning and it tended to form the basis for the post, telegraph and telephone monopolies in many European countries.

The institutions which ran the telegraphs, whether public or private, were partly responsible for the reluctance to recognise possibilities of the telephone. In its early days the telephone was expensive and not very reliable, and it did not provide a permanent record of the messages as did the telegraph. In both America and Great Britain attempts were made by the existing telegraph interests to curb the development of the telephone. In America the Western Union Telegraph Company backed rival patent claims in an attempt to squeeze the Bell Telephone Company out of existence, but failed. In Great Britain where the telegraph was a state monopoly the government tried to limit the expansion of inter-city trunk lines. In March 1892 the Postmaster General proposed to buy up all the existing telephone lines in the country. He wished, he said, to provide:

a system which would facilitate instead of retard the development of the monopoly which, although an ugly word, expresses a great interest of the country acquired at great cost.[4]

It was into this technical and institutional context that the 'wireless' was born at the end of the nineteenth century. What called forth a new form of telegraphy were the developments in naval armaments, in particular the fast Dreadnought class of battleship. The manoeuvrings of fleets had now overtaken the ability to communicate. The arms race of the late nineteenth century was thus the 'supervening social necessity', to use Brian Winston's phrase, which brought wireless telegraphy out of the laboratory to the stage of field trials.[5]

Technical Digression: Broadcast Transmission

At this point, a brief technical explanation, in terms which we hope are understandable to the non-technical reader, is needed.[6] It will help make sense of the account which follows of the arguments between the different factions urging their view of how the new medium should be developed, and, on an international plane, the debates of the International Telegraphic Union (ITU – the letters now stand for International Telecommunications Union).

The technology of radio transmission and the way radio waves behave (propagation) early on caused unexpected problems. It did not help that radio was at first regarded as an extension of the telegraph, a means of sending messages from point to point over a distance without wires. The fact that radio waves spread outwards in all directions from their point of origin/transmission and could be received by anyone with a receiver tuned to the appropriate frequency was accepted as useful in emergencies at sea, but seen as a nuisance from the military point of view.

Radio waves can be measured either by their *size* (wavelength) or by their *frequency* (by convention counted as the number of waves per second and named after Hertz, the German inventor who first demonstrated the existence of radio waves). Traditionally, wavelength has been used to label waves in the long, medium and short wavebands, while frequency (numbered in hertz and abbreviated Hz, MHz) is used to describe shorter waves (i.e. higher frequencies), beginning with VHF (see below). The radio-frequency spectrum is the complete range of radio frequencies, from the very long waves used for communication with submarines under water to x-rays and visible light. Only relatively small portions of this range are used for broadcasting, and which portions are used for what purposes is a matter of international agreement, recorded in the ITU Table of Frequency Allocations. Thus space must be found for commercial operation of telecommunication links, for 'land mobiles' (emergency services, taxis, etc.), for marine and aeronautical services and for military use.

The airwaves are at any one time and place limited in capacity. Neighbouring stations cannot broadcast on the same frequency without creating mutual interference, so some plan has to be agreed to use different frequencies in the same region of the world. The power with which a station transmits is also a factor in interference.

The trouble was, and is, that even a low-powered transmission on medium wave can cause problems. Medium waves, the area of the spectrum which was first exploited for broadcasting, extend far further at night than during the day, owing to the reflective properties of the ionosphere as it cools with the departure of the sunlight. Any medium wave listener tuning the dial after dark will have been either delighted or irritated by the intrusion on to the waveband of distant foreign stations that are not audible during the day. This means that the number of medium wave frequencies available for use round the clock in an area the size of Europe is limited. This discovery, painfully learned, was one of the first constraints on frequency allocation in Europe in the early 1920s. By then, however, it had been discovered to advantage that short waves, transmitted day or night, are also reflected by the ionosphere, and can be made to 'bounce' between earth and sky around the globe for long distances in relatively controllable directions. Short wave thus became the basis for international broadcasting.

The characteristics of the medium-wave band mean that overcrowding becomes worse at night. Broadcasting in the part of the spectrum known as VHF (Very High Frequency) avoids this problem, but, on both VHF and medium wave, power limitations and frequencies have to be agreed internationally under the aegis of the ITU. Within countries, governments assign frequencies to stations in accordance with the ITU Table of Frequency Allocations. Given adherence to transmission power limitations it is possible to re-use frequencies within a given area. It is also possible for one country to seek and be granted use on a 'permitted' basis of a frequency allotted to another provided no interference is caused.[7]

Signals broadcast on VHF (Very High Frequency) travel more or less in straight lines and are not subject to the night-time reflection that affects medium wave. From the beginning of the development of broadcasting in this part of the spectrum, a different method of superimposing the sound on the carrier signal was used – frequency modulation (FM) as opposed to the amplitude modulation (AM) used hitherto for medium- and long-wave transmission. In most parts of the world except Britain,[8] radio manufacturers and broadcasters have used the initials FM, rather than VHF, to denote this type of broadcasting, and as a consequence the terms are interchangeable in popular usage. FM/VHF occupies more space (bandwidth), but delivers a better signal, including stereo signals if required, and can be tuned to by receivers in a way that excludes unwanted transmissions. Thus FM/VHF is ideal for music broadcasting.

We can now return to the early years of the present century to see how the invention of wireless telegraphy was applied.

International Positions

As we have said, it was the use of wireless telegraphy at sea as a means of saving lives and controlling the movements of shipping, especially of naval fleets, that formed the general conception of the medium. Indeed, a growing understanding of its potential role as the key element in imperial communications underlay the discussions of the first international conferences which considered the new medium in 1903 and 1906 under the auspices of the ITU.

As the International Telegraphic Union, the ITU had been in existence since 1865 to resolve difficulties over technical standards and the passage of information across national frontiers. In the increasingly hostile international climate of the times, the great European powers keenly appreciated the importance of their commercial and military links with their respective colonies. In the event of war those who controlled the sea could cut the cable links of their enemies. This consideration explained both the ready support which governments gave to the new commercial undertakings, the British and Italian governments to Marconi, the Germans to Telefunken, and the self-interested positions adopted at the international conference table.

The ITU meetings of 1903 and 1906 had, then, to deal with two kinds of problem: the technical problem of frequency allocation in order to prevent interference, and the problems that arose from the Marconi Co's ruthless protection of its patents.

Radio was different from its technological predecessors in the crucial respect that it used frequency space and the distribution of the frequency spectrum has been used as the basis for different institutional arrangements. The fact that the foundations of international frequency agreements were laid at a time when a world war was looming and before broadcasting was dreamed of has had far-reaching consequences: the demands of civil authorities responsible for marine (and later, aeronautical) navigation and control, and above all those of the armed services have literally come first. It was not until 1927, seven years after the start of broadcasting in the USA and five after the formation of the British Broadcasting Company, that the ITU's consideration of the frequency spectrum formally admitted the claims of broadcasters.

Patent Tangles

Up to the outbreak of the war in Europe in 1914, the development of the medium of radio was hampered by a tangled web of patent law relating to various inventions, and the issues of monopoly associated with their ownership. When we use the term radio it connotes a single unitary phenomenon, but successful radio transmission and reception depended on a number of inventions. The development of the medium as a whole depended on all these inventions being applied at the same time, and by implication by a single institution. Unfortunately for rapid development, the patents for each of them tended to be held by a variety of individuals and companies, among which the Marconi company had achieved an early lead. It had negotiated extraordinarily restrictive contracts with some European governments and its exploitation of its near monopoly led to the absurd (and dangerous) situation where ships without Marconi apparatus and operators were not allowed to communicate with those carrying a rival's equipment. It seems likely that this monopoly contributed to the US government's determination to break the power of the company.

The First World War

The complicated saga of claims and counter-claims among inventors and their companies was suspended with the American entry into the First World War in 1917, and in Britain, more than in America, the production of valves was nearly wholly given over to wartime needs. In effect the government, at the same time as it banned amateur use of the airwaves effectively took over all the patents for its own use, while the US government told patent owners to register what they thought might be infringements with the courts.

It was not only the outbreak of the First World War which had concentrated attention on the potential of radio; the sinking of the Titanic and the use of radio by the combatants in the Russo-Japanese war had already focused both civil and military attention on the uses of radio at sea. So the United States Navy had merely to reorganise and set up the Naval Communications Service. On the day after the declaration of war in 1917 the Navy took over all the wireless stations in the United States. Not only did this have the effect of breaking the log jam in radio development caused by patent suits, it also gave the US government a heady taste of a monopoly of communication, as well as laying the foundations for the idea of cross-licensing which the navy later proposed as a solution to the problem of multiple patent ownership after the war.

The Services in Peacetime

The armed services in both countries gained considerable influence over the development of radio as a result of the war. After the war in Britain this power was used to block uses of the frequency spectrum which conflicted with military needs.

One of the most influential bodies in the early discussions of radio was the Imperial Communications Committee, an offshoot of the Committee of Imperial Defence, three of whose members represented each of the armed services, the rest came from the Treasury, the India Office, the Foreign Office, the Colonial Office, the Board of Trade and the Post Office. Not surprisingly therefore the Post Office was very conscious of the power of this committee and in 1922 the Postmaster General told the House of Commons that the whole question of broadcasting was being referred to it.

The kind of objections made by the British Armed Services are typified by a story which appeared in the Financier on 25 August 1920.[9] It reported that a pilot crossing the Channel in thick fog was trying to get weather and landing reports but could only hear a musical evening. The programmes referred to were those being put out by the Marconi Company, and they were criticised as a 'frivolous' use of the medium. The critics maintained that radio which could be a servant of mankind' was being treated as a toy.[10]

In the United States the navy had been and remained interested in any and all the inventions which looked likely to be useful. Before the outbreak of war they had tested systems from Marconi, De Forest and Fessenden among others. The Marconi system had interference problems, but what finally seems to have sabotaged the attempts to do a deal was the fact that, typically, the company wanted to rent rather than sell the apparatus. Understandably, the US government was unwilling to let so important a system remain under the control of a foreign company.

The Amateurs

The role of amateur radio enthusiasts was important since it was they who were most vociferously opposed to the state monopoly of radio and were largely responsible for jolting corporate conceptions of the uses of the medium.

Although early experiments with radio were carried out by Marconi and other companies, the state of development of the medium was such as to allow a number of amateurs to experiment too. The distinction so often made in the latter part of the twentieth century between professionals and amateurs (usually as a way of excluding amateurs) was not so sharply drawn in the early days of radio. The Wireless Society of London had been founded in 1913 and its members were interested in perfecting the medium and building their own apparatus and consequently they were knowledgeable about the possibilities it offered. Nor were they without influence: the Post Office itself included people who were experimenters, and at least one member of the Imperial Communications Committee which played such a crucial role in the early days of radio was a radio amateur.[11] Amateurs worked in their own laboratories, they could not be mystified by technical jargon, and many of them were articulate and in positions where they could oppose any attempt by the services to retain a complete monopoly over the use of radio.

The amateurs, then, could make a real contribution to radio in a number of ways. Some combined interest in the building and improvement of pieces of apparatus with a desire to transmit their own material. One of the acid tests of the fidelity of the signal was (and still is) music, so some amateurs put together their own 'programmes' of gramophone records. Although not all of them were interested in transmission, most would of course have an interest in reception. Even the least dedicated amateur, interested only in building receiving apparatus would naturally require something to receive on it.

After the war in Britain the societies complained to the Post Office about the Defence of the Realm Act which they maintained was preventing amateurs from contributing as effectively as they might to the development of radio. The official response was that the Post Office was responsible for naval, military and civil interests and they all had to work in the same laboratory; wireless should be seen as an object of scientific research, not as a source of personal pleasure, but as Briggs notes it was not a distinction which had much meaning in the real world. The 'scientific' amateurs may well have wanted to listen to music because it was a good test of their apparatus, but in practice it was difficult to distinguish between these people and those who wanted music for pleasure. Certainly licences were only granted to people of 'good character', and references were required; the licensing system was not a rubber stamp as it is today.

Apart from their pretensions to scientific respectability, the amateurs enjoyed another advantage in the eyes of the Post Office, and that was simply that they were by definition not part of a commercial company. Throughout the early history of radio the Post Office's suspicion of commercial companies and its discomfort at having to deal with them is a leitmotif, and one which with other factors led to the formation of a monopolistic broadcasting service. Hence although it sometimes seemed an uphill struggle the Wireless Societies were pushing on an open door because the Post Office found it less difficult to grant licences to amateurs than to commercial concerns.

The veto on broadcasting after the war was lifted because of a petition, organised by the wireless societies, which, among other things, said, 'It is therefore, primarily, to serve the scientific purpose of improving the receiving arrangements that we desire to have telephony included.'[12]

Meanwhile in the United States, in November 1918 a bill was introduced into the House of Representatives and the Senate which proposed experimental and technical schools for radio training, but made no mention of amateur stations. The government still retained control of communications, and the American amateurs were not slow to attack the bill. The National Wireless Association claimed that the bill 'frankly and unreservedly gives the Government permanent possession of radio and its unrestricted operation'.[13] The Secretary of the Navy said, 'that having demonstrated during the war the excellent service and the necessity of unified ownership, we should not lose the advantage of it in peace.'[14] However the opposition was such that at the beginning of 1919 the Congressional committee threw the bill out.

Recap

Thus far then the history of radio on both sides of the Atlantic is similar: conflicts centred around patents and frequencies. The state saw radio as a useful instrument of war and governance and was keen to see it developed. Marconi and Telefunken were quick to exploit European governments' desire to control the new medium of communication and the restrictive agreements they entered added to American suspicion. The American government used the war to break the patents deadlock which was hampering progress. With the hold of monopoly capital thus loosened, the necessary inventions could all be brought together, the development of the hardware became more straightforward, and the American state seems to have been as anxious as the British to retain control of the airwaves for its own purposes. The eventual freeing of sectors of the frequency spectrum was in some measure due to the representations made by amateurs in both countries. At this point it became possible for broadcasting to exist, and it is now that the histories start to diverge. We follow them respectively in Chapters 3 and 4.

Frequency Policy in Modern Times

We have seen that the use of frequencies lay at the root of the

early arguments between the state and the 'amateurs'. As broadcasting and other uses of radio have proliferated, the arguments
have drawn in the other actors involved – manufacturers, broadcasters, listeners, commercial users of airspace and the other
departments of government besides broadcasting's original sponsor, the Post Office or its equivalent. Though this has added
bureaucratic complication, the basic issues remain the same, and
we move to modern times to illustrate what one BBC Director-
General described as the 'inescapable connection between
frequency policy, receiver distribution policy and programme
potentialities'.[15]

The first point to note, remembering our earlier technical di-
gression, is that it is a matter for individual governments, while
conforming to ITU agreements, to decide how broadcasting frequencies are assigned within a country. Thus a given waveband
may be filled by a powerful transmitter covering a large geographical area such as a nation-state, or by a number of less powerful
stations covering smaller areas.

The large geographical extent of the USA and a tradition that
favoured individual commercial or city initiatives against federal
planning, i.e. a free market, ensured maximum use of frequencies
in the major cities and a relative deprivation in rural areas – a
deprivation which was to be exploited when the television era
dawned by cable companies bringing in the distant city signals.
The Federal Radio Commission (see Chapter 3) came on the scene
in 1927 only after economic imperative, rather than any national
plan, had created networks. The Commission's successor, the
Federal Communications Commission (FCC), has ever since
maintained a policy that seeks wherever possible to fill frequency
space rather than find reasons to deny its use. It is aided in the
process by Constitutional Amendments and a Freedom of Information Act.

The exact opposite is true of Britain. An Official Secrets Act,
passed (1911) in the very period we have been considering when
military interests dominated the infant technology, sets the tone. It
is part of an even older civil service tradition, which continues to
this day, of being economical with the truth and has habituated a
British public uncomplainingly to accept a shortage of information. On this side of the Atlantic, the onus is on the citizen to show
cause why s/he should use the frequency spectrum at all.

When broadcasting started, the Post Office, itself a master of procrastination, was inferior as a government department to the War Ministry. The Postmaster General was not usually of Cabinet rank, and the post had no less than seven incumbents in the crucial years 1921–4. Half a century later, the transfer of responsibility for broadcasting to the Home Office (1974), which divided technical supervision with the Department of Trade and Industry, at least gave broadcasting a Cabinet voice, though one which was accorded a low priority and was uneasily associated with law and order. In an age when control of weapons and intelligence depends on telecommunications, the military stake in communications remains an overridingly influential one. Not only does the military control 36 per cent of spectrum space, but the actual frequencies included in its fiefdom are an official secret. The long arm of military intelligence has extended to the vetting of BBC staff and, as the BBC found to its cost in 1987, to the censorship of programmes to do with spy satellites and the secret service.

Engineering perfectionism is an important factor. British broadcasting policy was originally shaped by John Reith, the BBC's first chief executive, who determined to provide a national service under unified control. So the first separate, local stations were soon connected to London by telephone links and 'simultaneous broadcasting' (what we would now call live networking) was achieved by 1924. This system was replaced by a national service originating in the powerful long-wave transmitter at Daventry. The service was boosted in the regions by transmitters which could also originate the alternative Regional Service on different frequencies, an alternative that was important to enable Reith to pre-empt charges that the BBC was abusing its monopoly and to defuse calls for competition. The system assumed relatively few, high-powered transmitters each giving coverage over a wide area.

Reith had to struggle against military interests to secure the frequencies he wanted.[16] Once successful, he was marvellously supported by his engineers who set about attempting to deliver the ideal that the notion of public service required: that any broadcast service designed to serve a given area should be receivable by everyone in that area. It was logical and socially just, but necessarily excluded a degree of choice, as later generations began to discover when competition and low-cost technology suggested another way of ordering things. However, the engineers' loyal and dogged pursuit of the public service ideal set in motion a dynamic in which engineering standards became an end in themselves, an immutable 'given' in an arena in which, as we have seen, official secrecy excluded the possibility of public enlightenment or debate. The traditional lofty indifference to technology among top people (Reith was a notable exception) has contributed to the vicious circle. The engineers have been allowed to indulge themselves because they are still after all only 'electricians'.

On the manufacturing front, the story is also one of good intentions too often baulked by inept economic and trade policies at governmental level. The manufacturers of course were in at the beginning, forming the consortium which made up the British Broadcasting Company. The official BBC symbol was stamped on the licenced receivers the public was supposed to buy, thus bringing the Company its income. The system broke down because so many listeners built their own receivers from parts, most of which had entered the country from abroad.

The licence fee system was then devised which freed the BBC and the manufacturers to go their separate ways, but a close connection had to be maintained as new services, wavelengths and improved transmission technology demanded reciprocal changes in the receiver industry.

In the inter-war period, the swiftly expanding domestic market and guaranteed access to the Empire allowed the industry to thrive. On the whole the stability of the BBC and its monopoly position served to maintain it in a reasonable state till the outbreak of the Second World War in 1939. During the war, government contracts, particularly those concerned with radar, provided a huge boost for the industry which emerged into peacetime as an electronics industry, interested in and capable of developing television as well as radio. Britain's weak economic position in the post-war period was both an obstacle and a challenge to growth. Raw materials were in short supply, earning dollars a national priority. In this critical period, military considerations continued to intrude: in 1949, BBC planning for television received a boost when Ministry of Supply officials expressed their concern that the radio and electronics industry should be kept in 'an efficient state for defence purposes'.[17] For radio sets, 1951 was the peak year, with $2\frac{1}{4}$ million produced, a third of them for export. Thereafter the major industrial effort went towards satisfying the domestic television boom.[18]

From this point onwards, the health of the electronics industry and its export-earning capacity figured in government calculations concerning broadcasting policy. Increasingly, competition from Japan and the newly industrialised countries of the Far East undercut British prices. It was not, however, easy, even after the Department of Trade and Industry (DTI) was brought into the picture in 1974, to assemble such calculations across departmental boundaries into an overall policy – as witness the confusion in the Thatcher government's cable and satellite plans caused by the rivalry between the Home Office and the DTI.

But we are concerned with radio, and since the age of television radio, the poor relation, has suffered a comparative neglect that amounts to planning blight. The intertwined story of VHF and local radio is a good illustration of the problem.

VHF and Local Radio

By the end of the Second World War the technology for VHF/FM had considerably improved. At that point North American regulators faced fewer geographical and political constraints in frequency allocation than their counterparts in Europe. In 1945, the FCC assigned 20 FM channels in Band II (the part of the spectrum allocated for broadcasting and covering 88–108 MHz) for non-commercial use. Europe had to wait until an agreement which followed a conference in Stockholm in 1952.

In the USA, VHF/FM took off slowly and for a number of years was an unregarded backwater with interesting consequences as we shall see in Chapter 3. But in contrast to Britain, the FM band was 'freed' to develop separate programming. In 1964, the FCC ordered AM-FM licence holders serving populations over 100 000 to stop simulcasting and broadcast original programming on FM for at least half their airtime. By this historic decision, FM radio was able to take off, assisted by an extraordinary convergence of music, radical politics and youth culture.[19]

BBC engineers had been experimenting with VHF since 1946[20] and had already begun to plan for a national VHF network. The Beveridge Report,[21] published in 1951, contained more original ideas about the use of VHF than its successor, the Pilkington Report, a decade later. Beveridge noted that while the purpose of the VHF development being carried out by the BBC was to complete the satisfactory reach of existing BBC services, 'there is . . . a quite different object, which appears to us equally important – that of making possible a greater diversity and independence of programmes'. Beveridge urged an early experiment, and after wondering whether independent bodies, such as 'a Local Authority, a University or a specially formed voluntary agency' might not be in a better position to innovate, came down in favour of obliging the BBC to set up local stations. This was in line with the main recommendation of the report that the BBC should retain its monopoly. In the event, however, it was Selwyn Lloyd's famous minority recommendation which received the attention and the limelight, and radio took a back seat as ITV was introduced.

After the Stockholm conference BBC engineers went ahead with the development of a VHF network, eventually completing the work in 1965. The BBC planned for high-power transmitters using a form of aerial configuration (horizontal polarisation) which assumed fixed reception on the outside of homes, not having anticipated its unsuitability for reception in cars or by the small portable transistorised receivers which were coming on the market in increasing numbers from the late 1950s.

Meanwhile the three national services (Home, Light and the Third Programme) continued to be broadcast on medium and long wave at the same time as they were transmitted on the gradually expanding VHF network.

It was now that local radio entered the policy calculations. The Pilkington Report (1962) had supported the BBC's plan for a large number of small local stations, but once again the radio initiative was shelved in favour of television – the development of BBC2 took priority. However the arrival of the North Sea pirates from 1964 speeded plans for an appropriate response from the BBC: the creation of Radio 1 and the deployment of local radio was the answer.

For local radio, the BBC plan had been for a main service on VHF with supplementary daytime support simulcast on medium wave.[22] After the success of the first eight BBC local radio stations (from 1967), broadcasting on VHF only, the Labour government in 1969 authorised the development of a total of 40 stations, also on VHF only. With the return the following year of a Conservative government committed to commercial radio, the BBC had to fight hard to retain local radio at all. Finally, it was allowed to go ahead and introduce up to 20 stations, all 20 being allowed medium wave as well as VHF, to the considerable relief of BBC local radio staff, who had found their programme reach limited by the low level of VHF set ownership.[23]

Commercial local radio was to be developed by the Independent Television Authority, renamed Independent Broadcasting Authority (IBA), as a series of 60 Independent Local Radio (ILR) stations. These too were to be allowed to simulcast on VHF and medium wave, the latter frequencies being made available partly from cutting down on the BBC plan and partly through the use of directional aerials which allowed frequencies assigned elsewhere to be re-used in the targeted locations without interference to the primary user. Directional aerials were an expensive solution (and incidentally contributed to the high cost of the rental ILR companies paid to the IBA) to the dilemma Chataway, the Minister of Posts and Telecommunications, was in: how to find the frequencies to implement the Conservatives' election promise of commercial radio in the face of well-organised BBC resistance. Lord Hill, an experienced broadcaster and former Conservative Minister, was BBC Chairman at the time. In his memoirs he records how in 1970 he was pressed by Chataway on the matter of frequencies. No spare frequency could be found to accommodate commercial needs without affecting the BBC's existing services and a desperate search for another began. Hill gave the BBC's Chief Engineer four days to find one. 'The computers began to hum and by Tuesday the appropriate wavelength was found'[24] – a good example of how 'shortage of frequencies' evaporates given political will.

British listeners therefore had little incentive to tune to VHF: the programmes they were used to could be found in the old places on the dial. Those who bought the new 'trannies' got poor reception on VHF owing to horizontal polarisation and often found there was no long-wave tuning band at all, since imported receivers were made mainly for Far Eastern and American markets where long wave is not used for broadcasting.[25]

As for Radio 1, the pop music channel created to win young listeners back to the BBC after the Marine Offences Act had disposed of their favourite pirates, it would have been a 'feasible decision' in the judgement of Charles Curran, the BBC's Director-General at the time, to have started it on VHF only, in the 'hope that the young audience, prepared to spend money, would buy VHF receivers to patronise the service'. But this was overruled at a political level for fear that piracy would continue to be heard on the medium-wave receivers that at the time still dominated the market.[26]

It was to be twenty years before the BBC, under pressure from a Conservative Green Paper, was converted to the view that simul-casting was a wasteful use of frequencies. Then, once again, the BBC proposed a VHF only Radio 1 in the expectation that 'the young, more technologically mobile, will find VHF faster'.[27] Up till then, a commitment to simulcasting (as well, it must be said, the frequency straightjacket into which successive governments forced the BBC) inevitably and constantly led the Corporation, to the intense irritation of listeners, to 'split' services so that, for example, cricket commentaries invaded Radio 3's medium-wave music programme, and Schools programmes interrupted the flow of Radio 4 VHF, forcing listeners to retune to find the programme of their choice.

Belatedly, during 1986, the Home Office gave permission for a limited experiment in six ILR stations for split frequency broadcasting.[28] More significantly, after the 1987 Green Paper openly urged the end of simulcasting, the IBA began to give routine approval for 'splitting'. Later that year, in a move clearly designed to show willing and meet the Green Paper proposals to deprive it of two frequencies, the BBC announced plans to re-shape its services. It proposed an end to simulcasting and splitting; that all four networks should be available on VHF; and that the possibility should be investigated of maintaining separate services on the remaining long- and medium-wave positions. The Home Secretary's announcement of January 1988 confirmed the Green Paper proposals for setting up three national commercial networks and hundreds of small local stations. (See Chapter 10 for further details and discussion.)

Decisions on frequency assignment have up till now always been the result of negotiation behind closed doors between the BBC and Whitehall officials, joined by ITA/IBA representatives from 1954 in respect of television, and from 1972 in respect to radio. The existence of regular meetings to plan local radio was not publicly revealed until the enquiry of the Select Committee on Nationalised Industries (SCNI) in 1978.[29] Thereafter the Home Office Local Radio Working Party (HOLRWP) became slightly more visible, but still inaccessible on any regular basis to any public interests except the broadcasters. The concept of the frequency spectrum as a public resource in which planning applications, submitted by others besides the established broadcasters, could be scrutinised in a public forum was glimpsed by Beveridge, and is certainly accepted in Australia. It is possible that the deregulation and expansion of non-BBC local radio may in future admit a wider range of representation to the frequency planning table. But the conclusion must be that in Britain, lack of foresight in engineering planning, coupled with no apparent policy at all over receiver distribution, and timidity in trying to 'split' frequencies (that is, carry different programming on MW, LW and VHF) has prevented diversity and obstructed progress in radio. Had any of Radio 1, Radio 3 or local radio been provided on VHF only (as the BBC at different times proposed) listeners would have had an incentive to buy, and manufacturers to produce, cheap effective VHF sets. De-regulation – and pre-emptive moves by AM/FM stations towards providing distinct services on their two frequencies – is likely to change that.

Chapter 3

Free For All: The American Model

In this chapter we focus on the formative period of American radio, 1919–34. US radio moved quickly from being state dominated to a commercial medium. The state's suspicion of British imperialism and monopoly laid the ground for breaking the patent deadlock and from then on commercial interests spearheaded the medium's development. Popular interest in amateur experiment forced the switch from broadcasting as a way of selling sets to broadcasting as a means of publicity, and the development proceeded without much concern for either frequency planning or public service. Radio adjusted successfully to its displacement by television and the American model had a worldwide influence.

Towards Long-Distance Communications

That broadcasting should develop as a capitalist enterprise, a vehicle for advertising and commercial expansion, is not surprising in a country that by the end of the First World War led the world in industrial production. What is curious is the sequence of steps by which it became so, the twists and turns which took the medium out of the hands of the state and the military and emphasised its universal entertainment value as against its long-distance communication role.

For Marconi's obsession with long-distance, point-to-point communication was shared by influential American experimenters and dominated government thinking even before the war. In 1903 President Theodore Roosevelt and King Edward VII had exchanged morse code messages across the Atlantic using Marconi stations.

Before the discovery that short waves could use the ionosphere to bounce messages with ease around the globe, these transoceanic attempts required enormous levels of electrical power. A key device to facilitate this was the alternator developed in the General Electric Company (GEC)'s laboratories by Ernst Alexanderson and used by Fessenden in his famous first voice transmission of Christmas Day, 1906. On a visit to the GEC laboratories in 1915, Marconi was sufficiently impressed by the Alexanderson alternator to offer a multi-million dollar deal by which his company would gain exclusive use of it, while GEC retained manufacturing rights. Before the full deal could be finalised Marconi was recalled for wartime service by the Italian government, but GEC delivered one 50 000-watt alternator to the Marconi station in New Jersey. On the US entry into the war in 1917, it was taken over and developed by the Navy which used it the following year to broadcast President Wilson's Fourteen Point peace proposals to Europe. Some of these broadcasts were addressed directly to the German wireless station at Nauen, near Berlin, and received immediate acknowledgement. It was the first time there had been direct communication between the Allies and Germany since the British had cut the submarine cables in 1914. An improved, more powerful version of the Alexanderson alternator kept President Wilson in touch with the White House when he sailed to the Paris peace conference in 1919.

At the highest level, then, the significance of the device had registered: here was a means for nation to speak to nation as well as to end British control of cable traffic. When, therefore, the Marconi Company renewed its approaches to GEC, Franklin D. Roosevelt, Acting Secretary for the Navy, was quickly informed by Owen D. Young, the senior GEC executive who had dealt with Marconi in 1915. Roosevelt instructed GEC not to close any deal with Marconi, communicated his concern to the Presidential delegation in Paris, and received authority to intervene on the US government's behalf. His representative, Admiral Bullard, Director of Naval Communications, lost no time in meeting Young and the board of GEC.

Like other companies which had prospered by wartime sales to the armed forces, GEC was anxious to secure peacetime contracts and would in other circumstances have welcomed the Marconi deal. But Bullard argued that if the company sold the alternator and other devices to Marconi it would 'fix in British hands a substantial monopoly of world communications'. GEC agreed but pointed out that no American company was able to buy these expensive pieces of equipment.

The navy and the state therefore faced a dilemma very similar to the one which was to confront the British Post Office when broadcasting first began in Britain. They had to choose between a state monopoly or a company (and in the case of the United States) a foreign company having a monopoly over radio. For Admiral Bullard the way out of the dilemma was to organise an American company powerful enough to withstand Marconi commercially.

Not surprisingly Bullard suggested that GEC itself should form the nucleus of such a company. He overcame their objections that they were not interested in the field of long-distance communications by pointing out that if they boosted communications it would automatically help them in their main business which was to sell more equipment.

Creating a Commercial Giant

The task which fell to GEC of creating an American radio corporation faced formidable obstacles. The necessary patents were still scattered among GEC's rivals, but in one way post-war nationalism made the most formidable of these rivals easy meat. The American Marconi Company was seen as a branch of the British company even though it was mostly American owned, because it had in the past followed the policy of its parent company. The American directors were willing to sell their shares to GEC; in any case, at this time, the Navy still retained its wartime control of the Marconi stations. The problem was to persuade the parent company to relinquish its holdings. The American General Manager realised that the state and public opinion were ranged against his company and he undertook to go to Britain to persuade the British company to sell its American interests. The parent company must also have realised that it could not win this battle and in September 1919 agreed to sell.

As soon as this hurdle had been overcome the way was clear for the formation of the Radio Corporation of America. The American Marconi Company exchanged shares in the RCA for its own assets of radio stations, equipment, patent rights and goodwill. Nevertheless there were still outstanding problems in the matter of patents without which RCA would have been unable to operate.

These were overcome by a device thought up by officials of the Navy Department termed a cross-licensing agreement, and the first of these agreements was executed on the same day as the merger between the American Marconi Company and RCA, 20 November 1919. The first agreement gave RCA the rights to the inventions and patents of GEC and established GEC's reciprocal rights in present and future patents which RCA might own. The arrangement of course established monopoly in all but name. RCA also allowed a limited measure of government influence in its affairs and the following provision appeared in its bye-laws:

> The corporation may permit a representative of the Government of the United States the right of discussion and presentation in the board of the Government's views and interests concerning matters coming before the board.[1]

Admiral Bullard was appointed the US government representative on the RCA board, of which Owen D. Young became Chair. The staff of American Marconi transferred to RCA and with them David Sarnoff as Commercial Manager. It was Sarnoff who had caught the public eye in 1912 when, as a junior Marconi operator based in New York, he stayed at his post for 72 hours receiving news of the Titanic disaster. More significantly, it was Sarnoff who, as early as 1916, had proposed the use of radio as 'a household utility. The idea is to bring music into the house by wireless.'[2] The American Marconi Co. had rejected the idea.

Now RCA was now free to build up the business of international wireless traffic. It took in the American Telephone and Telegraph Company (AT&T) as a partner, and through the energetic dealings of Owen D. Young it forestalled British, French and German interests from control of concessions in South America, and began negotiating rights in Europe and the Far East.

A Domestic Market Opens Up

The cross-licensing agreement may have cut the patents knot which was holding back radio development, but it was not to everybody's taste. In particular it did not please those companies who were not part of the web of cross-licensing agreements. The Westinghouse Electrical and Manufacturing Company just like GEC had found the end of the war meant a sudden decline in the sales of its products, the chief of which was the vacuum tube. Westinghouse also took note of GEC's negotiations with the American Marconi Company and resolved to try to make their own alliance with companies owning useful patents in the field of radio. Being based in Pittsburgh they first of all looked at Fessenden's old company, the International Radio Telegraph Company (IRTC) and offered to buy the Fessenden patents. This offer was turned down, so Westinghouse offered a cross-licensing agreement, and financial backing which is what the smaller company lacked. Agreement was secured and Westinghouse imagined that it could now join the big league in long distance radio communications.

However its international nature was threatened as the company president discovered when he went to Europe to arrange radio traffic agreements with companies there: RCA had got there first. Thus the reach of the IRTC was confined to areas where traffic was less intense than the Atlantic. Westinghouse had bought the rights to expensive equipment, but could not use it in the most profitable arena. Their search continued for useful patents and some idea that would expand the market for the equipment for which they now held the rights. They bought Armstrong's superheterodyne patent, authorised one of their researchers, Zworykin, to continue the television experiments he had begun in pre-war Russia, and unsuccessfully pursued the idea of broadcasting a news service to ships at sea.

It was Dr Conrad, a Westinghouse employee and keen radio amateur, who noticed the interest in broadcasting which had revived since the lifting of government restrictions after the war. By 1920 he had established a wide circle of amateurs with whom he was in touch, and he arranged regular broadcasts in his spare time so that members of the group could amaze their friends. The gramophone records he needed for his twice-weekly two-hour broadcasts were supplied by a local record dealer in return for an on-air mention of his store. The publicity attracted custom. Other stores latched on to the idea as a way of advertising radio sets. Soon several stores were reaping the benefit of the broadcasts by the Conrad family. One of them, advertising radio sets in the *Pittsburgh Sun*, mentioned the Conrad concerts. The ad. caught the eye of the vice-President of Westinghouse who summoned his employee to his office the next day.

He had come to the conclusion, he later recalled,

> that the efforts that were then being made to develop radio telephony as a confidential means of communication were wrong, and that instead its field was really one of wide publicity, in fact, the only means of instantaneous communication ever devised.[3]

Their intentions still fixed on expanding the market for their product, Westinghouse applied to the Department of Commerce for a licence. A station was located at the top of the tallest building of the Westinghouse plant. Simple receiving sets were distributed, and KDKA started by broadcasting the election results of November 1920 with the co-operation of the Pittsburgh Post which passed on the results to the station by telephone. After this the station established a regular broadcasting schedule in the evenings.

It soon became clear that there needed to be some variety in the broadcasts, and the Westinghouse band was pressed into service to leaven the diet of recorded music. A broadcast from a local auditorium produced resonance problems which tortured their listeners' ears and so, in what must have been one of the first outside broadcasts, the band performed in a tent.

The Radio Boom

The effect of KDKA's broadcasts in the last weeks of 1920 was immense: newspaper comment was widespread and continued, stores opened radio departments, across the country people obtained parts and assembled sets, licence applications to the Department of Commerce began to increase. Westinghouse itself constructed several 500-watt transmitters and installed them in its

factories in Newark, Chicago and Springfield, Mass., where the
first crystal receivers were being produced. More important for the
company, it obtained admission as a 20 per cent shareholder to
RCA whose founding partners were reeling from the shock of the
Westinghouse publicity coup. RCA, which had taken United Fruit
on board as a partner, now disposed of some two thousand
patents, which effectively armed the corporation for engagement
in the business of international wireless traffic. What RCA could
not afford to overlook was the new turn of events which promised
a lucrative domestic market. However, the patent arrangements
had not anticipated the possibility that amateurs would assemble
sets from parts on a scale which quite markedly affected the
potential sales of the RCA partners. It was the same problem the
BBC was to face a few years later, but the American solution was
different because the issue of state versus commercial control had
already been decided. A determined effort was made to stamp out
amateur patent evasion by a series of lawsuits, and the prosecution
of this campaign, together with a drive on the production of
receivers for domestic use was one of the chief concerns of the new
RCA General Manager, the far-sighted David Sarnoff, appointed
in 1921.

That year saw the beginnings of different types of broadcast:
sport – the Demsey–Carpentier boxing title fight, and the baseball
World Series; music – concerts in New Jersey and opera in Chicago. Twenty-eight licences were issued under the old 1912 Act by
the Department of Commerce.

But the year of the boom was 1922. By the end of it 670 stations
were licensed. All were allotted the same frequency and told to
work out arrangements with their neighbours. Amateurs and
industry-sponsored stations clashed, bargained, time-shared and
fought each other with escalating transmission power. Already by
the start of the year the prospect of chaos had prompted the
Secretary of Commerce, Herbert Hoover, to convene in Washington the nation's first-ever radio conference. Hoover invited the
industry to advise him whether further powers were needed besides those available to him under the 1912 law. There was no
doubt about the answer. As Hoover remarked, 'this is one of the
few instances where the country is unanimous in its desire for
regulation'.[4] The conference was attended by an observer from the
British Post Office, F.J. Brown. That he should have witnessed

this phase of radio and the attendant discussion was of immense significance for the development of British broadcasting, for his report and advice to the authorities in London was influential in shaping the British attitude to regulation and monopoly.

Advertising Appears

1922 also saw another development. Until now, the RCA partners' main motive for involvement was the sale of equipment; broadcasting was simply a way to promote sales. The patent agreements underlying RCA's formation specified which partner could sell what. AT&T owned the rights and cables for national and international telephone and telegraph services. Denied by the RCA agreement the right to sell receivers, AT&T hit on the idea of what it called 'toll broadcasting' – the use of studio time in return for payment. Hoover's statement at the first Radio conference that 'it is inconceivable we should allow so great a possibility for service . . . to be drowned in advertising matter'[5] had met with general agreement. So AT&T described their scheme as an 'experiment . . . to see whether there are people who desire the right to talk to the public and at the same time tell the public something it would like to hear'.[6] The company claimed it had received many requests for such a service, but it was not until some months after their announcement, on 28 August 1922, that the first 'programme' was broadcast from the AT&T New York station, WEAF. The Queensboro Corporation paid fifty dollars for a ten-minute message promoting the sale of apartments. The build-up of revenue from subsequent messages was slow in coming, but as the idea began to catch on, four effects gradually became noticeable: 1) artists and musicians who had hitherto given their services free began to ask for fees; 2) AT&T began to use its long-distance lines to bring broadcast material to WEAF and at the same time deny the use of them to the stations of others in the RCA group; 3) further, the lines were used to link together AT&T stations in a package that was more attractive to advertisers – i.e. the embryonic appearance of networking; 4) adverse public reaction to on-air advertisements began to mount. Radio Broadcast magazine talked of 'driblets of advertisements . . . floating through the ether every day . . . concerts . . . seasoned here and there with a dash of advertising paprika . . . every little classic number has a slogan all its own'.[7] The dissatisfaction with advertising was to reach a crisis in 1927, by which time the industry had discovered which side its bread was buttered – there was no going back. But in these early days, few people in a business 'conceived in haste and executed without thought for the future' as one contemporary account admitted,[8] had given much thought to the question of how broadcasting should be paid for.

Financing Broadcasting

RCA's Sarnoff, was, as usual, an exception. He appears on a number of occasions to have urged that the industry should cooperate in operating broadcasting as a public service, financed by a levy on the sale of equipment.[9] Since the industry was torn by rival accusations of patent infringement and monopoly trust building, his scheme evidently did not get much support. But he went on to argue that broadcasting should be seen in the same light as libraries, museums and educational institutions, and, with the recent examples of Carnegie and Rockefeller in mind, suggested that it could be supported by philanthropic grant.[10]

This idea was one of a number discussed in the first issue of Radio Broadcast in May 1922. The editor had already concluded that the boom in radio set purchase was not going to pay indefinitely for broadcasting. Other ideas discussed in the article were finance from city authorities, and public subscription. Both were in fact tried. The City Council of New York, in the face of industry opposition and federal suspicion, established WNYC. And a significant, though relatively numerically small, grouping of educational stations in universities and colleges funded by states was to remain the core of a lobby for non-profit broadcasting through the 1930s and 1940s. Public subscription was also tried, in New York and Kansas City, but failed.[11] A quarter of a century later the idea took a firmer hold in the pioneering work of the Pacifica Foundation (see Chapter 7).

Radio took hold as an institution in 1923 and 1924, participating in many key aspects of public life and inserting itself ever more closely into the home. The opening of Congress was broadcast for the first time in 1923, and in the 1924 Presidential election campaign Coolidge's use of the 26-station AT&T chain was thought to have contributed to his success. Though the first attempts at audience research, using national telephone surveys, did not begin until 1929, the sales figures for sets and parts over the period are an indication of the rapid growth in use of the medium.

Year	Dollars in millions
1925	430
1926	506
1927	425.6
1928	650.5
1929	842.5[12]

Steps Towards the American System

By this time the melting-pot contained all the elements which were to fuse together to form the American broadcast model. The steps by which this occurred may be summarised as follows:

(1) Established to safeguard military interests and to wrest control of international wireless traffic from European and particularly British control, an alliance of major corporations, RCA, is jolted by amateur experiment and its popular reception into entering the market for domestic receivers.

(2) The RCA group carves up the market amongst its own members. Its use of patent suits to block the small-scale entrepreneurial response to the radio craze earns it enemies who see these corporate manoevres as an attack on the liberty of the individual.

(3) Congress is unable to agree on measures to authorise federal regulation. Hoover deems himself mandated by the industry and acts to allocate frequencies and transmission powers.

(4) The future for broadcasting funding seems increasingly to lie in advertising, despite listener opposition. The beginnings of networking, at this time known as 'chain broadcasting', respond to the commercial logic of advertising.

(5) Competition within the RCA group intensifies and when AT& T breaks the agreement by marketing receivers, its partners bring the dispute to arbitration.

(6) At the same time the Federal Trade Commission gave notice

of hearings to investigate whether the RCA monopoly constituted a violation of anti-trust laws.

The outcome of complex negotiation and compromise was, by January 1926, the formation of a new company, the National Broadcasting Company (NBC), which avoided illegality and was owned by RCA, General Electric and Westinghouse. NBC would enter into a long-term agreement with AT&T for use of the latter's wire networks. In fact NBC launched two networks in January 1927, the Red and the Blue. (The Blue became the American Broadcasting Company – ABC – in 1942 after RCA were forced to relinquish their holdings following the FCC Report on Chain Broadcasting – see p. 45 below.)

Regulation

But also in 1926, a High Court judgement ruled that Hoover had exceeded his powers in his frequency allocations. The result was renewed chaos in the airwaves as stations arbitrarily increased power, shifted frequency and started up without licences. The chaos produced pressure for swift legislation and the Radio Act of 1927 was passed in January, creating the Federal Radio Commission, required to consider the 'public interest, convenience and necessity' in its licence awards. The FRC was authorised to make 'special regulations applicable to . . . chain broadcasting' – the Act's only reference to networking. At this time, of 732 stations broadcasting, less than a hundred were affiliated to networks, but their importance was growing. The same year a third network was formed – the Columbia Phonograph Broadcasting System (shortened to CBS after Columbia Phonograph's shares were bought out).

The FRC was originally appointed for one year to bring order to the frequency chaos. It was soon obvious that there was a more permanent role for it and the Commission continued till it was replaced by the Federal Communications Commission (FCC) when the 1934 Communications Act became law. Much of the 1934 Act was taken from the earlier legislation, and the FRC established precedents important for its successor's operation.

For example, Commissioner Caldwell said in Congressional hearings in 1928:

Each station occupying a desirable channel should be kept on its toes to produce and present the best possible programs and, if any station slips from that high standard, another station which is putting on programs of a better standard should have the right to contest the first station's position and after hearing full testimony, to replace it.[13]

Three years later on a visit to America, Reith tested this position in a meeting with the FRC.

> I asked if they had the power to put stations off the air if they felt it was not in the public interest to leave them there. He [Chairman General Saltzman] said they had, but it was an embarassing question.

Reith repeated the question to the other members of the Commission:

> There were surely many stations not serving any useful purpose. They seemed amused at the idea they should assert themselves.[14]

Reith's typically forthright interrogation had no doubt caught the Commissioners off guard, for the public rhetoric of the industry's official member organisation, the National Association of Broadcasters (NAB), stated in 1934 that 'it is the manifest duty of the licensing authority . . . to determine whether or not the applicant is rendering, or can render an adequate public service.' Public service was defined as including programmes covering education, religion, trade union and agricultural affairs. 'Over a period of seven years,' the NAB statement continued, 'this has been the principal test which the Commission has applied in dealing with broadcast applications.'[15]

The 1934 Act

But this was 1934. In the short time since 1927, the stock market crash and the Depression had shaken confidence in the infallibility of the free market system, while the arrival to the Presidency of Roosevelt, prepared in his New Deal policy to use widespread federal initiatives, inclined industry to look to government not just for temporary relief but for some sort of more permanent partnership.

Drawing on the language of the 1927 Act, the 1934 Act spoke of broadcast licences providing for the 'use' of channels 'but not the ownership thereof'. It was concerned, like its predecessor, that neither the Commission nor licensees should have powers of censorship nor interfere with the right of free speech. It required the FCC, in effect, to produce a frequency plan, and to

> study new uses for radio, provide for experimental uses of frequencies and generally encourage the larger and more effective use of radio in the public interest.[16]

In this area the Act allowed the possibility that the FCC could go further:

> The Commission shall study the proposal that Congress by statute allocate fixed percentages of radio broadcasting facilities to particular types or kinds of non-profit radio programs or to persons identified with particular types of non-profit activities.[17]

But the FCC decided not to use this discretion, judging that 'commercial stations are now responsible under the law to render a public service and the tendency of this proposal would be to lessen this responsibility'.[18]

Thus fifteen years from the birth of American radio legislation confirmed the system which, in Barnouw's words, 'made the salesman the trustee of the public interest, with minimal supervision by a commission'.[19] What is surprising is that the 1934 Act contained no amplification to take account of networking, merely repeating verbatim the 1927 Act's reference to 'special regulations applicable to chain broadcasting'. (A fourth network, Mutual, began in 1934, but operated as the name implies more as a co-operative organisation among stations than a New York-based hierarchy.)

Networking

To complete the picture of the American system at this stage it is worth noting what was involved in this, the most important feature of American broadcasting. Barnouw notes five effects of networking's earliest stages:

(1) As NBC developed prestigious New York-produced programmes for networking, sale of airtime locally became easier to obtain.
(2) Long-distance listening declined. In the early days many local stations had observed a weekly 'Silent Night' to allow listeners to search the dial and indulge their choice of distant stations. Now network pressure on affiliated stations swept listener protests aside and duplicated programmes on most stations at peak hours.
(3) Local talent, dropped in favour of high quality network shows, disappeared.
(4) NBC's artist bureau squeezed out the small talent agencies and began to monopolise the talent supply business.
(5) Advertising agencies acquired a commanding position through the double commissions they obtained on each deal – from the networks for arranging the sale of airtime and from the sponsors for securing a slot. By 1932, agencies had moved into programme production and network approval of their programmes became a formality.[20]

Networking is basically concerned with putting a maximum number of stations or affiliates (in a later evolutionary stage, a particular group of stations or time segments) at the disposal of an advertiser/sponsor. The transaction is between an advertiser/sponsor and the network company: the sponsored programme, then, costs nothing to the affiliate. In the early days of the system, some additional hours of programming were offered free to the affiliate as an inducement. These would be unsponsored and thus free to be 'sold' locally. More recently the inducement – indeed, the basis – of networking is a payment from network to affiliate. The network thus secures a guaranteed base for national advertisers, while the affiliate gets high budget programming it could not otherwise afford.

The early stages of the process saw a struggle between the three networks to acquire affiliates in the large cities and coast to coast. In return for the network payment, affiliates agreed to be bound by stringent conditions. *Exclusive* affiliation obliged the station not to carry any programme from another network. *Territorial exclusivity* meant that if an affiliate declined a network offering no other station in the area could take it either. *Option time* meant that networks obtained an option on all key segments of an affiliate's time so that, if necessary, planned local programming had to be cleared at short notice to give way to a networked programme. Affiliates might be bound contractually for long periods of time, and in certain situations had to accept a reduction of the network payment. This applied particularly to use of recorded material and needs a brief explanation.

After the use of gramophone records by the pioneering stations, live musical performances became the hallmark of the network show, and recordings, or transcriptions as they were called, were frowned on as inferior. However, in the late 1920s transcription services developed and the idea of syndication gave them a boost. The famous comic show *Amos 'n Andy* pioneered syndication in 1928. Before it became so popular that it was bought up for (live) networking by NBC, *Amos 'n Andy* was made available in recorded form to some 30 stations who were allowed to use it subsequent to its first live transmission. It became a tactic for local stations to attract national advertising by offering popular transcriptions in competition with the networks' live shows. To prevent this, NBC drew up contracts stipulating that if an affiliate undercut the network advertising rate, NBC would lower the station payment accordingly.

FCC Pressure

Such contractual arrangements limited listener choice and worked against the diversity and provision of minority programming which the 1934 Act had intended. An FCC survey in 1938 of the 700 stations then broadcasting showed that only 15.3 per cent of output was devoted to 'talk programs' (serials, variety, news and sport were counted separately), and in a follow-up survey of stations in Buffalo, New York, this category was found to include only 11.9 per cent of 'public affairs' programming.

Paul Lazarsfeld, a member of the Frankfurt School who after his arrival in the USA became a pioneer of audience research, cites these figures, concluding:

A program must be entertaining and so it avoids anything depressing enough to call for social criticism; it must not alienate its listeners, and hence caters to the prejudices of the audience; it avoids specialisation, so that as large an audience as possible will be assured; in order to please everyone it tries to steer clear of controversial issues. Add to this the nightmare of all broadcasters, that the listener is free to tune in to competing stations whenever he pleases, and you have a picture of radio as a stupendous technical achievement with a strongly conservative tendency in all social matters.[21]

Disquiet with the situation culminated, in 1941, in an FCC Report on Chain Broadcasting in which the restrictive practices of the networks were made public, and the extent of RCA's monopoly was indicted: not only did it control two networks through NBC, the Red and the Blue, but in a process of vertical integration it had taken up dominant positions in the field of talent supply and the recording and film industries. (It was as a result of this report that NBC was forced to divest itself of the Blue network which became ABC.)

A further FCC report in 1946, 'Public Service Responsibility of Broadcast Licensees', known as The Blue Book, criticised the disparities between licensees' promise and performance, the lack of adequate local service and of the discussion of public affairs. Shortly, the arrival of television was to shift the spotlight, and the finance, on to the new medium and change radio drastically. But the shortcomings of the commercial system as a whole continued to be felt and the formal introduction of public broadcasting in the 1960s, together with the growth of community radio in the same period, is an acknowledgement of them. We look at listener-sponsored radio in Chapter 7, and complete this sketch the American system by tracing the origins of public broadcasting and the rise of music radio in the television age.

Public Broadcasting: Origins

There were some notable successes in American radio in the 1930s: the variety shows which grew out of the collapse of vaudeville theatre in the Depression, CBS's March of Time which broke new ground in current affairs and as an innovative use of the medium, the Mercury Theatre which developed radio drama and the talent of Orson Welles; Roosevelt himself whose Fireside Chats showed a far better understanding of the paradoxical intimacy of this mass medium than any other contemporary world leader.

The sector that had to admit disappointment in this period was educational broadcasting.[22] Scores of educational stations had surrendered or sold their licences in the mid to late 1920s, frustrated by the frequency chaos and unable to sustain the politicking necessary to survive. The few that remained formed the National Committee for Education on Radio to lobby for improved access. The NCER's high point was the inclusion in the 1934 Act of the subsection of Paragraph 307, quoted earlier, which asked the FCC to consider setting aside a percentage of frequencies for non-profit use. As we have seen, the FCC decided against this and by the end of the 1930s a mere dozen stations survived mostly with daytime only, low-power licences.

In 1940, the FCC made its first FM allocations and reserved five channels for non-commercial use. In the 1945 re-allocation on the band (88–108MHz) still used today, twenty channels were so reserved. The concession was of little immediate use to educationists because the market in FM receivers was so slow to develop. To assist them financially, the FCC in 1948 ruled that educational stations could operate on a transmitter power of 10 watts or less. The hope was that local interest would encourage colleges and universities to boost their power. This did not occur, though the numbers of stations slowly increased; by 1969 there were 384 FM licensees and 28 AM.

Public Television

In the 1950s, with attention on television, the Ford Foundation took the initiative in creating funds to assist the educational lobby to gain a foothold in the TV frequency spectrum and to make programmes. Through its support the Educational Television and Radio Center was set up in 1952. Ten years later radio was dropped from the title and was only with difficulty re-inserted in the later crucial stage of legislation. This came about as a result of the Carnegie Commission on Educational Television, set up with President Johnson's backing in 1965. The Commission's twelve recommendations set the framework for a Corporation for Public Television. Last minute lobbying by the National Association of Educational Broadcasters got the title and remit changed to Broadcasting. The Public Broadcasting Act of 1967 established the Corporation for Public Broadcasting (CPB) to help develop public television and radio stations, and programming of 'high quality, diversity, creativity, excellence and innovation'.

CPB and National Public Radio

The CPB acts as the recipient of public funds and as a means to insulate public broadcasters from, in the Act's words, 'extraneous interference and control'. Its support for television operates through the Public Broadcasting Service (PBS) and for radio through National Public Radio (NPR). NPR was incorporated in 1970 to act as a programme producer in collaboration with stations. Its first offering was a tape of twenty concerts by the Los Angeles Philharmonic and its first live programme was to carry the Senate Foreign Relations Committee hearings on Vietnam in 1971. In May of the same year 104 NPR member stations took the first broadcast of a 90-minute daily news programme *All Things Considered* which runs to this day.

As early as 1969, the CPB announced a six-year plan to try to raise the standard of educational radio. In its present form this ties funding to minimum criteria regarding levels of transmission power, hours of programming (18 hours per day, 365 days a year), numbers of staff (5 full-time equivalent), and technical and production standards. In 1986, 297 stations qualified for CPB support. The implications of this funding strategy are discussed in Chapter 7. In the last few years in the context of an increasingly beleaguered financial environment created by an administration which does not favour the public funding of this sector, stations have had to depend more and more on their own fund-raising initiatives, trading services and fees with NPR in a structure based on their annual revenue.

Adjustment to Television

In the late 1940s and early 1950s, radio materially assisted television's rebirth: radio profits paid for television's development, then 'video killed the radio star' and swallowed almost whole the national advertising cake. The radio networks cut their advertising rates to stay in business, and the result was increasingly to lose affiliates who found they were better off using local DJs to play locally popular records interspersed with community information and local news.

As local stations adapted for survival they researched the times and tastes that would appeal to advertisers, since the mass audience and evening prime-time now belonged to television. At the same time the growth of suburbs and increase in car ownership and use created radio's own twice daily prime time − drive time. Teenagers with money to spend could not find in the (white) ballads that headed the network charts the pace and excitement they wanted to dance to: they bought black music, and, observing the trend, stations began to play rhythm 'n blues for white audiences. Stations serving black audiences also increased, though as yet few were black-owned. Meanwhile the record industry plagiarised and 'cleaned up' versions of black hits which filled the juke-boxes and were played out on air. This was the start of rock 'n roll, given a push by the film Blackboard Jungle (1955) with its chart-topping 'Rock Around the Clock' and then overtaken by the Elvis Presley phenomenon.

So began the close association of the record companies and the radio stations which resulted in the playlist, based on the charts published weekly in national trade papers, themselves based on sales. As Frith remarks,

> There is obviously a circular argument involved: a record on the playlist has a good chance of being popular; a record not on it has hardly a hope − hence the recurring temptation of payola.[23]

Payola was a term which described the practice of record companies paying DJs or programme controllers to broadcast their records. The American payola scandal came to a head with a Federal Trade Commission and Congressional enquiries in 1960, and later that year an amendment to the Communications Act outlawed the practice. Scandal also hit the ratings measurement business and again Congressional intervention was necessary. Standardisation resulted and within ten years the emergence of Arbitron as leader in the field of audience ratings.

Meanwhile, precise demographic surveys allowed formatting to develop and deliver targeted sections of the audience to the advertiser: Top 40, MOR (Middle of the Road), Beautiful Music, Disco, Country, All News, Jazz, Classical and Black music were among the formats that were separated out in the search for markets as stations multiplied in the 1960s.

The FCC decision to end simulcasting (see Chapter 2) freed FM at a crucial time for a generation which used music as a key symbol of cultural and political protest. Thousands of young people were turning to FM on both educational and commercial stations. Dylan, the Rolling Stones, groups like Jefferson Airplane and the Doors were largely ignored at this time by AM radio and TV. Despite the growth in stereo album sales and the growth in the number of FM stations which followed the FCC decision, for some time FM remained 'underground radio'.[24] Without the pressure of the Top 40 format which limited plays to a maximum of three minutes in a mix of advertisements and chat, FM was ideal for the longer and more elaborate pieces rock musicians were beginning to compose. Gradually 'progressive FM' became safe enough for commercial exploitation and 'album-oriented rock' (AOR) was adopted as a money-making format. As a sign in one station put it, 'The Age of Aquarius is over – and now it's time to kick ass.'

Conclusion: American Influence

It has not been the intention of this chapter to summarise the entire history of American radio, only to sketch the main features and determinants of what has been a highly influential model. We have touched on modern developments to show how radio adapted to counter its displacement by television, and how public broadcasting was introduced to make good deficiencies in the system. In view of the hostile climate in which public broadcasting presently operates, its introduction in America may turn out to have been a relatively short-lived result of a particular conjunction of political and social circumstances.

To say that the American model has been influential is not to describe some accidental pattern. The spread of influence was the direct result of diplomatic and commercial dealings, some of which were described at the beginning of the chapter. They are part of the cultural and economic domination of the US which has been a feature of global history in the post-war period. The path of US influence over broadcasting is clearly shown in the list of countries which adopted the commercial broadcasting system (and their start dates) in the 1920s and 1930s: Argentina, Brazil and Chile (all 1922), Costa Rica and the Philippines (both 1924), Cuba (1925), Colombia (1928), Mexico (1929), Venezuela (1930), Peru (1932), Ecuador (1937). The worldwide involvement of US armed forces in the Second World War left its mark if anything more strongly. The Armed Forces Radio Service (AFRS) was set up in 1942 to bring American programming to troops stationed overseas. In Britain AFN (the American Forces Network) was first heard in 1943 over low-powered transmitters sited in American bases up and down the country.[25] Though the programmes only reached a small proportion of the population, they gave thousands of teen-agers their first direct taste of American music and programme style and laid the ground for Radio Luxembourg's successful post-war return. By 1945, the AFRS had 800 outlets round the world each relaying over 40 hours of American programmes a week.[26]

Chapter 4

They Know They Can Trust Us: The Public Service Model

Origins

Most of the activity which led up to the establishment of broadcasting in Britain took place in 1922, after the Americans had demonstrated the possibilities of broadcasting. Before then the British had still to fight the issues arising from the armed services' reluctance to give up the frequency space they had used during the war.

The ban on amateur experiments as they were called was lifted in 1919. The Marconi Company proceeded to use its transmitter at Chelmsford to broadcast music and entertainment to the amateurs whose response enabled them to get a fair idea of the range of the apparatus. The Daily Mail was among the newspapers that took an interest in these novelties and it was Lord Northcliffe's suggestion that Dame Nellie Melba should give a broadcast. Her performance on 15 June 1920 was heard all over Europe and caught the popular imagination. But a few months later the Post Office stopped transmissions on the grounds that they were interfering with important communications. It was to be nearly two years before the ban was lifted after the petition made by the amateurs to the Post Office described in Chapter 2. Peter Eckersley, one of the radio pioneers who became Chief Engineer at the BBC compared this attitude unfavourably with the attitude to Conrad's experiments in the US, and the red flag which used to precede motor cars.

It was Eckersley who as head of the experimental section of Marconi was the main driving force in the new station, 2ET, authorised by the Post Office at Writtle. The first broadcast was in February 1922. Eckersley himself added wit and humour to the largely impromptu musical evenings which took place in a club atmosphere much appreciated by their amateur audience. During the summer, Metropolitan Vickers started experimental transmissions from 2ZY in Manchester, and Western Electric, after a trial in London, moved to Birmingham where 5IT began broadcasts a week before the formation of the British Broadcasting Company.

'Shortage of Frequencies'

In April 1922 the then Postmaster General, announcing to the House of Commons that the question of broadcasting was to be referred to the Imperial Communications Committee, said that, in contrast to the situation in America, 'what we are now doing at the beginning is to lay down very drastic regulations indeed for the control of wireless broadcasting'.[1] For the British Post Office the crucial question was the one of wavelengths; how were they to be allocated between the interested parties which included amateur experimenters, commercial wireless telegraph companies, ships and the armed services. The Wireless Sub-Committee of the ICC had before it the petition from the Wireless Society of London asking that companies be allowed to transmit weather reports and news and heard a report from F.J. Brown on his visit to America. Speaking for the Post Office he gave the view that only bona fide set manufacturers should be involved with broadcasting, and that 'clashing' of wavelengths had to be avoided.

The plan drawn up by the committee provided for one single wavelength – 440 metres – and restricted the power of the stations to 1.5 kilowatts (about the power of the average local radio station in the UK nowadays). Advertising was prohibited, as was any sort of sponsorship, and news which had not already appeared in newspapers could not be broadcast. The subject matter of broadcasting would be limited to music, education, religion and entertainment and broadcasting should be restricted to between 5 o'clock and midnight – drastic regulation indeed.

The restriction reflected the views of the armed services, and not surprisingly attracted a lot of protest from the radio companies which wanted to broadcast. Two of the largest, Marconi and Metropolitan Vickers, were invited to the next committee meeting, and made it clear that a single wavelength was totally unsatisfactory.

The response from the Committee was to suggest that the companies should collaborate and operate in a wider space of spectrum – the 350–400 metre band, where, the Marconi Company had suggested, half a dozen or so frequencies could be found. This initial approach reflected the two major concerns of the Post Office, a desire to avoid monopoly and to achieve efficiency. The dominance of the Marconi Company, its position as the sole contractor for the Imperial Wireless Scheme and its reputation for hard bargains had given good cause for concern on this first point. Equally the Post Office did not want to be put in the invidious position of having to select the most suitable among a number of firms. They were of course placed in this position precisely because they could not or would not find more space for broadcasting in the frequency band.

One Company

It was within these constraints that the discussions with the companies began in May 1922. At the first meeting a number of technical limitations on power, hours and wavelengths were set out by the Post Office, and at the end of that meeting the set manufacturers were asked to go away and prepare 'a cooperative scheme, or at the most two such schemes, for consideration by the Post Office authorities'.[2] One thing on which they all agreed was the need for protection from foreign competition in the sale of sets, and that was why they wanted broadcasting to be authorised without delay.

After considerable negotiation the set manufacturers reached an agreement that there should be one company. The chairman would be neutral, eight of the radio stations were to be built by Marconi, and the new company should decide who was to build the other two and that Marconi would not use its patents to prevent anybody else building them. The rules of membership of the new company stipulated that only British sets could be sold by members, that they should pay 10 per cent of the wholesale net selling price to the company and provide a deposit of £100 to the company. The British Broadcasting Company was formed in October 1922. Its advertisement for the chief executive posts caught the eye of John Reith, who had to ask his friends what the word 'broadcasting' meant. He was appointed General Manager in December, and was 'immediately involved in an almost overwhelming intensity and complexity of activity with problems of which I had had no previous experience. Copyright and performing right; Marconi patents; associations of concert artists, authors, playwrights, composers, music publishers, theatre managers, wireless manufacturers.[3]

Extending the Service

On the technical front, in the hands of Eckersley, the service was developed. It was at this time impossible to transmit further than 25 miles for reception by crystal receivers or 100 miles for valve sets, so the first British broadcasting was local.[4] Nine stations were set up in London, Manchester, Birmingham, Newcastle, Glasgow, Cardiff, Aberdeen, Bournemouth and Belfast, each with an effective service area of about twenty miles in radius. These local populations constituted the first audiences and they each heard a service designed specially for them and using a large measure of local talent.

Eckersley's account of this period is interesting in showing how different expressions of local feeling were held to cancel each other out and used to justify the universal introduction of a service from London. Sheffield was the first place to complain of poor reception – from Manchester, its nearest station. The solution proposed by the BBC was to bring the Manchester programme by telephone wire to Sheffield where it would be re-transmitted over a relay. The experiment met with bitter criticism from the civic authorities of Sheffield who wanted their own local service. On hearing that this was impossible within the BBC's budget, they opted to receive London's rather than Manchester's programmes. As Eckersley observed, 'this meant a longer telephone wire but a shorter argument', so Sheffield got its way, along with ten other places that demanded relay stations which took the London programme. After much protest, they were also allowed to broadcast about an hour a day of local programming.[5]

The original set of local services thus gave way to London by means of 'simultaneous broadcasting' or networking, using Post Office telephone trunk routes. Ceremonial openings were held in provincial towns and cities where the mayor's speech would be followed by the chimes of Big Ben, brought live by a 'technical miracle' admired with very little realisation that it marked the extension of metropolitan authority.

By 1924 Eckersley had already conceived the means to implement the idea of regional broadcasting which was put into effect five years later. It was the logical conclusion of Reith's policy of centralisation and it answered the critics of monopoly by providing an alternative service to the main National Programme broadcast from Daventry. Powerful long-wave transmission of the National Service was the technical solution to the problem of how most economically to reach remote rural areas, dispensing with the need to instal numbers of medium-wave transmitters linked by the telephone network. From 1929, the National Programme was complemented by six separate Regional services for London and the South-East, Birmingham and the Midlands, the North of England, Scotland, Wales and the West of England, and Northern Ireland.

Constitution

These extensions to the service, as well as the programme development described below, took place against a background of intense discussion between the set manufacturers and the Post Office to which Reith found time to make sustained and influential contributions. Meanwhile Postmasters-General came and went: the system was introduced, in Reith's words, 'while the watchmen slept'.[6]

The first stage concerned the finances of the Company and was the subject of a public enquiry by the Sykes Committee. The original agreement had been that two sorts of licences could be bought from the Post Office by listeners, both for ten shillings, half of the fee being passed on to the BBC. One sort of licence would be for sets manufactured by members of the BBC consortium and stamped with the BBC symbol. The other would be for experimenters, allowing them to build sets from components. After broadcasts began, so many listeners bought experimental licences and assembled their own sets that the manufacturers complained they were getting no benefit from the arrangement. The Sykes Committee, reporting in October 1923, rejected advertising as a solution, and recommended the abolition of the 10 per cent tariff and one licence to cover all types of use, this to finance the broadcasting activities of the BBC. From now on the increase in set ownership was to provide the manufacturers' revenue and the Company itself was freed 'to be run as a public service instead of an appendage of the trade . . . [whose] own interests would thereby best be served'.[7] The BBC's licence was renewed till the end of 1926.

The Crawford Committee, appointed in 1925, was asked to advise what should happen after as to 'the proper scope of the broadcasting service, and as to management, control and finance thereof'. Crawford recommended that the monopoly of broadcasting should be retained. ('Monopoly', it should be noted, had shifted in meaning since fear of a *commercial* monopoly had led to the idea of a manufacturers' consortium.) The commercial company should be replaced by a public corporation, licensed for ten years and 'acting as a trustee for the national interest in broadcasting'. A board of governors should be appointed by the government to serve for five years. Parliament should grant maximum freedom to the Corporation which should be allowed to broadcast (what had hitherto been prevented) discussion of controversial matters.

The particular solution devised by the British state for the control of broadcasting, while fitting the European pattern of centralised control of posts and telegraphy, followed a recent British tradition of the public corporation as a means of conducting public services or sharing public resources. The wartime experience of rationing and centralisation had convinced an important section of opinion among politicians and civil servants that market forces needed to be controlled by an agency operating at arm's length from government.[8]

The main substance of Crawford's recommendations was endorsed by the government. The BBC was given a Royal Charter like the Royal Academy and the Bank of England; the government retained the power to order the BBC not to transmit particular programmes or to carry programmes the government desired. Reith, appointed by the King in Council (i.e. by the Prime Minister advised by Ministers and officials) as the new Director-

General, had to battle to secure the right to broadcast controversial matters.

His position and that of the BBC had been greatly strengthened
by what happened during the General Strike in May 1926. During
the strike, when for nine days all newspapers except the government's British Gazette were closed, the BBC broadcast news
bulletins for the first time during the day which were listened to by
millions. (Hitherto, the newspaper lobby had successfully confined
BBC news till after seven in the evening.) The bulletins had to pass
the censor and Reith was not allowed to reveal the extent to which
the BBC's autonomy was limited. That its credibility was not
completely destroyed by a government take-over was largely due
to his vigilant diplomacy. On the other hand, in the eyes of the
Labour Opposition (no representative of which was allowed to
broadcast), the strikers and large section of the working-class, the
BBC had clearly shown whose side it was on. 'They want to be
able to say that they did not commandeer us,' Reith wrote in his
diary, 'but they know they can trust us not be really impartial.'

For fifty years, government control of the BBC operated along
lines set by this precedent. There were occasions that amounted to
interference and censorship, but they were managed behind the
scenes without recourse to the formal and public exercise of the
powers set out in the Licence.

For the time being at least, a constant increase in the number of
licences taken out by the public guaranteed a steadily rising
income for the BBC. 'Assured finance' was one of the four
fundamentals which, according to Reith in a famous passage in his
autobiography, 'enabled the BBC to make of broadcasting what
no other country in the world has made of it.' The others were
'public service motive, sense of moral obligation . . . and the brute
force of monopoly'.[9]

'"Publicists",' Eckersley states in typically robust style, 'those
who explain everything to the public by simple inaccuracies say
that the creation of the BBC was a "far-sighted measure of
sociological planning". In fact, it was nothing of the sort; the
BBC was formed as the expedient solution of a technical problem; it owes its existence solely to the scarcity of wavelengths.
This wavelength shortage is the fundamental disadvantage of
wireless.'[10]

There is some truth in Eckersley's crisp summation, but it is not the whole truth. Frequency shortage underlay the Post Office's concern about broadcasting but it could have solved that problem in different ways, either by time-sharing or with regional or local services. The Imperial Communications Committee might have been a little more generous with its allocation of frequencies for broadcasting in the first place. The fact that none of these things did happen led to the creation of the British Broadcasting Company, thence the British Broadcasting Corporation and the whole edifice of what has come to be known as Public Service Broadcasting.

The manufacturers of wireless receivers, a central part of the original initiative, were content with these developments. In Reith, their former chief executive, they had a contact which ensured the maintenance of a satisfactory relationship with the BBC. They were kept closely in touch with the BBC's technical changes which meant the gradual elimination of home-made devices, some crude and some ingeniously sophisticated, in favour of standardised products specially designed to give priority to the BBC's signals. Thus a combination of technological and administrative factors can be seen to have effected successive changes in the radio audiences from the first undisciplined 'air-fishers' to the creation of what Reith called 'the great audience'.

Public Service

The conception of the audience constrained by technology is one of the four components identified by Briggs as making up Reith's ideal of public service broadcasting. They were, first, that the BBC did not aim for profit. Second, it strove to extend its service to the whole population. Third, 'unified control' was the guiding principle, not sectional pressure or regional initiative. Fourth, 'there is an emphasis on the "public" or the series of "publics" which together consitute "the great audience". The "publics" are treated with respect, not as nameless aggregates with statistically measurable preferences, "targets" for the programme sponsor, but as living audiences capable of growth and development."[11] The National Programme and the alternative which the Regional Programme was at any time meant to offer were the means for this growth and development.

The Programme Schedules

What was provided for this audience? The early days of high-spirited improvisation in Savoy Hill and local initiative outside of London settled surprisingly quickly into patterns which were to grow into long-standing traditions – in music, drama, talks, variety, education and children's programmes.

At the start in 1922, there were 31 staff at Savoy Hill; the number had grown to 700 by the time of the move to Broadcasting House ten years later. By this time there was a conscious effort to plan schedules, and layers of administrative staff, between producers and Reith's top-level Control Board, had been taken on to implement the plans. Faced with the problems of catering for many tastes within one National channel, the planners tried to vary the menu. Hilda Matheson, the BBC's first Head of Talks, wrote in 1933 after her departure from the BBC, of the need for 'Some due proportion of the familiar and the novel . . . the right balance of regular and unexpected items, the appropriate hours for different types of programmes.'[12] The BBC held out longer than most other organisations against the discipline of the strict timetable. Not dependent as commercial broadcasting was on holding the audience for every second in order to please advertisers or thwart competitors, the BBC used the ticking of a clock to mark intervals in which listeners were expected to compose their minds for a change of mood, or tune into the news without the irritation of catching the tail-end of an unwanted programme.

News bulletins, especially the main evening news with its regular Big Ben chimes, were the spearhead of regularity which began to change the easy-going nature of continuity. News had become of increasing importance to the BBC and its audience since the daytime bulletins of the General Strike. Listening to the news became a habit around which household routines were organised. Gradually BBC schedulers adopted regularity and more exact timing in other parts of the day as well. Foucault has noted the importance of the timetable in controlling the activity of academic students and industrial workers.[13] The first of the mass media to be time-bound, radio imposed on its listeners the rhythms of the industrial age, and with its increasingly minute division of time, implicitly upheld the notion of scientific precision and predictability. In this, radio, according to Scannell, was fulfilling its primary task as one of the first of the national broadcasting organisations – 'the mediation of modernity'; in its insertion into domestic routines and in its celebration of national rituals for a community of listeners no less important for being 'imagined' in the minds of each,[14] this newest of the mass media was attempting 'the normalisation of the public sphere and the socialisation of the private sphere'.[15]

Specialist Programmes

From the earliest days regular items in the schedules had included talks, drama, religion, music, variety and special programmes for women, for farmers and fishing communities, for schools and adult education listening groups, and for children.

There was a Women's Hour in the London programme of Savoy Hill from early on,[16] and a Women's Advisory Committee, one of a range of advisory committees, met between January 1924 and September 1925 when it was discontinued on the grounds that the title Women's Hour no longer existed and only one women's talk was then being broadcast.[17] (In 1946, the title was revived for the famous programme which runs to this day.)

In its early years the BBC considered itself an enlightened employer of women. 'They should be as eligible as men for promotion. There is no reason why a woman should not be a Station Director,' wrote Reith in 1926. This attitude changed with the widespread unemployment of the 1930s.[18] Female staff who married were expected to resign, and a long-running skirmish developed between the BBC and the cheaper newspapers, always keen to sensationalise the steps of women towards equality, over the comings and goings of women announcers. Though in the Second World War the BBC, like other employers, took on a large number of women in jobs previously reserved for men, female announcers continued to pose problems for a male-dominated Corporation[19] (see below under *Accent*). A few women were, however, prominent in key programme positions in the early period, chief among them Mary Somerville, the architect of schools programmes, and Hilda Matheson herself, who in her book vigorously asserts the benefit to women of both specialist and general radio programming.[20]

Schools programmes are interesting as an area where an educational advisory committee, organised conditions of reception and the combination of teachers' and visiting BBC staff reports constituted what soon became a precisely organised feedback system. This careful foundation was laid by Mary Somerville whose pioneering 'study of broadcasting from the receiving end rather than from the transmitting end revolutionised the use of the medium as an educational instrument'.[21] Adult education programmes were remarkable for the successful organisation of the audience whose response was deemed an essential part of the process of education. Adult listening groups were a feature of this process in the 1930s. They were inspired by proposals in *New Ventures in Broadcasting* (1928), a report produced by a BBC Committee chaired by Sir Henry Hadow, whose name is usually given to the Board of Education's important report *The Education of the Adolescent* (1927). The appearance of the BBC's weekly, *The Listener*, which reprinted the main educational talks, and the appointment of specialist Education Officers in the Regions were two other developments of the time which stimulated the growth of interest in radio among those concerned with working-class education. By the winter of 1930/1, over a thousand listening groups had formed, but though the majority survived till the war, the BBC disbanded its Central Council for Broadcast Adult Education in 1934 and diverted its resources into schools broadcasting where partnership with the authorities on the ground was more easily achieved.

Children were the first section of the audience to be organised at the listening end – in Radio Circles which anticipated Radio Luxembourg's Ovaltiney's by a decade or more. The 'Uncles' and 'Aunts' of Children's Hour were, to start with in London, BBC executives taking time off from their duties to have fun around the microphone. Their mode of address was decidedly middle class and their literate audience loved them, rewarding them with a 'jolly mailbag' that was answered on air till it became unmanageably large.[22]

Music Policy

The BBC's music policy exemplified Reithian paternalism as well as any other programme area – 'the great missionary element in broadcasting' as one senior official described it. The developments of policy in this period have been examined in detail by other writers.[23] Two quotations from early policy makers give a flavour of how they conceived of their duty to their listeners. C.A. Lewis complained in 1924 that listeners demanding more light music had not 'studied our problem'. 'This music doesn't wear. It cannot be repeated, whereas good music lasts, mellows and gains fresh beauties at every hearing.'[24]

Nine years later, Matheson, who acknowledged the BBC's achievement in educating public taste for classical music, used the same tone:

> If programmes contain a large proportion of music that is deliberately background music – trifling tea-time sentimentality – broadcasting will tend to encourage the passive half-hearted listening which will soon destroy itself.[25]

Listening had to be, according to Matheson, an active experience, the pleasures had to be earned. The point was lost on those who looked for something after a day's work or at weekends. In fact, the failure of the BBC to satisfy popular musical tastes had, by the late 1930s, driven listeners in their thousands to Radio Luxembourg and Radio Normandy, especially on Sundays when the dance music and variety of the foreign stations attracted the largest audience in the country. Radio Normandy in particular, exploiting the BBC's late morning start, went hard for advertisers who would sponsor breakfast-time programmes to reach 'the mass of working men and women'.[26] A Radio Normandy survey of 1938 showed that this policy attracted two thirds of those listening before 11:30a.m.[27]

Accent

The BBC kept a sharp eye, or ear, on the speech used at the microphone. The accent and intonations of its announcers conveyed the authority and the self-confidence of the class that controlled the airwaves as surely as the evening dress that was compulsory uniform. Wilfred Pickles, who 'pioneered' a regional accent (Yorkshire) as a North Region announcer before the Second World War and graduated to the national Home Service news in 1941, recalls with admiration a more typical colleague who 'had most of the qualities the BBC looked for; he was steady, correct, just a voice without emotion, and his announcements were precisely right in every detail, cold and without feeling'.[28]

As Kumar[29] and Cardiff[30] have shown, the BBC needed to insist on a certain style in its continuity announcing and news-reading: voices at such moments had to speak for the BBC and impersonality sounded like neutrality. By contrast, according to the *Sunday Dispatch* in an accurate comment on BBC policy, 'critics consider that women have never been able to achieve the impersonal touch. When there was a triumph or disaster to report they were apt to reflect it in the tone of their voices.'[31]

Regional accents were allowed and encouraged in variety shows, and comedians could always raise a laugh by guying the straight announcer with the posh accent. A Northumberland reader of Basil Maine's broadcasting column in the *Sunday Times* complained of 'the Mayfair dialect . . . rawl for royal, hahr ap for higher up . . . railly quaht for really quiet'.[32]

Perhaps more significant was a point raised by the Wireless League in 1928. While praising 'the BBC's efforts to inculcate a desire for the King's English' the League pointed out that the prohibition of colloquialisms in scripts worked against 'a spontaneous effect'.[33]

Scripting Talks

In fact, to write scripts that sounded spontaneous was a skill that few speakers were able to grasp at first.[34] Hilda Matheson produced H.G. Wells's first talk and tells how, armed with a carefully prepared manuscript, Wells was greeted at his local station by the signalman who promised to listen in that evening. Wells had prepared a talk for an audience he'd imagined as nationwide. On the train he rewrote his script so as to address the signalman. The revised talk was, in Matheson's judgement, brilliantly effective.

Matheson had been brought in by Reith in 1928 to be Head of Talks after the government had at last been persuaded to lift the ban on controversy. Her Bloomsbury connections brought in a host of the Great and the Good, and she resigned on principle when Reith refused to let Harold Nicolson praise Joyce's *Ulysses*.[35]

Controversial or not, all talks had to be scripted. This precaution gave the BBC more control.

> 'In some stations,' Reith had written to Station Directors in 1924, 'I see periodically men down to speak whose status, either professionally or socially and whose qualifications to speak, seem doubtful. It should be an honour in every sense of the word for a man to speak from any broadcasting station, and only those who have a claim to be heard above their fellows on any particular subject in the locality should be put on a programme.'[36]

With a policy of this kind, and with an insistence on scripts, even for discussions, speakers were not surprisingly drawn from a narrow range of class and educational background. But even the carefully controlled output of Talks was lost to the National Programme's audience when the Department was disbanded in 1935 as part of Reith's clean-up in the approach to the government's Ullswater Committee which would advise whether or not to renew the BBC's Licence for a further ten years from 1937.

It was different, however, in the Regions, especially North Region, the Siberia to which Reith had banished the left-wing producer, E.A. Harding, after embarrassing complaints about one of his programmes. Harding recruited a group of talented writers and performers who included Joan Littlewood and Ewan McColl. Their work more faithfully attempted to bring working-class culture and voice to the microphone. Here at the edge of the BBC's empire there was less distance between producers and listeners. If it was the business of the BBC regions 'to express the everyday life of the region, its daily work, its past, its attitude of mind, and above all the quality of the people', as Grace Wyndham Goldie wrote in 1939,[37] then what was broadcast in the North was a truer reflection of that audience, less the paternalistic mediation of the London-based National Programme.

The different programme ingredients of the National Programme make a revealing statement of the broadcasters' 'sociocultural universe' and speak volumes about how they conceived of the audience as a whole.[38] What was not broadcast is equally significant, and in the BBC's case grew in significance as the popularity of commercial conceptions of popular entertainment, available from abroad in Radio Luxembourg (from 1934) and Radio Normandy, forced the BBC to revise its own.

Listening: the Cultural and Political Context

How did all this strike the listeners? The relations between the first broadcasters and their audiences were important in structuring a pattern that was to last for many decades. Once set it was a pattern sustained by corporate and bureaucratic precedent and reproduced by countless habits and assumptions embedded in the professional practices of broadcasters and the day-to-day lives of listeners.

Inevitably other contemporary forms of public cultural exchange influenced the way the first listeners were addressed and in their turn responded. The cinema, the theatre and opera, the variety playhouse, the lecture and the concert hall had established traditions and created expectations. The popular press, broadcasting's competitor in the news field, had become successful in organising the popularity of sporting events, and royal and state occasions whose presentation for public consumption was the very stuff of their business, and on which broadcasting felt compelled to eavesdrop. In time, broadcasting was to fill out this calendar with outside broadcasts from theatres, churches, concert halls, stadiums and streets, orchestrating the celebration of a 'single corporate national life available to all'.[39] The 'imagined community', in Benedict Anderson's phrase,[40] became a public that was national.

The broadcasting relationship with the audience must also be seen as part of that process of privatisation which, for increasing millions in industrialised Europe and North America, instated the home as source and symbol, of leisure, a refuge which turned mass consumption into a private and family experience. In this context, the wireless set took its place with the phonograph, the refrigerator and the motor car as symbols of success. The process was to continue, as we shall see in Chapter 5, in the relative affluence of working class families in 1950s Britain.

The classes which aspired to and could afford these status symbols, the Babbits of middle America and the cosy married couples of the Punch cartoon, *c.*1930, were important targets of state and capital in the period which saw the start of broadcasting.

War in Europe had shaken the system of inherited wealth and privilege on which society rested. The Russian revolution stood as an uncomfortable reminder of the power of organised labour when provoked by autocratic rule. Having failed to crush the new Soviet government by military means, the Western capitalist countries turned inwards to put their own houses in order, struggling to maintain economic stability and increase domestic wealth as an insurance against civil unrest. The beginnings of broadcasting, the moment when, as we have seen, the medium was prised from the hands of the military by corporate interest and amateur enthusiasm, must be seen against a background in which Western governments understood that the leadership of the dominant socio-cultural order had to be won by consent, not force: 'when you have the mind, why bother to chop off the head?'[41]

Listening: the Domestic Context

In the early days the voices and sounds that were plucked from the airwaves had a quality of magic about them. They seemed to float in like free spirits summoned by the hands and ears that tuned the receiver. Filson Young, who later was hired by the BBC as their resident radio critic, wrote in 1924 of his 'little magic cabinet by means of which on the manipulation of certain knobs and plugs, I am nightly in communication with the wonders or inanities of the ether.'[42]

In some ways, this illusion of listener control had substance: the haphazard growth in the understanding of radio transmission and propagation meant that broadcasters were often not at all clear how far their messages reached and therefore what was the extent and nature of their audiences. There was, too, more nearly an equality of status and technical system between senders and receivers so that the latter felt themselves to be free agents in control of what they heard. Brecht's dream of connecting listeners rather than isolating them was (as it still is) perfectly feasible.[43]

At home, as in the studios, men were usually in control of the technology, for the construction of wireless sets and their constant adaptation and improvement quickly became a popular and well-promoted male hobby. Before the ownership of sets became commonplace, group listening was common.

A Programme Report for the BBC Board in 1926 noted that loudspeaker listening, 'now increasing rapidly', resulted in less concentration by listeners than by those using headphones.[44] Nevertheless, 'air-fishing' for distant stations and the ingenuities associated with teasing signals from a 'cat's whisker' gave way to valve technology and the loudspeaker, as the BBC for its part extended the service and became more efficient in its transmission. Under Reith's regime, listeners were expected to be discriminating, to switch off rather than to listen 'on tap', to make dates with their favourite programmes. 'Don't expect broadcasting to entertain you all the time,' pleaded C.A. Lewis. 'After all, there are many other diversions! . . . Familiarity breeds contempt.'[45] This advice, as Scannell has pointed out, misunderstood the characteristics of the medium, treating radio as an *occasional* resource like the theatre or the cinema. Always on tap, like a domestic utility, it eventually exerted its own logic of continuous flow.[46]

Audience Feedback

The BBC itself and the *Radio Times* received voluminous correspondence which was noted and replied to, even if not always acted on – although most contained favourable comment. Occasionally there were broadcast appeals for response. Val Gielgud, later to become Head of Drama made one in 1924:

> We have to admit we are hideously in the dark, for we simply cannot know what sort of listeners have liked most, or what sort of plays listeners most wish to hear. Most listeners belong to that great majority of average opinion who feel, it is rather self-assertive to write letters to a public body like the BBC.

Gielgud received 12 726 letters in answer to this; only 323 were critically adverse. Generally they were supportive of the conventional rather than the avant-garde in radio drama production. Gielgud concluded that 'The play listening audience is not by any means confined to one class, for my correspondents ranged from deep-sea fishermen and factory hands at one end of the scale to retired Brigadier-Generals at the other.'[47] Whether such methods reached 'the great majority of average opinion' is another matter.

Kenneth Baily, writing in the *Radio Pictorial* in April 1937, made
the point that

> A large section of the audience never writes letters at all.
> Another large section is under the impression that it is useless to
> write. The section of the population which is not really a
> letter-writing one is at the same time the one which values
> broadcasting probably more than any other kind of entertain-
> ment or knowledge.[48]

Listener Organisations

A number of listener organisations were active till the end of the
1920s. The Wireless League and the Radio Association both had
local branches which gathered criticisms and ideas and tried to
exert pressure on the BBC. The Wireless League gave evidence to
the Crawford Committee, suggesting ways in which the BBC
Governing Board could be more democratically representative of
the listening public. Their suggestions were not taken up, and the
fact that Crawford's recommendations *were* implemented took
away the main purpose of the organisations.[49] It was not until 1937
that the BBC instituted audience research.[50] To have undertaken a
deliberate polling of views, such as the *Daily Mail* attempted in a
ballot of its readers in 1927, would have told the BBC what the
public wanted. The Corporation did not need the *Daily Mail* to tell
it that the answer was dance music and variety. It was precisely for
this reason that Reith was not in the business of giving the public
what it wanted: 'Few know what they want, and very few what
they need . . . Better to overestimate the mentality of the public
than underestimate it.'[51]

Britain: A Tradition of Public Service

Reith's personal contribution to the founding principles of the
BBC has been well documented and rightly emphasised. But while
his style was idiosyncratic, his general approach was not untypical
of the public servant of his day and the staff he recruited were
drawn from the same educational and social background as those

who still 'served' the peoples of an Empire. Burns comments that the BBC 'was developed under Reith into a kind of domestic diplomatic service, representing the British – or what he saw as the best of the British – to the British'.[52] Young and overwhelmingly male, they were described by Matheson as including

> a high proportion of those who served in the war but who, often on account of some awkward versatility, or of some form of fastidiousness, idealism or general restlessness, never settled down to any humdrum profession after the war was over.[53]

Lionel Fielden, one of this first cohort, talks of 'the same feeling of dedication and hope which had characterised the League of Nations in its earliest days.'[54]

Before long, this dash and dedication settled down to be codified in a professionalism which turned its back on the cosy relationship which Eckersley enjoyed with his first audience and expected the listeners to take their listening seriously. In his study of the modern BBC Burns has convincingly shown that an aloofness from clients' wishes and a corresponding diagnosis of needs, irrespective of expressed wishes or demand, is the hallmark of a certain type of service professional. Broadcasters share the claim to know 'what the public needs' with, for example, the medical and legal professions, where success and reputation are mediated through the judgement of professional colleagues, not of clients. This was broadly the attitude adopted by the BBC from the start and it has remained an enduring legacy of Reith's time.

Summary

We have traced the means by which the early BBC distanced itself from its audiences both geographically and culturally. We have seen how from a local and regional service the BBC changed into a national one which purveyed an elite culture with the avowed intention of converting the masses to it. This period was the heyday of the public service model, and as we shall see the war was the catalyst which led to change. Nevertheless it was during these pre-war days that the public service model became firmly established and although it has been modified it remains influential as the basis on which British and other broadcasting systems have been founded for half a century.

It is possible to trace public service broadcasting's antecedents back to the way in which the telegraphs were run on both sides of the Atlantic: public utilities in Europe and private in the US. From the very beginning of broadcasting there were two implicitly (though by no means necessarily) opposed models. Most Western broadcasting has tended to focus around these two poles both of which in their purest forms have positioned the audience as receivers rather than transmitters. Later in the book we shall be considering an approach which questions this positioning and attempts to instate the audience as subject-participant. First, we look at the response of the public service model to commercial pressure and some of its consequent modifications.

Chapter 5

Catering for Calibans: The BBC's Response to Competition

It is only by commercial competition that the BBC's version of public service broadcasting has been significantly dented. This chapter will examine two moments of change in BBC radio when the Corporation had to bow to popular demand. It will discuss the changing conceptions of the audience occasioned by war and post-war affluence in an attempt to locate and explain the two major structural changes in BBC network radio. In 1939/40 the BBC reacted to criticism from an independently formed collectivity – the British Expeditionary Force – by researching tastes and changing programmes accordingly. In the 1960s the recognition by others of the marketing possibilities of a relatively affluent market segment, the youth market, persuaded the BBC to move to 'generic radio'. In both cases the audiences had the model of commercial radio with which to compare the BBC's output.

The BBC in Wartime

We have seen how the First World War gave a boost to the development of radio, and it is often assumed that the Second World War 'popularised' the BBC. Certainly the BBC softened the rather severe paternalism of its early days, but the process started earlier, in the later 1930s, in the increased awareness, demanded by producers and supplied by the first research, of the differentiated needs and tastes in the audience.[1] Nevertheless the

71

war certainly concentrated the minds of BBC programme-makers on the needs of a new type of audience and weaned them away from the idea that radio was essentially a home-based medium.

The BBC's role in wartime had been considered by a committee in 1938 which assumed that listeners needed 'news . . . official statements and instruction of all sorts'.[2] Entertainment and other programmes were not completely ruled out, but they were to take a back seat. Later committees conceived of audience needs in a slightly different way and looked at programming form the point of view of 'the maintenance of public morale'. The Regional Service was to be closed down in case its localised transmitters inadvertently aided enemy aircraft as direction-finders.

After the rapid fall of Poland to the Nazi forces in September 1939, the first months of the war saw very little activity: this was the so-called 'phoney war'. The BBC doubled the number of news bulletins, official announcements proliferated, and Ministers broadcast pep talks. While the BBC did what it saw as its duty, air-raid precautions enforced the shut-down of theatres, cinemas and concert halls. This officially imposed gloom soon attracted criticism from listeners and the press who argued that if all other forms of entertainment were to be forbidden and people forced to stay at home, the least the BBC could do was to provide some diversion.

But it was not only the lack of entertainment on the radio which was causing concern, it was the quality of the information which was being broadcast. There were two problems: first, the fact that there wasn't much to report, and, secondly, the attitude of the Ministry of Information, which, as is so often the case with ministries bearing that title, saw its main task as restricting the flow of information. Changes were made between October and December 1939, reaching what Briggs calls an 'acceptable pattern' in the last four weeks of the year.

The news department had to deal with complaints from the Foreign Office as well as the Ministry of Information and tried to convince both of them of the need for the BBC to retain its integrity. (Nevertheless, news editors were, as a result, cautious about using the medium to its full effect, for example in the use of actuality recordings.[3])

The public was prepared to accept that sometimes information had to be witheld. Its main concern, however, focused on the overall mix of programmes. The press campaign against the BBC's output in the first weeks of the war prompted the BBC's Control Board to agree that 'we shall need guidance from Listener Research even more urgently than in time of peace'.[4]

Listener Research

The BBC had set up a Listener Research Unit in 1936. One reason for this development – and the new approaches which resulted – was the competition provided by commercial radio. Two independent surveys in 1935 showed 61 per cent of set-owning families listened to commercial radio. The following year another survey claimed that Radio Normandy was followed by a morning audience of 400 000 households and 750 000 in the evening, 900 000 listened to Paris, and just under a million to Radio Luxembourg.[5]

Soon after the start of the war the British Expeditionary Force had crossed the Channel to help the French defend their Maginot Line against Germany, and in the calm that was to last until May 1940, the authorities were concerned that there was very little to occupy the troops' spare time. They listened to the radio, and their listening was not confined to the BBC. Although Radio Luxembourg had closed down at the outbreak of war, Radio Internationale, broadcasting from Fécamp, managed from London and with J. Walter Thompson handling its advertising, kept up a lively service directed to the BEF until after Christmas 1939. When the BBC started an experimental programme in January 1940 its planners found that their programmes were being compared unfavourably with Radio Internationale.

> 'Depraved as the taste of the soldier may be' The Chief of the Imperial General Staff wrote to the BBC, 'he knows what he wants and I can give you my opinion that such a programme as that in *The Radio Times* of January 30th will not satisfy him.'[6]

Other generals joined in the criticism and the BBC sent one of its former public relations officers, A.P. Ryan, to tour the camps and billets and find out what the troops thought of what they heard. Thus the accident of war presented the BBC with a sociological gift, a unique chance to study group listening as an extension of their new listener research. Nothing like it had been attempted since Mary Somerville toured the schools of Kent in 1924, and the outcome was to be equally significant.

Listening in the Ranks

Ryan's report made it quite clear that if programmes were to be shaped by the same policies as in peacetime, they would fail. 'The troops won't mind if a proportion of good serious stuff is included in their programme out of deference to policy views as to what constitutes good balance. They won't mind – *and they won't listen.*'[7] The reaction of this captive sample allowed the BBC planners at last to grasp the circumstances in which their programmes were received. Whereas they had imagined the audience was 'listening in', they now began to learn that most people were neither able nor willing to devote the kind of attention that many of the programmes demanded. Radio, they were beginning to learn, was used as background in many situations.

This 'sample' was to a large extent a 'citizen's army' – the same citizen's army which is thought to have been at the root of the political changes which happened after the war. It was made up of men who would not normally have chosen to enlist, less bound than regulars by regimental commitment, more ready to laugh at authority whenever they got the chance. Listening to the radio in groups in their off-duty periods, they tended to be critical of the programmes as a way of reaffirming group identity. They certainly constituted a thoughtful, often vociferous audience for the BBC's first experiment in popular programming. What had proved significant was that the collectivity in question was characterised by a coherence and self-consciousness which till then no peacetime audience had possessed. It had also heard commercial radio and thus had separate standards by which to judge the BBC's output.

The BBC could not, and did not ignore the messages it received from correspondents in the forces. Many of them sound patronising to modern ears, and frequently also betray a surprise at the perceptiveness of 'the men'. Some in the BBC realised that these comments might apply to civilian audiences too. The Forces Programme was the result. From mid-February 1940 it was put on a regular footing, broadcasting from early in the morning to late at night. It proved very popular both with the army and the general public.

For the war had changed the listening situation of the civilian audience, and programmes such as 'Workers' Playtime' explicitly acknowledged this. The complementary scheduling of the Home and Forces Programmes caused the BBC difficulties: listeners could avoid the talks and features in the Home Service by tuning to the Forces Programme. 'The problem is eased by the fact that whatever the BBC may decide to do, listeners cannot be compelled to listen', admitted the BBC Yearbook.[8]

Here we can see that the paternalism has not entirely disappeared, but it is tempered with a recognition that choice meant that the audience could not be educated as it had supposedly been in the days when the 'brute force of monopoly' was intact. This kind of reasoning together with the figures from audience research helped to dissolve some of the missionary enthusiasm of the pre-war BBC, but the reports from the front pointed towards another lesson: that audiences could listen 'actively'.

The information about the reception of its programmes which was available to the BBC during the war was unique, and during the war the Corporation continued to respond to it.

Wartime Programming: the News

One of the consequences of wartime was that broadcasting became a largely national affair and not surprisingly the most popular programme during the war was the national news. If ever a community of sentiment could be claimed for radio programmes, a time when the listeners might feel that they had some sort of common purpose, it was during the news. The Second World War, in common with many another war is often remembered as a time of unequalled comradeship. It is a sociological commonplace that external conflict increases internal co-operation – a theme to which we shall return when we discuss locality. The mass media have a role to play in giving expression to feelings such as these, and the nation gathering around its radio sets at 9 o'clock every night was one such expression.

Despite the limitations under which it had to operate the BBC news gained a reputation at home and abroad as the most reliable source of information. It gained this reputation in spite of a shaky start in the early days of the war, and perhaps because in those early days when the victories were German and the defeats British and allied, BBC news did not try to deny the bad news. Had the BBC attempted to deny the seriousness of the situation the country faced at the beginning of the war its reputation might not have had the foundations on which to build in the years that followed.

The BBC's wartime reputation was also helped by the fact that German radio was more propagandist, tending to minimise German setbacks and trumpet their victories. It would be naïve to claim that any state broadcasting system would tell the truth during this or any other war, but truth is relative, and the BBC's version was truer than German radio's. For example it has been estimated[9] that during the 'Battle of Britain' the British overstated the number of enemy planes shot down by 55 per cent and the Germans by 234 per cent.

Finally, of course, the BBC was on the right side. Not only was it on the side that won, but much of its broadcasting was aimed at countries occupied by the Nazis where any service that opposed them was assured a sympathetic hearing.

The BBC's wartime news service was crucial to its high post-war reputation, especially overseas, but the Corporation's reputation with the British public depended, as has been indicated already, on other elements in the output.

Wartime Talk

Some of the most popular programmes caused worries either at the Ministry of Information or within the BBC itself. The Brains Trust was after the News, the most popular spoken word programme, consisting of a series of questions which were sent in and put up for discussion by a 'team'. It caused anxiety in both camps, even occasioning a memorandum requesting the programme to 'avoid all questions involving religion, political philosophy or vague generalities'. Questions about whether the team would advocate having a moral philosopher in the cabinet, what conditions were likely to be a year after the war and about the profit motive were all disallowed. Briggs describes the Brains Trust, and ITMA, a comedy show, as 'supremely unofficial'.[10] ITMA (It's that man again), like many popular shows poked fun at the red tape and the acronyms which were such a feature of wartime life, and by refusing to take the BBC or any other bureaucracy seriously endeared itself to its audience.

Another programme which upset some members of the government and the Corporation, but delighted the audience were the talks by the novelist J.B. Priestley. He had as a BBC memo put it 'definite social and political views',[11] and questions were raised as to the influence he wielded in the country. By 1943 the Governors produced a brief for the Minister of Information which proclaimed that 'The policy of the governors is that the microphone is not the place in wartime for persons antagonistic to the war effort.'[12]

Prime Minister Winston Churchill's opposition to discussion of post-war policy and the Beveridge Report (published in 1942, and outlining proposals which became the basis of the welfare state),[13] indicates that the BBC was gagged even on issues which could not be construed as bearing on national security. ITMA might poke fun at wartime red tape and 'His Fatuity the Minister for Social Hilarity', J.B. Priestley, might be allowed his populist commentaries, and the news might tell fewer lies than the opposition, but the state and the BBC itself kept a tight rein on what went out over the air, and reserved a special vigilance for certain issues, as well as certain areas of output.

Wartime Entertainment

The BBC's vigilance in the more narrowly defined area of culture did not relax either, and it had especial problems when the Americans joined the war. The Forces Programme began to include American shows in its light entertainment, and after 1943 AFN could be overheard broadcasting from numerous American bases in Britain. The Director of the General Overseas Service recognised that most British troops liked American records, but Haley, then editor-in-chief, said that 'in the entertainment field it is essential to ensure that the use of . . . American serial broadcasts such as Bob Hope, Jack Benny and other programmes does not become a Frankenstein'.[14]

The Variety Department of the BBC which spent the war in Bangor in North Wales had to suffer much criticism from the uninformed; 'vulgarity', 'filth' and 'tripe' were recurrent themes, usually articulated by people who did not themselves listen to variety. For them, the fact that it was the most popular aspect of BBC programming did not make any difference, the criticisms rested on essentially paternalistic notions of taste and what the public ought to like.

Music was a particular target for this type of criticism. It was not only MPs but BBC staff who felt that there was a need for more 'vigorous' and less 'sentimental' music. A committee was set up to work out a new policy for dance music, and it wanted 'the elimination of crooning, sentimental numbers, drivelling words, slush, innuendos, and so on'.[15] According to Sir Arthur Bliss who had brief spell in charge of music at the BBC

> The ideal method of broadcasting throughout this country would be to have three separate channels. Available for citizens worth fighting for would be two contrasted services. For the Calibans . . . a continual stream of noise and nonsense put on by untouchables with the use of records.[16]

Post-war: the Third Programme

After the war the needs and requirements of the audience were again conceived of in terms of the family and the individual. Apart from programmes such as Worker's Playtime which survived the war, programming did not on the whole recognise that sections of the peacetime audience might form a community of sentiment in a similar way to the forces during the war. The BBC recognised different tastes in terms of high, middle and lowbrow, by the creation after the war of the Third Programme, the Home Service and the Light Programme (in place of the Forces Programme) respectively.

The Third Programme was the pinnacle of that 'cultural pyramid' which Haley, now Director-General, imagined, in a bizarre metaphor, 'slowly aspiring upwards' with the listener 'being induced through the years increasingly to discriminate in favour of the things that are more worthwhile'.[17] At its birth, the Third Programme imbibed the atmosphere of the Oxbridge High Table,[18] reflecting as a result, in the words of one critic, 'a concept of culture more nearly suited to the social structure of Great

Britain in the late eighteenth century than to that of the 1950s'.[19] This concept implied a cultural continuum which had not changed in its essentials from that which informed the pre-war paternalist BBC. It assumed that each member of the audience could be placed, as on a cultural ladder, somewhere on this continuum. It could not conceive of quite different cultural needs or expressions. There were areas of culture which were beneath the bottom rung – jazz and most popular music for example. This essentially linear perception which allowed for progression and improvement on the part of the audience was still a powerful element in the BBC's ideology, making it difficult for it to recognise and deal with the cultural requirements of the generation born just after the war.

The BBC in the 1950s and 1960s

Like the war the 1960s is commonly thought to have been a decade of change in many spheres and BBC radio was forced (there is no other word for it) to respond to the challenge of pirate radio playing non-stop pop music. The underlying changes may be sought, in the previous decade, in the ideas about marketing which were reflected not only in the media and the marketplace but, according to some, in sociological and political thinking during the 1950s.

Between 1951 and 1958 real wages rose by 20 per cent and many more manual workers were starting to buy their own homes. The decline in support for the Labour Party in the same period suggested that affluence was eroding the class-consciousness of a working class which was becoming more home-oriented. Instead of going out to pubs and clubs where class solidarity was renewed people were staying in to watch television or perhaps improve the homes they had bought.

But TV was only one of the diversions which made the people more home-oriented and supposedly middle-class; consumer durables, home improvement and more holidays all played their part. The invasion of new popular cultural forms into public spaces marked the dividing-point between the generations. In a passage in *Uses of Literacy* (written between 1952 and 1956) Richard Hoggart writes of 'the juke-box boys . . . who spend their evenings listening in harshly-lighted milk-bars to the "nickelodeons". . .

The records seem to be changed about once a fortnight by the hiring firm; almost all are American; almost all are "vocals" and the styles of singing much advanced beyond what is normally heard on the Light Programme of the BBC.' Hoggart's disapproving eye had seen the future, precisely if unknowingly recording the trend which was to undermine his treasured BBC.[20]

The campaign for commercial television in the 1950s in the UK has itself been attributed to changes within the Conservative party which led to the erosion of traditional Tory paternalism by a more hard-headed and businesslike approach. According to this thesis the back-benchers who used Selwyn Lloyd's minority report to the Beveridge Committee (1951) to persuade a relatively reluctant government to introduce commercial television were a new breed, coming as they did not from the landowning upper classes, but the commercial middle classes with a stake in the worlds of advertising and public relations.

The Discovery of the Teenage Consumer

By the end of the 1950s, Hoggart's 'juke-box boys' had been spotted by the advertising business and their newly recognised spending power became a force to be reckoned with. In 1959 the London Press Exchange published a short monograph by M. Abrams, one of the pioneers of applied social research in Great Britain. Entitled *The Teenage Consumer*, it set out in a few pages some salient facts about the generation born during and just after the war. Their real earnings compared with just before the war had increased by 50 per cent, and most of this money was spent on entertainment. He noted that teenagers were looking for goods which were, as he put it 'highly charged emotionally'. Their spending, Abrams wrote, 'is distinctive teenage spending for distinctive teenage ends in a distinctive teenage world'.[21]

This market changed rapidly in its composition and its likes and dislikes. At this stage it was distinctively working class and Abrams made an observation which predicted some of the 'working class heroes' who were to emerge in the 1960s:

The aesthetic of the teenage market is essentially a working class aesthetic and probably only entrepreneurs of working class origin will have a 'natural' understanding of the needs of this market.[22]

He also observed that whereas the US market had been catering for this group for some time, the war had not given British industry much experience of it, hence British teenagers had turned to US products.

In this short booklet we can see some of the salient characteristics of popular culture in the 1960s prefigured. Although the idea of the teenager was to become subsumed under the category of youth as the decade advanced, the marketing possibilities, especially in entertainment began to be explored and exploited.

The mass media were of course to assume increasing importance as a vehicle for disseminating popular cultural products, but from the point of view of this book what is striking about *The Teenage Consumer* is that radio isn't mentioned. Most teenage entertainment took place outside the home, so the cinema was very popular, television less so. There were few magazines aimed specifically at the young, and all those mentioned by Abrams were aimed at a female audience, and at the 'bedroom culture' since analysed by Frith.[23]

The Role of Music

Nobody who grew up during the 1960s or since needs convincing of the centrality of popular music during their youth. Of course popular music has played a significant role in the experience of other generations too, but rock 'n roll seems to have been qualitatively different.

All music is evocative in the sense that, like smell it has the capacity to anchor experience and evoke memories in a more direct way than the other, perhaps better-analysed, senses. Popular music especially is uniquely connected to the body through dance and generally associated with youth. But during the 1960s rock 'n roll became much more central to the existence of the young and since then music has become a way of 'fictionalising' everyday life, 'the almost narcotic abuse of sound by the young betrays a desire to make life into fiction'.[24] Rock music became an all-pervasive accompaniment to the lives of young people whatever their class. It was woven into their work and their ideology as well as their leisure: it became the sound track for their lives.[25]

Whereas American radio had been using popular music as its main offering from the beginning, the BBC had not. Rock music was seen as a 'minority' taste rather than something eminently suited to radio, and it took a long time and extraordinary circumstances before the BBC would abandon its notions of what radio ought to be in favour of what an increasingly large and vocal section of its audience wanted it to be.

The rise of rock 'n roll took place about the time battery-operated portable radios and record players became widely available. The transistor radio came on the market at the end of the 1950s. Through the decade the station most young people were listening to was Radio Luxembourg, whose Top Twenty on Sundays nights gave them what the BBC ignored.

Many young people used radio rock as a way of appropriating space in public as well as in private. Young people in modern industrial society need to set themselves apart from their parents both culturally and physically, and since the last world war and until recently their earnings have given them ways of doing that. Music can be used to shut out the home even when in it: the teenage record player is a familiar separating device, and music is of course central to dancing. Music, then, was particularly effective as a barrier, as a form of distinction and cultural identity, and an extra-domestic activity in the context of the home-centered affluent workers' families.

Another factor noted by commentators was that the music of the time, rock and roll, had a different sort of appeal from previous popular music. Laing writes that whereas previous popular songs addressed themselves to each member of the audience individually, early rock music especially addressed the audience collectively giving its young audiences 'a sense of themselves as a group, something enhanced by the hostility towards rock and roll of most older people'.[26]

It has been argued by Frith[27] that rock came to signify various forms of rebellion to different segments of its audience. He suggests that for the middle classes rock was 'a way into working-class adolescence; rock offers the fantasy of a community of risk'[28] and that student culture played a similar role in the lives of the working-class, suggesting the fantasy of a life of self-exploration, art and sex. The power of rock then derives in part from the fact that it can fuse these different fantasies together. The differences in taste within the young audience have become more apparent with time. This is partly because marketing to an undifferentiated mass market is a hit and miss affair (reflected in the term used for successful singles and popularised by the BBC TV programme Jukebox Jury), so any segmentation of that market makes life easier for the producers. However as might be expected any differentiation was blurred in the early days of rock 'n roll. Frith suggests that there was a golden age of teenage music from 1964–7 ending in a moment when pop became rock and the music became a form of expression for all young people: 'rock had become an art form which bound a community'.[29] Thereafter the market showed signs of differentiation into pop which was for the mainstream teenage taste, and rock which was more elaborate and aimed at the middle class/student market.

Frith's golden age was a time when the French government was shaken by an unlikely and (not surprisingly as it turned out) temporary alliance between students and workers, and British and American universities were disrupted by prolonged protests against the perceived undemocratic nature of their structures as well as the war in Vietnam. Rock music formed the (usually loud) background to the activities of young people from the west whether making love at Woodstock or making war in Vietnam.[30]

Above all however the music was and remains associated with opposition, and the conjunction between pirate radio and the rise of rock 'n roll only served to underline the fact that radio itself could become a part of protest. Pirates: the very name they were given by the establishment was romantic and appealing and their blatantly commercial motives were somewhat obscured by their oppositional stance.

The Pirates

The non-commercial BBC may have been slow to respond to the trends foreseen and exploited by advertisers and the market, but others saw the opportunity. One of the pioneers of pirate radio, Ronan O'Rahilly, discovered that the commercial stations and the record companies were (in their own ways) as rigid as the BBC when it came to the new music. Baron[31] recounts how O'Rahilly found that a recording he himself had made of Georgie Fame was rejected by EMI, Decca, Pye and Phillips, and that between them these companies controlled 90 per cent of the record market. He made his own acetate to take to Radio Luxemburg, but discovered that almost all their airtime was taken up by shows sponsored by these same companies. The BBC had one programme a week of popular music, but it concentrated on established artists, so the opportunities for innovation in the UK were severely limited.

O'Rahilly found backers from the UK, Ireland and Switzerland and launched Radio Caroline, a pirate radio station broadcasting from a ship in international waters to the UK mainland. Others were not slow to follow and pirate stations on board ships and offshore installations proliferated in the mid-1960s. By the end of 1965 the pirates had an estimated 15 million listeners tuning in regularly, and an NOP poll in 1966 estimated that 45 per cent of the population listened either to an offshore station or to Radio Luxembourg during any week.

After only 18 months on air, and despite its dubious legal status, Radio Caroline was grossing £750 000 in advertising revenue. Radio London got £200 000 worth of advertising contracts after only two months, and by March 1966 its income was running at about £70 000 per month: pirate radio was clearly a success.

Its success had become an increasing embarrassment to the BBC and to the politicians. As a direct response to the threat in July 1964 the BBC negotiated more 'needle time' with the recording industry and increased its broadcasting hours to cover the late night – early morning hours of the morning period favoured by the young audience, which did not, however, repay the gesture by forsaking the pirates. The Labour government's majority was slender and neither it nor the opposition wanted to alienate young voters. This meant that the 1964 election campaign ignored the issue of the popular but illegal pirates. However the 1966 election did give Labour a larger majority which meant that the government had to bite the bullet and do something about the pirates.

It was helped in this potentially unpopular decision by the piratical behaviour of the pirates. Added to the natural hazards of operating on the high seas which were responsible for damaging and in one case grounding the ships were the extreme methods used by some people operating stations. A fort in the Thames estuary was attacked and stripped of its equipment by a rival group, and following this one of the chief protagonists was shot by another at a cottage in rural Essex.

Another aspect of the pirates' behaviour which did little to endear them to the government of the day especially, and may have disquieted other politicians, was the fact that they had accepted political advertising, at that time unheard of in Britain. As might be expected the pirates were used by Conservative politicians in local elections, and other parties (for example the Scottish National Party) threatened to use them. The pirates had already blotted their copybook with the Labour Party during the 1966 general election because of their anti-Labour stance which was no doubt prompted by the entirely accurate presumption that any Labour government would bring legislation against them.

So, on 14 August 1967, the Maritime etc. Broadcasting (Offences) Act came into force, and it stopped the pirates in their tracks. It became an offence for any Briton to operate broadcasting apparatus without a licence or to arrange for it to be done. It also became illegal to provide any goods to such stations or to take part in broadcasts made by them. The Act could not prevent pirate stations being operated and supplied by nationals from other countries, but it did mean British advertising was denied them.

The pirates had however made the BBC realise that there was a large and important section of the audience which it was ignoring, and they were instrumental in changing the face of British radio. Not only did the BBC have to cater for the demand for popular music, but the pressure for local commercial broadcasting became more organised with the formation of the Local Radio Association in 1964.

The pirates were the recognition in radio terms of the commercial potential of the teenage audience. They had shown that there was money to be made by advertisers and record companies as well as broadcasters. Their very illegality lent them a romantic and rebellious aura which appealed to their young audience and which the BBC could not emulate: as the opposition spokesman on radio, Paul (later Sir Paul) Bryan said 'When the BBC try to imitate this type of programme it is like the Postmaster General (the minister in charge of broadcasting) or myself going to a teenage dance. We should either be too merry or too dull.'

The BBC's Reaction

Apart from the re-scheduling of hours mentioned above, the BBC's first main response was an oblique attack, one which it could be argued eventually resulted in a form of legitimation for commercial radio interests: local radio. This was not an entirely new departure for the BBC, but it seems likely that it was brought out of the cupboard as a diversion from the success of the pirates. The Corporation, through its Director of Radio, Frank Gillard, had carried out a number of experiments in local broadcasting in the early years of the 1960s which had been important in persuading the Pilkington Committee of the need for a full-scale development. The recommendation was not taken up by the government, but local radio assumed prominence a few years later because it was mentioned by the Postmaster General in December 1965 in the context of a Commons attack on the pirates. (For a fuller consideration of local radio see the next chapter.)

Another more direct challenge was mounted the following year in June when the PMG stated that the BBC was considering setting up a new network which would provide continuous light music (the term still reflected the post-war notion of popular music). At the end of 1966 the government issued a White Paper which gave the go-ahead for the BBC to start a network of local stations and to create a popular music network. The new configuration of BBC national radio started operating on 30 September 1967 with Radio 1 as the popular music station.

Radio's Place

It is easy, especially with hindsight to criticise the slowness of the BBC's response to the demand for rock music, but it was not only the corporation which had a rather jaundiced view of the phenomenon as a minority taste. As we have seen the notion of public service demanded that radio serve the whole audience, and young people were a minority of the 'great audience'. In the eyes of the BBC mandarins in the 1950s rock music could be seen as a fad which would die down as its audience aged.

The last time the BBC had reacted to audience demands by making significant changes was during the war. The message from the troops was clear, and the BBC responded. How different were the 1950s teenagers from the BEF. Far from being 'our boys' fighting for us, they were widely regarded as delinquents fighting against society. Furthermore the cultural coherence of the new generation went largely unrecognised at least until the advent of the 'swinging sixties'. Young people and hence their tastes were criticised and marginalised until their commercial potential became more widely recognised. Even when the commercial possibilities of the young were being exploited to the full, BBC radio, insulated as it was against the commercial world did not feel compelled to respond.

As a result, to the young, the BBC's image seemed more and more staid. The BBC was often referred to as 'Auntie' and was seen as part of what was referred to as 'the establishment' during the 1960s. Even though BBC television of the period produced a good few of the cultural landmarks which typify the 1960s, radio's reluctance to join in the fun helped to maintain that image. Even when it finally capitulated and produced 'Wonderful Radio One', the pop music channel, many felt that it was simply an act, auntie trying to be trendy, and all a bit embarrassing really.

Proponents of the free market might want to argue that it was commercial competition which forced the BBC to change, but it is not quite that simple. Certainly Fécamp and the pirates provided British audiences with a taste of a different kind of radio more oriented to popular music, but the coherence of those audiences was also significant.

As we have seen the BBC initially saw the audience as clay to be moulded rather than a market to be exploited. The idea was that the audience should adapt to the programmes rather than the other way round. During the Second World War radio broadcasting came into its own with most people reliant on radio for up-to-date news of what was happening. The war followed closely on the establishment of audience research, and the BEF provided a captive audience. The BBC soon learned that its serious diet was universally disliked and it took particular trouble to find out what was wanted by a nation at war.

It was the combination of the Calibans and their exploitation by commercial radio which prompted the major changes in BBC programmes. During the war and in the 1960s the BBC was confronted with audiences whose tastes it could not ignore.

Public service broadcasting emerged in a new guise. Public service ideals influenced the structure of local radio and eventually made it difficult to create a viable commercial system. In the end however it was commercial local radio which helped to indicate some of the flaws in the notion of local radio. We therefore need to examine the idea of local radio and its operation in the UK to see how it came about and why it has not worked in the way it was intended to work.

Chapter 6

Serving Neighbourhood and Nation: British Local Radio

While the BBC had been obliged for some decades to take account of a demand for a more popular style and content in radio, the 1960s saw an intensification of commercial pressure on European broadcasting systems as a whole, along with, as one commentator has noted, trends towards specialisation, decentralisation and democratisation.[1] In this chapter we examine the hopes and realities of British local radio, and analyse the rhetoric that accompanied its beginnings and justified its subsequent adaptation to changed circumstances.

The History

It is not an easy history to uncover. Partly, this is because there is no account, official or otherwise, that foregrounds radio, includes both BBC and Independent Local Radio (ILR), and charts the succession of opportunities, promises and disappointments surrounding the medium.[2] The managers of radio, not usually themselves in control of events since power passed to television, have nevertheless colluded in a rewriting of history that justifies the present arrangements at any particular time. For most of the period in question, television was the focus of public attention while for successive governments issues relating to broadcasting and communications rarely pushed their way on to the agenda.

Within the BBC, radio was subordinate to television, and local radio, 'set up in idealism and run on enthusiasm', as one Managing Director of Radio admitted, rated lowest of all. Wheeled out to help dress the rhetoric of localism when occasion demanded, it was at best forgotten, at worst cut and diluted. On the commercial side, compromise and arrested development have limited the medium's appeal to advertisers.

Yet the 'localness' of local radio has always been part of its appeal. In an age of big business and increasing centralisation in government, there is ideological mileage in the idea of locality. Certainly local radio brought the BBC closer to the people, and helped justify the claim 'serving neighbourhood and nation'.[3] Commercial radio spoke to many of the same concerns by, as it put it 'serving the community', or, in another slogan, providing 'public service without public expenditure'. The idea of service and the connotations of unity carried in words such as 'nation', 'neighbourhood' and 'community' serve to underline the fact that local radio was conceived of as part of public service broadcasting.

'Community' itself in this history exemplifies the 'struggle for the sign'. Harnessed to the cause of local radio in the early days, it was then contested by the community radio movement which introduced the idea of 'community of interest'. That variant was built into the language of the cancelled Home Office experiment but finally in the 1987 Green Paper community was elided, without discussion, with small-scale commercial radio. In the following sections we argue that the conception of local radio which has governed the formation of both networks is both sociologically and commercially suspect.

The Meaning of Community

Discussion of the meaning of community has become a minor industry among sociologists, but in the context of local radio has attracted less attention. Community, as one of us has remarked elsewhere[4] is something of a weasel word used to mean all things to all people, and it requires some examination.

The association of community with locality is a relatively new idea.[5] In part it can be attributed to a nearly universal longing for the supposed certainties of a past (usually rural) society where loyalty, belief and kin provided a shield against the wickedness of the wide world. The enduring ties in this ideal community were the basis for mutual help and understanding, and the community looked after its own. The type of community this ideal draws on is one where everybody is engaged in a main (usually primary) industry, and the modern industrial or post-industrial equivalent is often the mining community where generations stay in the same village to work down the pit. In such contexts a degree of solidarity is exhibited which is remarkable in industrial societies, and which is held to be a mark of the thriving community. This particular type of romanticism, noted by successive sociological commentators,[6] has equated the basis for the sense of solidarity (primary industry located in one place) with the notion of community, and the association has been reinforced by the community studies tradition. In the UK at least this tradition predated the documentary film movement in its presentation of the facts of working class life to the middle classes. Rowntree and his successors who documented the life of the poor in London and York illuminated that solidarity in the face of poverty which is the hallmark of community.

The Second World War recreated a sense of community: the common enemy helped to paper over some of the divisions created by class but could not hide the fact that it was a single class that had had to endure the poverty and disease of the slums. The politics of the post-war period and the rebuilding of bombed cities attempted to recreate this sense of community by bringing together a variety of social and income groups. As has frequently been noted,[7] however, much of this sense of community derives from the insider versus the outsider. Mutual help and a sense of belonging spring more from common overarching aims than from geographical proximity, whether 'natural' or created.

It was in this post-war period that community studies flourished. Young and Willmott's classic study *Family and Kinship in East London*[8] celebrated the mutual help and community feeling of the Londoners who had braved the blitz and showed how rehousing threatened this community. Such studies tended by their nature to be geographically restricted, and in spite, or perhaps because of them, the idea of community remained wedded to locality, even when the social divisions within these areas were uncovered.

Once those divisions did become clear, the search for explanation led sociologists to look at the distribution of power and property within the communities they were studying. The realities of class divisions in localities where people no longer worked in primary industries, but commuted to work in service industries has, since the 1960s, led to a more realistic notion of modern geographical communities. A good example of this can be found in the rural communities which provide such a powerful symbol of the myth of community. The rural village is for many the ideal tight-knit community, but as agriculture has become less labour intensive, empty housing in the villages has been bought up by the middle class service industry workers searching for the world they think they have lost. Two consequences further undermine the old ties: the local working class is unable to compete for the housing and has to move away, destroying the historical continuity which is part of the notion of community solidarity; and the newcomers' view of the locality as a site for leisure comes in conflict with farming interests for whom it is a factor of production.[9]

Nevertheless outside sociological circles the equation between localness and a sense of community went largely unquestioned. Radio was appropriating the myth for its own purposes at the very time (the 1960s) when sociologists had the ammunition to explode it.

Radio and 'Community'

After the war the BBC was closely associated with the community feeling created by conflict. Yet both the introduction of the Forces Programme in 1940, and of the Third Programme in 1946 were recognition of separate 'taste publics' needing to be served. The separations were confirmed in the post-war Home/Light/Third arrangement, and Jean Seaton has shown how this parallels the equally reactionary implementation of the tri-partite school system designed by the 1944 Education Act. Interestingly, that famous piece of legislation has enjoyed the same mythic reputation as the BBC's wartime record, but with hindsight can be seen as representing 'a new recognition of class and the fragmentation of culture'.[10]

Next came the Beveridge Report of 1951 which, as we have seen, made proposals for local radio. The Conservative government which inherited the Beveridge recommendations was finally persuaded to concentrate on the introduction of commercial television, and, as a result, radio development languished. By the time the Pilkington Committee came to consider radio in 1962,[11] three successive Conservative election victories and the commercial success of ITV had encouraged a lobby for commercial radio. With a Committee highly critical of commercial television this lobby counted for less than the BBC's concrete plan for 250 stations, backed by recent successful experiment. The Conservative government, its political credibility weakening in the last period of Macmillan's leadership, chose to ignore Pilkington's local radio proposals, concentrating instead on strengthening the ITA to curb what Pilkington saw as the excesses of ITV, and giving the BBC the responsibility of developing a second TV channel (BBC 2).

With ITV temporarily in bad odour and the political tide running Labour's way – in October 1964 Harold Wilson won the General Election – the commercial radio lobby judged that a national profile might meet too much opposition, and it coalesced as the *Local* Radio Association. Though the Conservatives in opposition gave tacit support to the pirates, the LRA did not want to be associated with illegality or rampant commercialism and capitalised on a climate which favoured decentralisation and the reassertion of local and regional culture. The success of the BBC's closed circuit experiments had helped to create the climate for local radio, and the commercial lobby saw it as an ideological flag of convenience. In the long run this ideological cover was to create economic problems for ILR network, but in the shorter term up until its creation in the early 1970s the notion of localism with all its connotations proved very useful.

Ironically this also was the very period when, as we have seen, other cultural and economic realities were asserting themselves. In national radio terms one of the most significant divisions was to be by age, not geography. Whilst radio was being fixed into a local mould, at least part of its audience, and an important part, was already defining itself in terms which had little to do with locality and more to do with common interests.

Pilkington on Local Radio

What reinforced the direction local radio took was the thinking in the Pilkington Report. As so often happens in reports of this kind, though its structural recommendations were ignored, its philosophy was taken on board. It is worth looking more closely at the steps by which Pilkington reached a conclusion in favour of public service broadcasting at local level.

The Committee found no evidence of great public demand for local radio, adding in a much quoted aside, 'Yet, if people do not know what they are missing, they cannot be said not to want it.'[12] Its own definition distinguished between a large number of stations serving one locality and a situation where 'the material broadcast by a local station would, for a sufficient part of the broadcasting day, be of particular interest to the locality served by that station rather than to other localities'. The latter, it thought, was the right definition of local broadcasting. It followed that local programming would grow out of the life of the community, but such material, the Committee forecast, would be unlikely to fill the broadcasting day. There would be need for 'fill-in' material, provided from central sources and then networked. The BBC could switch into its other networks, but for commercial local radio this would raise the possibility of local companies becoming affiliates of a network. Further, the report noted that, since recorded music would be the most likely 'fill-in' material, the cost of providing it would be a difficulty for small companies.

As far as advertising revenue was concerned, Pilkington was emphatic: the need to deliver an audience to the advertiser conflicted with the provision of the kind of broadcasting it deemed suitable for local radio. Under the BBC, 'since the service would be financed from licence revenue, there would be no obligation, express or implied, to pursue any objective other than that of the public service'.[13]

That Pilkington took any notice at all of local radio was due to Frank Gillard's persistence.[14] In its support for a BBC approach, as well as in its notion of what today would be called access broadcasting we can trace the results of his research in America and the closed-circuit experiments of the late 1950s. Pilkington's emphasis on the importance of ensuring that local organisations should play a full part in local broadcasting is echoed in a BBC document *Local Radio in the Public Interest* which expected that 'a great many new programme forms and techniques would quickly emerge, based on community participation'.[15] Universities, the churches and Citizens' Advice Bureaux would prepare their own programmes and bring them to the studio as packages. BBC staff would spend time training volunteers and the stations would provide transmission facilities. The BBC would have final editorial control, but, as the document says 'there is no particular mystique about the making of simple radio programmes'.

The BBC was finally allowed to start local radio following the Labour government's 1966 White Paper.[16] Thus UK local radio was born at a time when contemporary limitations on frequencies allowing only one service per locality meant that local radio had also to carry the baggage of public service which demanded that the whole audience be catered for. At the same time a climate of political decentralisation was conveniently harnessed to the shortage of frequencies to result in a local radio network with a commitment to serve the whole audience in a locality rather than different interests within it.

The Realities of BBC Local Radio

There are a number of reasons why, in the BBC's case, the original hopes for local radio were not fulfilled.

(1) The BBC, its options genuinely restricted by a shortage of frequencies, handicapped by some mistaken technical decisions early on, was above all restricted in budget – as a *whole* through the increasing extent to which it had to rely on government to raise the licence fee, and *within* the BBC by radio's poor status relative to television.

(2) After the initial period, it was BBC headquarters in London calling the tune, deciding the location of stations, allocating budgets and dealing cuts. Once when it mattered, London axed Durham (in the teeth of local opposition) and created Carlisle. And it was to London – and the glamour of television – that many local radio staff aspired.[17] To the distribution of power between centre and periphery must be added other factors which inhibited the fulfilment of local radio's promise as originally foreseen in the BBC's *Local Radio in the Public Interest*.

(3) The dominance of the newsroom in BBC local stations, and the importance attached to them by top BBC management (itself journalistic in background) as a potential source for national news. Journalistic ideology is at odds with the kind of community access foreseen in 1966.

(4) The agreements made nationally with broadcasting unions and holders of music rights both tied the hands of local managers and severely restricted the needletime available to them. On the union side, management's frequent threats and actual implementation of cuts created an understandable attitude of suspicion towards community access as a form of cheap labour.

(5) Whenever the BBC made cuts, local radio suffered disproportionately. For example the reduction of output by 25 per cent ordered in 1979 and the 10 per cent cuts of 1988/9 had the effect of closing down most of the evening access programming supervised by staff but produced, in the words of the 1966 document, by 'responsible local groups'. In, addition, the 1988–9 cuts resulted in the disappearance of posts in non-news areas like education and community programmes, provoking strong union protests.[18]

(6) 'The manager has the authority to decide what he broadcasts, so long as it is within the limits of his budget and the framework of the BBC's general policies.'[19] The language of a 1979 publicity leaflet is revealing. In vain for the BBC to protest that its station managers have autonomy when a system of recruitment and promotion[20] is designed to ensure that senior managers do not 'go native'.

Nevertheless, for a time in the mid 1970s, there were some encouraging initiatives within the BBC from the point of view of small-scale local radio. Some of these, like similar moves on the IBA's side,[21] were inspired both by the existence of the Annan Committee (1974–7), and by the need in the period after the publication of its Report[22] to make gestures that would win the favour of the Labour government.

In 1977, the BBC borrowed a mobile transmitter unit from Radio Telefis Eireann which had been using it in Ireland since 1974 in a regular programme of one- or two-week visits to rural communities. The BBC used the unit for a brief period in North Wales for VHF transmissions in Welsh. Sales of VHF receivers leapt and the success of the experiment showed that listening on VHF can be popularised given sufficient incentive. The next year, 1978, BBC Radio Wales used a low-powered medium-wave unit to tour four English-speaking locations. The response here too was enthusiastic but an important difference between the RTE and BBC operations was that RTE handed over editorial control to a local committee formed at a public meeting some three months before the mobile unit's scheduled arrival. The BBC staff retained control of their broadcasting. Subsequently, two opt-out stations were set up, Radio Clwyd and Radio Gwent.[23]

In Scotland, from 1977, the BBC created opt-outs, broadcasting a few hours a week in Orkney, Shetland and the Hebrides, the latter financed in partnership with the Western Isles Development Council. Each station used studios built at a tenth of the cost of standard-sized BBC local radio stations, and these operations have continued on a permanent basis.

In England, temporary arrangements allowed BBC Radio Bristol to set up a flood emergency service in Taunton Town Hall in the winter of 1977/8,[24] while for two and a half years a small Oxfordshire town, Thame, was allowed to contribute a regular half-hour weekly programme to BBC Radio Oxford.[25]

London

The huge size of London, with a population bigger than some European countries, has always created a special problem for BBC local radio. After the arrival of Capital and LBC in 1973, Radio London made a poor showing against the commercial opposition, though to some extent this was due to the station's patchy medium-wave coverage. Audience share was worst of all. BBC local stations (2.3 per cent in 1981[26]), and the first of a number of internal studies was commissioned in 1978 to investigate community radio possibilities in the capital, while the former Radio 1 DJ, Tony Blackburn was imported to boost the daytime ratings.[27]

The 1978 report, leaked early in 1979 was found to recommend a six-month experiment in which a BBC mobile unit should visit locations for two weeks at a time to prepare four days broadcasting from each. Alternative recommendations were for a city-wide station for the black and Asian communities and that the BBC should, in the wake of interest aroused by the mobile unit, give encouragement to independent, non-profit-making community radio stations in the form of provision of sustaining service, training, engineering advice and secondment of BBC staff.[28] No more

was heard of the report, though the last recommendation surfaced
in modified form in a proposal made later in the year at Edinburgh
by Aubrey Singer, BBC Managing Director of Radio, that a third
tier of community radio should be created.[29]

This proposal marked the limit of BBC interest in small-scale
radio. Thereafter the Conservative election victory shifted the
bargaining power within Whitehall's HOLRWP (see Chapter 2) to
the IBA and brought the Authority a lion's share of the frequencies. These enabled the IBA to set up twice the number of
stations compared to the BBC while the latter was compelled to
tailor the coat to fit the cloth with its 'county radio' conception
which had the effect of enlarging the coverage area of the system
as a whole.

So, where London was concerned, the BBC lost a chance to
sidestep in an innovative way the problem of the hugeness of its
coverage area. Some years later it again demonstrated that its
London station was too close to the centre to be really adventur-
ous: in 1985, another Managing Director's working party failed to
go through with a recommendation to turn Radio London into a
women's station.[30]

Meanwhile the black and Asian communities in London, about
to suffer more than any others from the harsh Thatcher climate,
were to become increasingly critical of their marginalisation in the
media – Radio London's Black Londoners, for all its increase in
hours, simply illustrated its critics point about 'ghetto' slots. The
interest in community radio was to pass to the GLC.

The Contradictions of Commercial Localism

The Pilkington Committee had felt that commercial radio would
be incompatible with public service broadcasting as the committee
understood and defined it. Looked at from the point of view of the
marketing or advertising executive a similar conclusion can be
reached. Whereas public service broadcasting starts off with an
idea of what the public needs, and recognises (indeed some would
say capitalises upon) the fact that it is difficult to find out what
audiences want, marketing tries to define a target audience. Modern marketing is used to design and redesign products so that they
appeal to consumers, and companies take care to research market

needs before launching new products. In the limiting case, public broadcasting starts with the product – the type of output it ought to produce – modern marketing with the market or the consumer, and the difference is crucial. Public service broadcasting is in the business of selling programmes (programmes which inform, educate and entertain) to audiences, commercial broadcasting in the business of selling audiences to advertisers.

If one is in the business of selling audiences, they too need to be packaged. If marketing planners have done their work properly they should have identified a particular market segment for their product, and what they are looking for is a medium which will deliver that segment to them. Some products for the mass market simply need to be advertised to the largest number of people possible, but there is a vast range of products where the market is more accurately identified. If a market is big enough it is often catered for by specialist magazines, and the launch of new technology such as home computers usually sees the birth (and often swift death) of a plethora of magazines which carry advertising for these products. In between these two extremes of the mass market and the product-defined medium there are a series of possible niches for commercial media, but increasingly they must be defined by the market, that is the audiences they can deliver to the advertisers.

Notions such as the 'great audience' and the unified nation which were current before, during and just after the Second World War helped to shape British broadcasting and they continue to influence, some would say hamper, its development. Much of the sociological, political and commercial evidence indicates that even if this notion of unification was ever more than a hegemonic myth, it no longer makes sense for any practical purposes to see Britain (or indeed any other advanced industrial society) in those terms.

Although the broadcasting planners of the late 1960s were convinced of the necessity of responding to stratification by age, radio has not been allowed to make itself much more discriminating in the audiences it attracts. The fact that the first commercial radio in Britain was local radio ensured that its commercial viability would be limited. Locality as it was defined only ever accidentally made sense in marketing terms and local advertisers had a tradition of using the local press. In contrast to many other countries, Britain introduced commercial radio *after* commercial television had accustomed advertisers to the richer medium. It was also established as *local* radio at a time when the local press was declining rapidly and it became clear that except in large cities, local radio would depend heavily on national advertising. Understandably national advertisers were not particularly enthusiastic about negotiating with a large number of separate companies so that much of the money to support the system came from national advertising sold nationally, just as Pilkington had predicted. Nevertheless, the fact that in Britain, unlike many other Western countries, commercial radio was introduced *after* commercial television made national advertising support harder to win.

For a long time commercial local radio in Britain existed on a knife edge. The most successful station, Capital Radio, the entertainment station for London, nearly foundered due to the recession created by the first oil crisis, and subsequent economic recession led in the early 1980s to stations closing down or succumbing to takeovers. Outside the large conurbations local radio managements started to recognise that whereas the region might be a viable marketing area for their product, the locality was not. Local radio was in effect a mass market medium whose viability was limited by its geographical reach: except in densely populated urban areas local stations could not deliver a large enough chunk of the audience to interest advertisers of products for the mass market. The commercial radio industry in the UK tends, predictably, to blame the regulating authority (the IBA) for many of its troubles, but the IBA is merely the instrument which embodies the contradictions inherent in the system as it stands.

During the 1960s the Local Radio Association had used the cover of localism only to discover in the 1980s that it had struck a somewhat Faustian bargain. At that point, a number of pressures coincided, enabling them to obtain a better deal. This latest phase of commercial radio, the Green Paper of 1987 and the government plans for radio announced in January 1988 are discussed in Chapter 10.

Commercial Radio: the Realities

Commercial radio has a fifteen-year record in Britain. How successful has it been in coping with the contradictions discussed above? Answers must be sought in programming, and in the operations of the regulatory system.

Both have been scrutinised in the work of *Local Radio Workshop* (LRW). The Annan Committee had received (and used) evidence from LRW strongly critical of Capital Radio, the London ILR franchise holder and 'flagship' of the system. LRW contrasted adversely the promises which Capital had made in its franchise bid with its performance. Drawing on American example in a period when FFC policy was at its most interventionist, the group made an important contribution to the response of the Community Communications Group (COMCOM) to the Annan Report.[31] In the years that followed, LRW was the main focus for the thrust of community radio campaigning directed at attempts to reform broadcasting practice. It produced impressively well-documented evidence to the SCNI investigating the IBA in the spring of 1978,[32] organised interventions at IBA public meetings which exposed the cosmetic and ineffective character of these consultations,[33] and analysed the programming on London's three 'local' radio stations with a network of monitoring groups.[34]

At the same time LRW assisted these and other groups to produce programmes in its small studio at Paddington, and attempted to get them accepted for broadcasting by Capital and BBC Radio London, with, for the most part, a lack of success which all too often confirmed their criticisms of the stations. LRW's work with non-professionals at first aroused the opposition of the broadcasting unions, but after they won the support of the Labour-controlled GLC their political credibility increased. Their influence can be traced in a clause inserted into the Broadcasting Act of 1981 which requires the IBA to introduce 'break-points' in ILR franchises and re-advertise them publicly every eight years.

Programming on Local Radio

LRW singled out the speech programming of the two commercial stations in London for particular criticism.

One of the virtues of speech programming is that it is relatively cheap when compared to the playing of records and the costs of 'needle-time'. Local stations use the *phone-in* more widely than the national networks and often point to it as an example of the community talking to itself. Many phone-ins feature 'swap-shops' and advice services which do meet some needs in a particular sense. Phone-ins are the most economical form of broadcasting since all they require is a presenter who is prepared to guide the discussion and deal with whoever wishes to call. The phone-in is perhaps the closest most stations get to access broadcasting allowing as it does public expression of normally private concerns, but callers are controlled by both mechanical and social means. The 'intimacy' of the phone-in is part of its appeal, and is taken to its logical conclusion with 'topless radio' dealing with emotional and sexual problems. This sense of eavesdropping is an essential part of the entertainment for many listeners. However programmes, or their presenters, set the limits to what may be said by their callers. According to Higgins and Moss[35] they have two aims: firstly to foster a sense of personal interaction with the caller and secondly to make the programme entertaining for the audience.

Other forms of speech programming require more staff time and are therefore more expensive. For example, *magazine programmes* featuring guests usually demand that the presenter do some minimal amount of research so that he or she can ask the right questions. Local radio budgets rarely stretch to producers, so the presenters generally have the responsibility of organising the contributors to their programmes.

The magazine programme which combines speech with music is often less expensive. The presenter, or ocassionally a producer, will set the programme up in advance. They can rely on the fact that in any given period publishers or record companies will have product to shift and will be promoting it by sending authors or artists on a tour of local radio stations.[36] Such programmes will also establish regular contributions from local agencies such as the Job Centre or the Citizens' Advice Bureaux which they can be reasonably sure will be broadcastable.

A striking feature of the speech on commercial radio is its sexist mode of address. Daytime listeners are presumed mainly to be women; certainly the DJs are almost without exeption men. Baehr and Ryan[37] showed how at the time of their study the assumptions made by ILR programme controllers, presenters and advertisers about the employment and domestic status of the female audience were considerably out of date. Karpf[38] has collected damning admissions of senior controllers and presenters about what they expect women want from male radio presenters. (Women DJs are still rare in daytime shows.) Male DJs, she points out, fit the role of 'romantic visitor' interrupting the lonely tasks of housework or childcare, or jokily supporting the daylong routines – and the sexual division of labour. Any attempt, such as a woman DJ might be inclined to make, to question such ideology would be unacceptable to a medium that depends on advertising for its revenue. So 'valium taken aurally' is, in Karpf's phrase, the standard form of a type of radio that situates women firmly in an apolitical domestic realm and blanks out the publicly political.

Probably the most expensive form of programming is *news*, and even the smallest ILR stations at present employ several journalists. Local news is the main platform on which the localness of local radio is based, and an IBA survey in 1980 showed that it was the main reason why people listened to their local ILR station.[39] However the news values are not essentially different from those of news processors everywhere except that most local news might be defined by default as events of no interest to people outside the area.[40]

The fact that local journalists are close to the sources they use can be a positive disadvantage. They know that they will have to deal with the same politicians and local authority officers for many years to come since local political landscapes tend to change less dramatically than the national. They cannot therefore afford to offend these sources, and the result is the somewhat bland coverage audiences have come to expect from local media.[41] Most local stations build their bulletins from a mixture of local and national news. The national news comes from the network services of either the BBC or IRN (Independent Radio News), and in many stations this contribution sets the tone of the news bulletins.

Social Action Broadcasting

If these forms of speech programming form a sort of continuum of control, ranging from the phone-in to the news, then social action broadcasting (i.e. output which encourages listeners to act) is local radio's most substantial claim to encouraging solidarity in the community. Local broadcasters have been careful to demarcate responsibilities in this area. They were, and remain, concerned that such output might upset the professionalism of their output by producing bad radio, placing an intolerable burden of work on them or somehow threatening their reputation for impartiality.[42]

The result of this concern with professionalism is that with some exceptions local organisations do not find it easy to use local radio in this way unless they form part of a national network such as the Church, or have already collaborated with other stations, in the manner, for example, of Community Service Volunteers (CSV) which has extensive connections through its Media Project with BBC and ILR stations. When one compares the resources available for news – and the strength of the newsroom's position in most ILR stations, a doubt must remain whether social action broadcasting does not provide 'a respectable alibi for commercial profit . . . A station may successfully recruit volunteers to help in social services, while doing nothing in its news and current affairs coverage to help listeners understand and question the political context in which cuts are being made by government in those same services.'[43]

Professional Barriers

The manner in which broadcasters reacted to social action broadcasting demonstrates why local radio in the UK has not been able to pioneer new forms of broadcasting. It is because notions of professionalism throughout local radio parallel those to be found in national networks, and they have exactly the same effect of distancing the public from the broadcasting process. Local broadcasters claim to be uniquely qualified to judge what is newsworthy, what the public want, and what is likely to make them switch off or stay listening. In the case of local broadcasting the result is a remarkable homogeneity in the product whichever local station you listen to. Even the local accents one might expect to hear introducing the rather bland musical diet give few clues about the location of the stations: blurred glottal post-punk speak has replaced the mid-atlantic accent once affected by aspiring music presenters. What used to be termed 'meaningful speech' which fills the gaps between the music and appears on the news tends to differ in stress and form from network radio only when, in its desire to ape the norm, it topples into self-parody.

For a medium which makes so much of its immediacy, radio in the UK has been noticeably shackled by its past. Local radio, with all its genuinely radical possibilities is mostly aspiring national radio: its content may be local, but its form is not. Increasingly from 1986, the commercial half of the duopoly began openly to drop the 'local' from its designation. Independent Radio (IR) and its ambitions are discussed in Chapter 10.

The Community Radio Movement: Origins[44]

The community radio campaign was a response to the failure of local radio in Britain. As elsewhere, it was *both* aimed at the reform of existing broadcasting structures and practice *and* at opening up a space for autonomous, locally-controlled stations. This second aim had its origins in the experience of community access at some of the cable TV stations surviving from the Conservative experiment launched in 1972.[45] The Annan Committee had been more impressed by these small-scale operations than the Labour Government and it was doubtless the Committee's influence which persuaded the Home Office, a year before the publication of the Annan Report, to licence five *cable* radio networks.[46] Annan had also absorbed from Canada and elsewhere the idea that co-operatives and non-profit trusts could directly involve communities in the ownership of radio stations.[47]

The Community Communications Group (COMCOM) was formed in the Spring of 1977. With funding from the Gulbenkian Foundation, it aimed initially to bring together the experience of community cable, make links with different sectors of the community arts movement and respond to the Annan Report. Its *Comments on Annan*[48] argued the case for a sector of community radio, co-existing with BBC and IBA local radio under Annan's proposed Local Broadcasting Authority. This proposal, which would have taken local radio away from the BBC and IBA, was predictably opposed and successfully disposed of by the duopoly. However, COMCOM's Local Radio Working Party continued to press the case for community radio and its evidence to the Parliamentary Select Committee on Nationalised Industries in 1978, along with LRW's, seems to have influenced the Committee's final recommendation that 'future plans for broadcasting in the UK should encompass the possibility of frequency assignments to provide very low-power transmission facilities for voluntary community radio services within small communities'.[49]

In 1979, COMCOM published its Community Broadcasting Charter, adapted from the American NFCB's station membership rules (see Chapter 7). The charter has since been modified by the Community Radio Association (see below) as a Code of Practice and is reprinted as Appendix B. By 1981 a slow-motion but official dialogue was in process between the Home Office Broadcasting Department and a coalition which included hospital, student and cable broadcasters, some pirates, a variety of sound/radio workshops and COMCOM. A series of conferences in different locations in Britain cemented this coalition under the name of the Community Radio Association which took over from COMCOM. One of the latter's final acts before being wound up was to give an initial grant to RELAY magazine, an editorial and production collective which, between 1981 and 1988, published news of community radio in Britain and overseas at quarterly intervals.

Meanwhile the Greater London Council began to have a significant effect on the trend towards more localised radio. The Left leadership which won power in 1981 developed an interventionist media policy from 1982 onwards, arguing that media impinged on several policy areas, including arts and recreation, and industry and employment. The GLC was also strongly committed to anti-racist, anti-sexist policies and a variety of groups in the field of arts and community politics received funding. For three years until the GLC was abolished by the Conservative government in 1986 the Community Radio Development Unit became the best resourced centre of information, advice, research and funding in the country. Its Local Radio Forum which met for the first time in October 1982 identified areas for intervention and research – the latter on foreign experience, frequency space in London and public attitudes to community radio[50] – and Afro-Carribean, Asian and other minority ethnic groups became prominent in the community radio debate as a result of GLC interest and funding.

The Community Radio 'Experiment'

Over the next two years a number of other developments occurred which strengthened the case for community radio. The government's plans for cable had accepted the principle and created the precedent of broadcasting by organisations other than the BBC and IBA (hitherto always raised as an objection to a separate sector of community radio). Land-based radio piracy was on the increase, despite the greater penalties imposed under the new Telecommunications Act. Some of these were small ephemeral operations, but a number, like those serving the Greek and other ethnic communities, were solidly-based commercial businesses with thriving advertising revenue. In 1984, Radio Jackie, which had by then been broadcasting from a South London suburb for fifteen years, produced a glossy brochure describing itself as 'small business radio' and criticising the costly and restrictive IBA regulations which prevented the licensing of 'literally hundreds' of small stations. This was a calculated appeal to a section of the Tory party which was pressing for deregulation. The IBA itself had been forced into a greater flexibility to save some of the weaker ILR stations from going bankrupt, and within ILR too there were calls for deregulation in language not unlike Radio Jackie's. This was not something either BBC or IBA top management favoured. With the government's Peacock Committee considering advertising as a source of revenue for the BBC, both saw it in their interest to make a firm stand against creeping deregulation and brought pressure to bear on the Home Office and the Department of Trade and Industry (DTI) to take stronger action against the pirates. Finally the efforts of the CRA succeeded in convincing the Home Office of the merits of a case which, politically, seemed to fit the traditional Tory belief in private enterprise while working in favour of the newer hawkish trend towards privatisation and deregulation.

In January 1985 the Home Secretary, Leon Brittan, spoke of the government's intention to permit community radio in some form and in July he announced the details of an experiment. In 21 locations from the Shetlands to Penzance he invited applications for two-year experimental licences which would be of two types: neighbourhood licences for transmission over a 5km radius, and 'community of interest' licences over 10km. Finance was to be through any combination of advertising, grants, subscription or donations. There was no requirement for programme content to be balanced, but stations could not be primarily religious or political in character. Existing media interests were to be allowed minority shareholdings. An advisory panel would assist the Home

Secretary in choosing the successful applicants and the intention was to run the experiment 'with the minimum of regulation'.

From the point of view of the CRA, there were a number of unsatisfactory features about the conditions of the experiment – a very short deadline for applications; no minority ethnic representation on the advisory panel (though two CRA officers had places); in London and other large conurbations, the 10km radius meant that ethnic broadcasters in different districts would not be able to link up. The CRA would also have liked to have seen its Code of Practice adopted by all applicants and a Community Broadcasting Trust set up which could raise and redistribute funding and have some supervisory role over the sector.

But the most serious drawback, the tentative and grudging nature of the experiment, was underlined when 286 applications were received for the 21 licences. Some of them were of a very high standard. Most represented many weeks of work in forming constitutions, identifying and planning premises, hiring staff and volunteers, writing engineering specifications, involving the participation of the community, fund-raising and publicity.

By January 1986 the Advisory Panel had passed its recommendations to the Home Secretary, Douglas Hurd, who had replaced Leon Brittan three months earlier. Now for the first time the government seemed to become aware of the political danger of granting a small number of licences, due to run through an election period, to groups not required to be 'balanced' in their broadcasting. Six months of silence passed, then in June 1986 the government announced the cancellation of the experiment, giving as the reason the need to digest the Peacock Report and incorporate the public debate on it and the Green Paper into a new policy for radio. A chorus of condemnation greeted the cancellation accompanied by statements of commitment to community radio from all the opposition parties.

Cardiff Broadcasting

We conclude the chapter with a case study of Cardiff Broadcasting (CBC). Much of the above account has dealt implicitly with the IBA over the period under consideration. As with the first years of ITV, the Authority was obliged to launch its commercial radio system at a time of economic recession, and became fixed in a protective, not to say complicit relationship with the service it was meant to regulate. The reverse was true of CBC and its fate is of interest in view of the currency given since the 1987 Green Paper to the 'motherhen' concept, in which it is suggested an IR station might take a community radio station under its wing. The Cardiff case illustrates the difficulty that can arise from mixing commercial aims with community radio principles. It matters also to set the record straight about Cardiff because it was an operation whose eventual failure has been used to discredit community radio as a concept.

The Cardiff radio franchise bid itself[51] was a brilliant success story. It was only later that things went wrong. The Labour government's White Paper of July 1978 intended the IBA to establish ILR stations which were 'diverse in character' to experiment with the Annan ideas about non-profit making trusts.[52] Cardiff had been next in line for an ILR station when Labour froze ILR development in 1974, and as many as five groups were ready to bid when the franchise was advertised late in 1978. CBC entered the competition as a latecomer when only five of the eleven weeks remained between the IBA's franchise advertisement and the closing deadline for applications.

The group had its origins in a coalition of community activists, arts administrators, broadcasters and journalists. A researcher was hired as full-time co-ordinator for the group with funds donated by Chapter Arts, a neighbourhood law centre and the South Wales Poverty Action Group. One of the co-ordinating group was on the national committee of COMCOM.

The group's approach committed it to open democratic accountability as much in the planning of the franchise application as in the running of the hoped-for station. The IBA's application format requires a searching set of questions to be answered on matters concerning programming, staffing, finance and engineering. Typical applications run to several hundred pages, and forty copies must be delivered to the IBA by the deadline – in itself a considerable cost in energy, time and money. In the commercial sector, consultancy firms were at the time charging fees of £20 000 to produce polished and detailed applications. CBC had to work out an entirely new concept, unprecedented in British broadcasting, in public and democratic consultation with a constituency which had to come to terms with itself as well as the novel subject matter of the project. Capital had to be raised, engineering and site plans prepared and programming proposals developed – all in five weeks.

The method used was a series of public meetings, a standing co-ordinating group and sub-groups working on the various areas of programming, finance, administration and publicity.

A packed first meeting, attended on a snowy January evening by over 300 individuals and group representatives, heard the idea explained, confirmed the co-ordinating group in office and set the agenda. A second meeting confirmed the proposed structure and announced forthcoming elections to the proposed Cardiff Radio Trust. A third meeting elected the members of the Trust.

By this time it was clear that it was not going to be possible to raise the £½m needed to convince the IBA of the company's viability, without going to orthodox business sources. The compromise proposed was that the Board of Directors of CBC should represent, half and half, conventional shareholding and the Cardiff Radio Trust.

The Trust was a non-profit-making company, whose Council of Management was elected half directly by the community and half by organisations in the transmission area. In the first elections, supervised by the Electoral Reform Society, 350 electors took part. In subsequent elections some 2000 people voted. The Council nominated six of its members to be Directors of the Board of the Company. The Trust had approximately 3 per cent of the overall share capital but 50 per cent voting rights in the Company. The Vice-Chairperson, Jane Hutt, was a founding member of the Trust. (She had a struggle to persuade her colleagues on the Board to address her correctly and the title was a joke in the male-dominated industry; it was after all a time when Lady Plowden was Chairman of the IBA.)

These arrangements proved acceptable to the IBA which, to the surprise of Cardiff and the industry generally, announced CBC to be the winner of the franchise in April 1979.

A year later the station went on air. In the interval the Trust had acquired staff; a Co-ordinator's salary was paid for by the main Company, an 'Action Desk' Co-ordinator by the Gulbenkian Foundation; other posts were funded through job creation schemes (later, the Equal Opportunities Commission and the Commission for Racial Equality funded full-time posts to encourage programming and policy related to their aims). The Trust launched a newsletter appropriately called *Have a Hand in What You Hear*, and organised an extensive series of workshops. These aimed to acquaint local groups, and any members of the public who applied, with the possibilities of access broadcasting, train them in the necessary skills and develop programmes. The Trust's Workshop Diary shows meetings throughout the winter of 1979/80 for young people, ethnic minorities, children, people with disabilities; and for groups interested in news, education, live music, sport and leisure, poetry and visual arts, religion and the theatre.

The Workshops developed skills and expectations which came into contact with a professional staff, appointed only in the last two months of the year of preparation, whose training and experience had not equipped them to handle such demands. It was an uneasy interface. At the same time the Board and top station management confronted the reality of having to try and make a profit – and repay loans – through advertising revenue. CBC's application had committed it to being a 'strongly speech-oriented station', but music is cheaper to programme and, broadcasting wisdom advised, more popular with an audience that must first be won to assure the station a sound financial start.

The resulting compromise pleased no one and a few months after the opening the station was in trouble with poor ratings and less than the anticipated advertising revenue. Management called in the National Broadcasting School, an organisation owned by Capital Radio and the IBA whose approach was conventionally professional. Changes were made, again taking the station further from its original community access principles, while still retaining a more than usual (for ILR) amount of daytime speech.

A year later, snow came to CBC's rescue as it often does for local stations. In the blizzards of January 1982 CBC became a lifeline for the area. New listeners discovered a station that was local *and* different. The May JICRAR ratings showed a 116 per cent leap in the audience. By the end of the year a new Managing Director, regarded as the most sympathetic of ILR controllers towards community access, was in post, drawing the comment from one Trust member 'If we can't make our ideas work under him we don't deserve to succeed.'[53]

Did they? An answer was attempted three years later by Simon White, Cardiff Radio Trust's Co-ordinator for the first five years.[54] In the period when access was established on a regular basis, it fell into two categories – the discrete access programmes scheduled in evening hours, and the access to the large daytime audience provided through Action Line. White writes, 'it is impossible to fill many hours [in the evening] . . . until you have created a large pool of skilled volunteers . . . Our experience is that a short weekly programme would fully stretch a small group.'

Action Line, on the other hand, was the main programme activity of the Trust. Though similar to the much smaller operations in other ILR stations, it was different because the Trust was committed to access as a founding principle and had structural power in the station. Whereas most radio staff were white, male and not locally committed, 'Action Desk staff introduced locally active women, paid and unpaid, into the radio station. People who wanted to be radio personalities were given a very low priority.'[55] The result was, as one voluntary group wrote of their production experience, 'we did not have to push to get recognised, CBC *wanted* us to have access to the airwaves'.[56] Within the traditional strip-programming format of the mid-morning show, Action Line would typically provide a scene-setting interview, a half-hour debate and a half-hour interview, What's On announcements and a report on audience feed-back. Women's health, peace, unemployment and Latin America were the subjects of special weeks in which the issue could be given prominence across the whole station schedule.

There were struggles with station staff to maintain this kind of editorial line, and, looking back, White concluded that

> although the Trust was very well integrated into what activists called 'the community' (trades' unions, pressure groups, community groups, etc.) it had no real resonance amongst the audience. Elections, public meetings, conferences, workshops, all the normal methods of 'community control' seemed slightly misplaced when compared to the efficacy of the medium itself to address hundreds of thousands of (passive) listeners.[57]

The fundamental problem was that the Trust's freedom of action 'was severely curtailed by the needs of the market'.[58]

The original compromise of a 50/50 split between community and commercial interests doomed the station to satisfy neither. As well, a total reliance on advertising revenue forced CBC more towards the conventional ILR mould.

The IBA's role was ambiguous: the high level of capitalisation required by the Authority, in part due to the unnecessarily stringent specifications demanded by its engineers was standard and was frequently criticised even by conventional ILR stations. The lack of any sympathetic specialist advice service from the IBA to community-based bids, and the total failure of the IBA and the government to develop what the IBA itself had suggested, namely 'initial capital grants for local radio trusts'[59] suggest that the IBA was never serious about non-profit franchises.

Subsequent events tend to confirm this. Encouraged by the success of the Cardiff bid, and ignoring the signals that followed the Conservatives' 1979 election success, groups up and down the country prepared community-based bids. Assisted in many cases by the Broadcasting Rights and Information Project, set up with Gulbenkian funding to help such bids,[60] and often helped by Cardiff veterans to improve on the Cardiff model, the documents produced by these groups make remarkable reading.

The IBA staff comments on them, prepared to save the time of Authority Members, reduced them to monotonous précis which lacked the vitality of the originals; the atmosphere and location of the IBA public meetings were not conducive to serious two-way discussion; the attitude of Authority Members in the formal interviews was reported variously as intimidating, acrimonious, distant or uninterested. At the interview for the Swindon franchise one Member fell asleep.[61]

The failures were in Aberdeen, Bristol, Coventry, Gwent, Leeds and Peterborough to name the most conspicuous. Other conventionally financed bids, such as those by groups in Swindon and Essex, used the Trust model to no avail. Moray Firth was the only success, and that a modified one.[62]

Amongst professional broadcasters the Cardiff experience had consequences more damaging to the community radio cause. The station's problems were seen, not as the fault of the IBA, but as due to the mistaken introduction of too much speech or community access. ILR management saw CBC as letting the side down. Nationally (though not in Cardiff) unions saw access as a threat. The IBA acted as if it were glad to be rid of what one commentator in the advertising industry described as 'a battered monument to the IBA's fatuity in the Plowden/Young era'.[63]

In the spring of 1985, at a low point in ILR's fortunes, CBC's neighbour, Gwent, ceased trading. Rather than re-advertise the Gwent franchise or allow CBC to take over and have fresh elections to put Gwent representatives on the CBC board, the IBA turned to Red Rose, an English station based in Preston which had already started to form a network by its acquisition of Aire, the Leeds ILR station. Red Rose was allowed to run Cardiff and Gwent as a single station, Red Dragon, whose Board included two community representatives elected by the shareholders rather than nominated by the Trust.

By this time it was questionable whether there was anything worth saving of the original concept. Prior to the takeover CBC had ceased financial support for the Trust whose input to programmes had substantially declined as a result. CBC's Chair, David Williams, who resigned before the merger, wrote, 'We were the offspring in many ways of the Annan Committee's report . . . written in the late 1970s . . . The realities of the 1980s when we came on air were very different .'[64] Penny Philcox, Action Desk Co-ordinator at CBC, comments,

> Whatever the access you have, the real impact depends on whether or not the community-based approach is represented at all levels of the station and management structure, from links with the community, recruiting policy, training resources to top management and policy making.

She concludes that where commitment of any of these levels is missing, as it was sometimes at management level 'it seriously undermines the scope of local (or community) radio to reflect and involve the full range of communities and interests it is supported to serve'.[65]

Jane Hutt had predicted as much in February 1980: 'We would have to move away from the commercial world to achieve something different and look to state-funded or publicly subscribed low-powered local stations for a more acceptable initiative.'[66]

Chapter 7

The Listener as Participant: North America and Australia

This chapter looks at a form of radio, eventually to be known as community radio in the USA and Canada, public radio in Australia, which re-instated the listener as subject-participant in a sharing of artistic and political power.

KPFA, Pacifica

In the beginning American radio was wild and free; then the 'toads' and the 'bores' took over and it became a desert. That is one view of radio's development in the USA, Lorenzo Milam's,[1] and it is certainly a view which expresses one of the motives leading to the creation of listener-supported radio in 1949. Translated, Milam's language recalls the Brechtian equality that reigned between the early broadcasters and their listeners, and their freedom to experiment; then the reduction of the audience to the role of passive consumer. It was in this broadcasting environment and against this sort of broadcasting that KPFA Pacifica made a stand.

The station which Lewis Hill and his colleagues in the Pacifica Foundation launched in 1949 – KPFA, Berkeley, California – survives to this day, the longest running example of non-profit, listener-supported radio in the world. Pacifica's name symbolises its commitment to the cause of peace for which several of its founders went to prison as conscientious objectors during the Second World War.

The Foundation aims to foster understanding between 'people of all nations, races and colours and creeds', study the causes of conflict, encourage 'the creative skills and energies of the community' and promote the 'distribution of public information'.[2]

The FM licence Pacifica was granted in 1949 was the first non-commercial licence that did *not* go to an educational or religious institution and was consequently important as a precedent. A precondition for this development was the FCC's far-sighted decision in 1945 to reserve 20 of the 100 available FM channels for non-commercial use.

Despite early financial crises which took KPFA off the air for several months in 1951/2 – problems in part caused by the temporary collapse of the FM receiver production industry, the station succeeded in fulfilling Pacifica's founding aims through diverse and original programming combined with a radical political stance which attracted the hostile attentions of the FCC and Senator McCarthy's Congressional Committee on un-American Activities.

Coming through this difficult period and with securer finances, Pacifica expanded to set up a group of fire stations, adding to KPFA, first KPFK in Los Angeles and WBAI in New York, later KPFT in Houston and finally WPFW in Washington DC. The Foundation now operates a News service, available to other non-commercial stations besides its own, while from Los Angeles a Programme service distributes by tape, cassette and satellite material from current production and from the Pacifica Archive. By 1982 the latter contained over 20 000 tapes in what must be one of the most remarkable collections of English-language programming outside the BBC.[3]

The key to the Pacifica programme philosophy is the relationship with and support from listeners. With no tradition in America of public service or licence fee payment, listeners in the San Francisco Bay area from 1949 onwards were offered a bargain that has continued to prove satisfactory – a service that deliberately attempts to satisfy needs unmet by other stations in return for a voluntary annual (and tax-deductible) subscription.

Over the years, by methods which have been adopted in most listener-supported radio stations, revenue from regular subscriptions has been supplemented through 'on-air marathons', benefits, concerts, sale of stickers, T-shirts, etc.

Listeners-sponsorship, daring then and much copied later,

rested on an attitude towards the audience which was unusual in America at the time. In a report written in 1957 just before he died, Hill described his philosophy:

> The much-argued characteristics of American radio which finds 'serious' subjects treated, if at all, in a way that will accommodate any degree of indolence in the listener, has arisen from the prior belief that the radio audience consists in numbers . . . The KPFA experiment set out to express an essentially opposite view. The audience was believed to consist of an individual, whose intention was to listen.[4]

In return for their subscriptions listener-sponsors received a copy of the monthly printed programme guide, *Folio*, and early KPFA on-air announcements urged a selective use of programmes, based on study of the guide, in tones very similar to the early BBC. Programming assumed such a selective approach on the part of the listener and was of the kind Liora Salter has described as 'revolving-door', 'tending to splinter the public as producer and audience, into distinct interest-groups'.[5]

This discrete programme format followed as a consequence of the use of listeners as producers. Listener sponsorship has always been matched by volunteer involvement. In the period described by Hill's 1957 report 12 paid staff were assisted by 30 volunteers, who came 'almost without exception, from the listening audience; which is to say, in cyclic fashion, from the programming. The program schedule and the physical operation were almost as much a product *of* the audience as a service to it.[6]

In 1986, there were 22 paid staff and 250 unpaid staff. Volunteers are recognised as 'unpaid staff' if they have been with the station a minimum of four months undertaking 20 hours of regular work in the station per month. This designation entitles the volunteers to attend and vote at staff meetings, and, by agreement of the Union of Electrical Workers which represents the paid staff, to have access to grievance procedures and participation in the union health plan. This union recognition underlines the fact that volunteers are not seen as cheap labour but as an essential element of listener participation.[7]

KPFA's Public Affairs Department is one of six; the others are concerned with Music, Drama and Literature, News, Third World and Woman's programming. The Public Affairs Department is run by the equivalent of two full-time staff and 60 unpaid staff. Its Director, Philip Maldari, explained the present-day extent of the Pacifica station's accountability to its listeners.

Each of the five stations has a local advisory board and the Foundation's National Advisory Board draws two members from each station board. At KPFA the station has a policy of soliciting membership from 'prominent or active members of the community to provide a balance of the sexual, ethnic and cultural diversity that exists in our community'.[8] Members serve two years and can be re-elected.

Unlike some of the (non-Pacifica) community radio stations that were set up in the wake of KPFA, the station is not owned by its listeners. The Pacifica Foundation is the licensee and appoints the Manager and paid staff. The station's advisory board's powers are limited to approving (or disapproving) the Manager's annual budget, and to agreeing (or disagreeing) with a decision by Pacifica's National Executive Director to hire or fire the Manager.

> Where we are forced to depend on our listeners for 80 per cent of our income – and we have $1m a year budget – you can't help but have that influence decision-making in programming. The bottom line is that we are accountable to our listeners to the extent that they will pay for the programming and when they stop paying for it we are out of business.[9]

America in the 1960s

For a long time, the Pacifica formula, exemplified in KPFA, KPFK and WBAI, remained unique. Pacifica excepted, non-commercial radio meant educational radio – college-based stations that existed to give communication students practice in radio journalism during the day with an in-fill of classical music and perhaps imported BBC drama and features.

Then came the 1960s. Through the decade civil rights, the Vietnam war and the women's movement became issues. The Pacifica stations were deeply embroiled in the politics but were too few to satisfy the musical tastes of a new musically-informed generation.

Lorenzo Milam, who had worked at KPFA, was both an admirer of the BBC and in tune with the times. Passionate about radio, he was also doggedly persistent in his dealings with the FCC bureaucracy from which he finally wrung an FM licence for a frequency in Seattle. He began broadcasting in 1962 under the call-sign KRAB and went on to set up other stations with equally idiosyncratic call-signs – KBOO in Portland, KTAO in Los Gastos, KCHU in Dallas, WORT in Madison and KDNA in St. Louis.

His book, *The Radio Papers*,[10] draws on articles he wrote for the programme guides of these stations and vividly evokes the atmosphere and philosophy of the period. For Milam the 'toads' were the commercial interests which had swallowed up American radio, the 'bores' were the educational stations training future broadcasters in the same mould. Repeatedly he appeals to the 'potentialities of radio' – the drama, poetry and political dissent which the established system ignored. As in the Pacifica stations, so in Milam's the volunteers were the lifeblood of the operation. Of KCHU before it opened, he wrote:

> It is a station which will try our ears. One which will revel in open access. One which will utilize an army of friends and volunteers to keep it alive, and ticking and *there*. The station will revive the art of early radio which was known as Local and Live . . . Here we have a center of experimenting with the feel and touch and dynamics of a city alive, alive to itself, through tapes and live talk and telephone beaming in from all sides: the voice of a city coming to feel itself through its own pulse . . . It will take awhile . . . It has to take some time for the people to get used to the idea that the walls are down, and that the microphone sits here open as the sun, ready to be talked to.

Community radio was still sufficiently unusual, the FM commercial still sufficiently undeveloped, for stations to be attractive because of their lack of structure, their programme of demystification. But meanwhile the Johnson administration was introducing structure to strengthen non-commercial broadcasting at the national level. At the very moment that the British government with its Marine Offences Act moved Canute-like to fend off the tide of commercial radio, the Federal Government was creating a space for public broadcasting.

But the financing criteria of the CPB (see Chapter 3) excluded many college stations and the slowly growing number of autonomous, low-budget radio stations that had followed the Pacifica and Milam initiatives. From their perspective NPR stations showed 'more concern for sizeable budget than service to the community, more attention to professionalism than participation of the public, more emphasis on the power of a station's signal than responsiveness to community needs'.[11]

The New Wave of Community Radio

Nevertheless, the smaller community radio stations were by now able to build on a body of experience and precedents bequeathed by the pioneers of the 1960s. Transmission technology had improved; there were more working examples of what it meant to be alternative, avoid formats, be 'local and live'; a common feature of management structures was the electorate of an annual assembly voting in a board which, as licensee, hired the paid staff, a repertoire of fund-raising strategies was shared and widened.[12]

In 1975, a group of fifteen stations and licence applicants came together to form the National Federation of Community Broadcasters (NFCB).

Under the NFCB's present rules membership is open to any station which

* is incorporated as not-for-profit organisation;
* is governed by a group broadly representative of the community it serves;
* has a stated and demonstrated commitment to the participation of women and Third World people in all aspects of its organisation and operation;
* has a stated and demonstrated commitment to access by the general public to the airwaves;
* provides or seeks to provide a service to the general public and not to any single group, organisation or institution;
* seeks to reflect a diverse range of culture and opinion found in its community through its broadcast operations.

(Article One, Section 1.01, NFCB Bylaws.)

NFCB, though its membership includes stations which receive CPB support, has always distanced itself from National Public Radio (NPR – see Chapter 3) by its emphasis on decentralisation. For many NFCB members NPR appears too close to government and corporate interests in its language and stance. For the NFCB, the key features of community radio can be summarised as: an element of *control* by the local community, typically in a board of management; a *commitment to community access*, especially for those normally excluded from the mass media: women, ethnic groups and people of colour, the elderly and young people. This policy implies the *use of volunteers*; in turn this requires *a training programme*; *paid staff and volunteers* should have a voice in policy, which implies: the *definition of a clear purpose* to which all can relate.

Besides assisting the development of community radio on the ground through a newsletter, training conferences, tape exchange and advice, the NFCB was remarkably successful in its national interventions. The times were indeed favourable. During the 1970s, the FCC was open to democratic pressure, one of its Commissioners, Nicholas Johnson, was an ally of the media reform movement, commercial franchise renewal was often challenged, and successive administrations were sympathetic to public broadcasting.

Community Radio in the 1980s

Some ten years later it is a different story. NFCB continues to be influential within public broadcasting and its membership has grown to 70, with 120 associate members. But the economic and political climate of Reaganism has taken its toll. At the local level, a general retreat from community activism as affected some stations in the loss of key staff with consequent loss of direction. All public radio has suffered a decline in listenership. At national level, deregulation is the order of the day. For the 8500 commercial stations this has meant that the FCC has relaxed its programme guidelines and is trusting to market forces to ensure sufficient amounts of public affairs and news programming.[13] For the nearly 1000 public stations, it has meant a decrease in public funding and a ready acquiescence on the FCC's part in the sector's increasing reliance on 'underwriting' (a limited form of commercial sponsorship) which threatens to blur the distinction between public and commercial broadcasting.

Among public broadcasters, the language of the market-place can be heard – programme product, targeting audiences, defining the market. Stations that in the 1970s were proud not to be format-bound, now strive for a 'seamlessness' to carry the audience through from one segment to another. NPR reflects the new realism in its call to double the audience within five years. A report of a 1986 Task Force, using an argument familiar to BBC planners, points out that 'if we fail to achieve an audience of significant size, public broadcasting loses not only its purpose but also its base of support and its legitimacy as a social institution'.[14] The report identifies poor management, inadequate staff salaries and training, a failure to define a market position or develop on-air promotion as causes of audience decline. In the small station, non-NPR sector too, a rigorous reassessment is in progress.

What is new, and marks a clear difference from the environment in which community radio first appeared, is that a highly diversified cultural industry, working through many outlets besides radio, is becoming skilled at identifying needs and satisfying them. Community radio stations have learned that listeners, even to alternative radio, can no longer be taken for granted. Two examples of this perception at work are to be found in WORT and KBOO.

WORT, Madison, Wisconsin, is a founder member of the NFCB. With a budget of $310 000 a year and 8 full-time equivalent paid staff it qualifies for CPB funding. From a very free and open structure at the start, WORT has evolved over the years to the point where its concern with 'audience development' has, its manager David LePage conceded, earned it the reputation of being 'at the commercial end of community radio'.[15] WORT achieves a 10 per cent weekly reach in a city of 400 000. Its FM competition includes two state-wide public and two commercial music stations. WORT concentrates on the local, Madison scene and its morning drive-time programme comes from a small restaurant which invites casual on-air access. A midday public affairs programme regularly includes phone-ins to studio guests.

The decision to accept 'non-commercial advertising' marked a major policy departure which was arrived at by stages. First a committee of volunteers, staff and Board members considered the question at length and finally recommended it to the Board. A year's negotiation ensued with different factions within the station to determine the exact rules. Next a six-month trial period launched the scheme and was evaluated by an internal group which reported regularly to station meetings as well as mailing a six-page letter and questionnaire to WORT's 4000 listener-sponsors, obtaining a 20 per cent response. The majority (80 per cent) said 'Do what you have to do to keep the programmes coming'; 10 per cent were against, and 10 per cent said advertising should have been accepted from the beginning. After that the change was accepted as permanent. A similar process is being undertaken to evaluate a suggested change in the programme schedule. The example shows that democratic processes need not be ignored even in a highly market-oriented station.

KBOO, Portland, Oregon, set in hand a similar reappraisal in the second half of 1986 and its Information Director's explanation in the Program Guide is worth quoting at length as a good summary of NFCB thinking in a competitive era.

> Despite evidence of growing audiences in some areas . . . we, like other public stations, have lost listeners overall. Our classical and jazz offerings are better than other stations, but unfortunately listeners are leaving us for those stations. It is no coincidence that when three other stations began providing classical music our classical support dropped off . . . Our past success has caught up with us in the form of competition.
>
> Reduced listener support means we must rely on more federal and private grants, underwriting and events for funding. Unchecked, these sources will force our programming to change if they begin to make up too large a proportion of our budget. As a community radio station, KBOO should stay primarily listener-supported . . . Listener support is the freest way we can support ourselves. Ignoring our declining listenership puts all our programming in jeopardy . . .
>
> The key is to design programming which we have good reason to believe will appeal to listeners. We have made significant strides in serving new audiences over the last few years (Childrens, Seniors, Latinos, Blacks, Gays, Disabled People). In fact, it is only through adding this programming that our audience hasn't dropped off more than it would have . . .
>
> We have never really thought of ourselves as competing. We had the idea of community radio as being so special that we were in a different category. But most of our listeners aren't looking for media salvation, they just want an oasis in the wasteland of Portland radio. Let's get them to the oasis and then try to change the way they think about the media.[16]

CANADA

Canada's population of $20\frac{1}{2}$ million occupies a huge country of 10 million square miles, but is mainly concentrated within 100 miles of the US border, the remainder living in small communities increasingly isolated the further North one goes. These facts have given communications a prominence in Canadian government planning that is found in few other countries. Despite this, American influence is inescapable. Cable, satellite and broadcast signals make it easy for most of the population to watch American TV, and American imports can be seen on Canadian channels in proportions which give the authorities cause for concern. A Federal Task Force report of 1987 made proposals designed to increase Canadian public broadcasting and production, as well as strengthen the hand of the Canadian Radio, Television and Telecommunications Commission (CRTC) in limiting American influence.

The CRTC itself, soon after its establishment in 1968, developed a policy for community programming on cable and welcomed the subsequent arrival of community radio. This takes three forms: *Native radio*, comprising some 139 stations, is found serving communities in the North. *Student radio*: 15 stations broadcast from university campuses with programming that includes material produced, and intended for reception by, communities in the area. *Community radio*, broadly along lines pioneered in the USA, is broadcast by 23 stations, all but two of them in Quebec where the political struggle for recognition of French language and culture inspired the birth of community video in the late 1960s, followed by community radio.

Less than 9 per cent of Canada's 1363 radio stations can be described as community radio stations. The majority are either commercial broadcasters or belong to the Canadian Broadcasting Corporation (CBC). Three quarters of the CBC's revenue comes from a licence fee and a quarter from advertising.

Vancouver Co-op Radio: a Case Study

Vancouver Co-op Radio (VCR or Co-op Radio; its call-sign, CFRO, is less commonly used) is the same age as a number of the stations which founded the American NFCB – it has been on air since March 1975 – and is in many respects very similar to them.

Sixteen people appeared before the CRTC at the Vancouver hearings in March 1974. They represented the 231 shareholders of a co-operative that had been formed a year before from two groups, Neighbourhood Radio which had plans to use cable for community access radio, and a group known as Muckrakers which, through press clippings service, provided research for local trade union and community groups.

One of the main planks of Co-op Radio's application was a critique of Vancouver's mainstream media environment. A population of over a million in the capital of British Columbia, located a few miles north of the US border, is served by two main newspapers, closely linked in ownership, and by broadcasting which is overwhelmingly commercial. CBC television and radio is outnumbered by Canadian commercial stations and by the many US stations that can be received off-air or by cable. (In the second half of the 1980s domestic satellite dishes were adding to the receivable signals; on the other hand, in recent years an Open University-style educational network has been set up by the provincial government.)

In 1974, as now, Co-op's programming proposals were intended to be a radical alternative to these mainstream outlets. From the CRTC's point of view, Co-op's radical stance was acceptable, even desirable, because it did something to counter the imbalance of Vancouver's media environment. The proposals made at the hearings had mostly a solid basis in the production experience of a coalition of programme-making groups, each formed round existing interest groups in the city. Representatives of news, women's, arts, literature, drama, legal, health, education, native, urban planning and trade union groups assisted in a presentation to the CRTC that is a model of planning for a community access broadcasting bid. It is as impressive in the detail of its paperwork as in the lucid extempore answers given to the Commissioners' questions and recorded in the CRTC transcript.

The CRTC was content at the hearing to satisfy itself that a decision-making process existed to take responsibility for programmes, that the revenue prospects were realistic, and that the structure proposed conformed to Canadian law.[17]

Structure

The legal structure proposed, and continued to this day, was a co-operative of shareholders (each with one vote, regardless of the number of shares bought) electing a nine-member Board whose three-year terms rotated to ensure continuity. The Board was the licence-holder, decided general policy and met monthly.

The daily running of the station has been overseen by different bodies during Co-op's existence. Their common feature has been the involvement of the programme-making groups and some kind of relationship to various committees responsible for administrative matters. Since 1981, the Board has taken a more active role and currently works through several committees composed of Board members, paid staff and elected volunteers to carry out the daily operations of the station. Currently the co-operative has over 2000 members, several hundred of whom attend the AGM.

It is worth mentioning that the original constitution provides for the Board to have an advisory board, but in a pungent critique of advisory bodies that the BBC might do well to note, Liora Salter said at the CRTC hearing 'We have decided not to do that. Because an advisory board are people who don't have defined responsibilities, who don't have accountability to anybody, and who do they represent and how come they get the right to advise?'[18]

Finance

From the start Co-op Radio wished to avoid dependence on government grants and aimed not to rely on any one source of money or programmes for more than 10 per cent of its budget. In fact, government job creation grants, linked to specific projects or programmes, and government contracts to research policy issues have from time to time played a useful, though not dominant, part in funding staff, and, through the overheads costed in such projects, the station as a whole. The largest source of funding is, and has been, the listeners in the form of memberships, donations and response to the annual on-air fund-raising marathon. Grants from private agencies and foundations, and special fund-raising events bring in further revenue.

Finally, there is programme sponsorship. From 1982, the station took the decision that each regular programme should take on responsibility for finding at least one sponsor. As the CRTC were told at the original hearing, 'we don't expect that every group we work with has the money, but we would like them to try to help find it'.[19]

Sponsors have their name, address, hours of business and a brief description of their product or service mentioned for $10 per announcement over a minimum 13-week period. Announcements may not be made by the programme's regular hosts. Sponsorship can be charged as tax-deductible and sponsors' names are listed in the programme guide. *Radio Waves* listed 34 sponsors in its July/August 1986 issue.

After some years of the crises which plague all community stations, Co-op Radio went 'into the black' early in 1983 and seems now to have achieved a plateau of stability. In assessing its financial state it must be remembered that the unpaid help of over a hundred regular volunteers amounts to a figure which probably matches the cash cost of the station, currently about $175 000 a year.

Staff[20]

Currently there are four and a half full-time paid posts at Co-op Radio. Staff work collectively, sharing the many administrative tasks. The posts are Station Co-ordinator responsible for membership, management, fundraising, publicity, liaising with the subscriber magazine *Radio Waves*; Programme Co-ordinator overseeing programme development, advanced training, community involvement; Volunteer Co-ordinator looking after volunteers working on programming and administration, organising orientation and basic skills courses. (The Volunteer Co-ordinator also helps organise a new Volunteer Committee which, it is hoped, will ease volunteers' feeling of alienation and isolation from the station infrastructure which has recently been a major issue.) Accountant responsible for finance, book-keeping, office management; and Engineer (half-time) co-ordinating equipment maintenance and development. There are also a number of contract jobs mainly related to sponsorship and the financing, production and distribution of *Radio Waves*.

Over two hundred volunteers fill out the responsibilities needed to keep a station on air 20 hours a day. Over the years, as in other stations which have weathered the cultural revolutions, the spells of inefficiency and even of despair, Co-op Radio has devised a system of 'appropriate bureaucracy' which enlists the participation of this crowd of people. It is currently embodied in a 45-page Handbook for Volunteers. Herein are listed station objectives, history, and systems dealing with funding and publicity; station structure is outlined together with studio, technical and administrative routines; there is a section on legal constraints on broadcasting, an appendix on voice production and a reading list for radio journalists. The rights and duties of volunteers are spelled out. All programme groups are required to put in two hours work a month for the station in areas *not* connected with their programme, and to take turns in cleaning up the old building that houses the station.

Programme groups have an obligation also to ensure that everyone in the group has taken relevant station training courses before being let loose on equipment or in the studio. To assist in this, Co-op Radio has produced a series of technical pamphlets, a manual on interviewing and a witty and well-illustrated *Basic Equipment Manual*.

Programmes and Programme Policy

The station's Programming Policy Statement describes Vancouver Co-op Radio as

> a community-based, non-commercial radio station that strives to provide programming that is non-sexist, non-racist and non-ageist. As a community-based station, programming is aimed primarily at people who do not now have access to established media. We endeavour to be accessible to artists, local performers, working people, as well as the economically, socially or politically disadvantaged . . . Our aim is to provide information that is not now available or easily accessible to the general public. This information is sometimes geared towards special interest groups and sometimes aimed at general audiences.

Currently sixty different programmes, some repeated, fill the schedule. They include 'Broadly Speaking', a women's hour,

'Radio Peace', 'The Rational' a public affairs programme, 'Eco-watch' about environmental issues, 'Union Made' – news and features about working people and union organisation, 'Coming Out' and 'The Lesbian Show', 'The Ether Patrol' – science fiction and fantasy radio, 'America Latina Al Dia', a bilingual news programme on Latin America and other programmes from Chinese, Punjabi- and Hindi- speaking, Armenian, Iranian, Italian and Native Canadian communities. The criteria for developing any particular strand of ethnic programming are, according to the Co-op Policy Statement: the relative size of the group in the listening area; whether or not it has an existing outlet; whether or not the proposed Co-op programme would be a significant alternative to an existing outlet; the content should 'reflect a positive and unifying view of a given ethnic community . . . [emphasising] the contemporary experience and culture of British Columbia ethnic populations'; material that is pre-recorded or based on government bulletins is unacceptable. Littman comments that this is a sensitive area: some groups are progressive and some are not.

Most of the English language spoken-word programming follows a magazine format with interviews interspersed with music, although people do experiment with discussion panels, phone-ins and 'soundscapes'. All the English spoken-word shows define themselves as collectives, although the degree of actual collectivity varies. Content varies widely depending on the levels of skill at any time for each show. The station attracts high quality music on disc and recorded at concerts: jazz, folk, classical and native. Presenters are specialists in their area and aim to contextualise the music within a group's culture. Rock and punk are mainly covered by a nearby University station.

Each show functions as an independent collective within the station. To apply for a show a group must submit a fairly vigorously evaluated proposal and demonstration tape. Once on air the station bureaucracy generally doesn't officially intervene unless things get very bad, for instance departing from the 'promise of performance'. Shows which have been initiated by the station tend not to thrive as long as the ones started by defined community groups.

It was originally the intention that a Quality Control and Listeners' Committee, with a changing membership of up to fifteen 'experienced programmers', should select one or two programmes per month for evaluation and discussion with the production group, but this has rarely happened in practice.

A Canadian study of June 1979[21] noted that music of all types accounted for 42 per cent of the output. Shortly afterwards, in a trend that continued for four years, the proportion of music exceeded 50 per cent.[22] This tendency was checked in late 1983 when the station decided to move back towards the original priorities.[23]

What is known of the audience? After eleven years, more than used to be, but surveys are confined to those who receive the programme guide and the response tends to come mainly from the committed public affairs audience. Production groups get feedback from their own listenership, and marathon appeals are a clear test of the pulling power of each programme.

Theoretical Analysis

It is rare for the experience of a community radio station to be subjected to theoretical analysis by someone intimately connected with it, but this is the case with Co-op Radio. One of its founders, Liora Salter, now teaching in the Communications Department of Simon Fraser University, has analysed[24] the conflicts and 'cultural revolutions' in which each generation of station leadership represented democracy as crystallized in one or other of what she calls 'the range of perspectives-in-conflict'. 'If the public, as producer or audience, experiences his or her situation on many different levels simultaneously, the conflicts within the station reflect part of an external reality' – a reality refracted by class and gender. Salter identifies the perspectives-in-conflict as three: those concerned with class, with participation and with process. 'Each perspective represents a skeletal analysis of society, some commentary on the role of the media, and a prescription for Co-op programming and organisational structure.'

Those who hold a 'class perspective' see themselves as journalists whose task is to uncover the nature of the economic relations which exploit an 'underclass' and which are masked by mainstream media. Co-op Radio's role, avoiding the 'instant news' which serves capitalism, is to provide news analysis that lays bare the decision-making process and facilitates political activity.

Those holding the 'participatory perspective' see the demand for participation as having in itself a radical effect. Co-op Radio is in part an issue-based organisation 'challenging the media portrayal of public events and intervening in matters of broadcast licensing policy'. The station should offer training and access, acting in a sense as co-worker with citizen, tenant and other groups. '*What* information groups choose to present is of secondary consideration.'

The 'process perspective' holds the view that mainstream media reinforce isolation by providing no means of response and by treating audience as commodities. From this perspective *how* things are done (the station's internal democratic structure) has radical consequences which are important in themselves.

Each perspective has a conservative aspect into which it is easy to slip, and each, Salter argues, on its own fails to account adequately for critical dimensions of experience.

A concentration on *participation* creates the kind of programme blocks that 'tend to splinter public, as producer and audience, into distinct interest groups . . . Public becomes a concept of aggregation . . . The hidden assumption . . . is a reformulated liberal pluralism . . . Community control, as an unthinking localism, masks conflicts within and between communities' and on a wider scale.

A concentration on *process* ties audience to producers 'by obligation generated in the importance of the issues being addressed'. The audience gets talked *at* rather than *with*, as if content could be dumped without reference to the contextualised interests of producer or audience.

Those with a *class* perspective have the special problem, according to Salter, that Co-op's membership is mainly middle-class and that the station had yet to develop an effective and continuous relationship with the labour unions at the time she wrote.

Salter's 'perspectives' may be incomplete as regards race and sexual politics, issues which have become more important since she wrote. And apart from other considerations, her account has almost certainly been outdated on points of fact by later 'cultural revolutions'. But her analysis has value as an explanatory principle, and she is careful to stress that it is an interpretation of *implicit* perspectives, not necessarily fully developed or articulated by those who work in the station at a particular time. In a telling observation, she remarks that 'to any new member, the history of the organisation begins with their discovery of it. In another sense, groups like Co-op Radio have multiple histories, each one tracing a different route through the organisation.'

Co-op radio works best, she suggests, when the perspectives are brought together. That the station should act as an 'organiser' is common ground among the holders of different perspectives, and so is a tendency to replace the notion of 'community' with that of 'constituency', viewed as 'people sharing multiple overlapping relationships in a system of power'.

The role of the producer, Salter suggests, is delicately balanced:

> Producers are drawn from the audience; they programme in concert with what they feel are audience needs and aspirations. They fail as organisers if they remain insiders to the audience relationship and continue to share the audience view of circumstance and potentiality. They also fail if they get cut off from the needs and aspirations of their audience as their audiences understand them.

To be able to succeed in this double role/double bind, functioning 'at the fulcrum of the producer–audience–issue relationship' is the special requirement of the community radio producer, and, Salter claims, only a precarious marginality allows success.

Comment

Beyond the individual 'programme constituency', it is worth considering the extent to which a station whose schedule links a number of such constituencies can provide a 'forum for in-movement and inter-movement debate . . . [to] ensure the linking up of issues, the challenging of ideas, actions and ideologies'. The claim was made by the producer of *Radio Peace* who pointed out that 'resistance to war, and to the use of nuclear weapons and nuclear energy, is impossible without resistance to sexism, to racism, to imperialism, to ageism and to violence as an everyday pervasive reality. So in providing a link for listeners between violence against women, the power of multinational corporations, the plight of native Canadians and indigenous people in other parts of the world, the wars in Central America and South African apartheid, Co-op Radio is providing the means for an analysis which mainstream media rarely offer and which can break through isolation.'[25]

AUSTRALIA

Australia was the first 'Western' country to establish community radio as a regular part of its broadcasting system, and it is in terms of system that the following brief survey is directed. Several Australian public radio stations (to give them their Australian label) are contemporaries of the founding American NFCB stations of the early 1970s, and their history, present structure and programming closely resemble features discussed in the section on US community radio. What is unusual is the institutionalisation of this type of radio in a system which, like Canada's, grew out of a British model and has a commercial sector more like that of the USA.

The Australian Broadcasting Commission (ABC) runs national radio and TV networks; commercial broadcasting, with a high concentration of ownership, is found mainly in the cities where it claims three quarters of the audience to ABC's one quarter. Till the early 1970s, the VHF Band II (88–108 MHz) was used for television, and it is as these frequencies have been cleared that more space has become available for public radio. In any case Australia's geographical isolation gives it an enviable freedom from foreign interference in medium-wave channels. A very large proportion of new citizens of non-Australian origin has created a pressure and a response in the area of broadcasting which helped put public radio in place. The effect on the Aboriginal population of Western settlement and the role of public broadcasting in helping to reinstate Aboriginal culture has parallels with trends in North America.

History

The first non-commercial, non-ABC radio had been experimental, low-power transmissions on university campuses, licensed under the Wireless Telegraphy Act. Next, under the Labour administration of Prime Minister Whitlam, two licences were granted in 1974 to 'fine' music (classical) societies in Sydney and Melbourne which had been pressing for several years to be allowed to broadcast. These apparently unthreatening demands for educational and classical music broadcasting led the way and did much to establish a respectable case for public broadcasting.[26]

But those who, in the same year, formed the Public Broadcasting Association of Australia (PBAA) aimed at more comprehen-
sive community access programming and many of the 12 licences
granted to educational institutions in the last throes of the Whitlam government went to PBAA supporters determined to em-
phasise the needs of the audience beyond the campus.

The incoming Liberal administration was faced with a *fait ac-
compli* and mounting pressure from minority ethnic communities
who saw public radio as a means access to broadcasting. The
government had inherited an ethnic/access station in Melbourne,
3ZZ, run by the ABC, and two ethnic stations, 2EA Sydney and
3EA Melbourne. In 1977 it ordered ABC to close down 3ZZ and
took over the two ethnic stations, actions which aroused strong
political protest and accusations of interference in the ABC's
independence.[27] Instead, the Special Broadcasting Service (SBS)
was set up to supervise ethnic broadcasting on radio and TV, and
2EA and 3EA were brought under the SBS with greatly increased
budgets.[28]

Whatever misgivings surrounded this change at the time, from
this point on the evolution of public broadcasting proceeded more
smoothly. A key moment was the policy statement of 5 April 1978
by Posts and Telecommunications Minister Staley. Announcing
that three categories of licence – E (educational), S (special
interest, e.g. music, sport, religion, with medium coverage area),
C (community, low coverage area in cities, medium elsewhere) –
would be now available, Staley gave strong positive endorsement
for public broadcasting:

> The Government sees public broadcasting as a force for diver-
> sity. Its role is to provide Australians with a range of choices
> which the national and commercial sectors are not able to
> provide . . . It is accepted that public broadcasters have a better
> appreciation of the interests, hence needs, of their broadcasting
> communities than anyone else, including government.

This policy represented a considerable achievement on the part
of the PBAA whose position from here on was increasingly stabil-
ised as representative of the sector to the point where, today, it
dispenses government funds to public broadcasters through the
Public Broadcasting Foundation (PBF). The arrangements made

for public broadcasting by the Liberals were confirmed by the succeeding Labour government. In 1986 there were 65 public radio stations broadcasting and another 150 groups expressing an interest in obtaining a licence.[29]

Licensing Procedure

An important feature of the licensing system is that the initiative comes from the community, which first deals with the Federal Department of Communications, supplying detailed proposals for financial, organisational and technical arrangements, backed by socio-economic research on the proposed service area. Test transmissions authorised by the DOC, usually over a weekend, allow groups to verify technical calculations, test community support and give volunteers a taste of operational conditions.

DOC approval will be based on a national frequency plan in which public radio's need for space is in principle assumed, alongside the claims of ABC and the commercial sector. If the DOC gives approval in a particular case, an intention to award a licence is announced and applications are invited. Public hearings are held by the Australian Broadcasting Tribunal (ABT) whose responsibility is the award of licences and their renewal at three-yearly intervals.

For community groups these two stages can take several years of effort during which local support has to be maintained and costs met – mainly through fund-raising locally, but limited pump-priming funds are in some cases available from the federal government via the PBF. Another hazard is that a broadly-based bid for a C (Community) licence can be overtaken by the case made by a special interest group for an S licence. From 1986, E (Educational) licences were no longer issued but will come under the S category. The present distribution is that two thirds of public radio licences are C category and a quarter S. The remainder are E or licensed originally under the Wireless Telegraphy Act.

Finance

Income for public radio grew steadily from $3m in 1981 to $7m in 1985. It comes from three main sources: listeners and local support; commercial sponsorship; federal and state government grants. In addition, a small number of stations (7 in 1985) receive a proportionately large amount of funding from the educational institutions that hold their licences, an amount which in 1985 was equal to a fifth of the income of the entire sector.

Federal grants totalling $1.2m were channelled through the PBF in 1985/6. Of this, 12 per cent went to Aboriginal broadcasting groups and 57 per cent to stations to enable the production of ethnic programmes. This was the year the SBS radio budget was transferred to the PBF which has argued that the amounts are considerably below what is needed to support the growing number of hours of ethnic and Aboriginal programming.

The main other source of federal funding is job creation schemes, whose disadvantage is the abrupt cut-off when the scheme ends. Other federal sources included the International Year of Youth, the Australia (Arts) Council and programmes for rural and Aboriginal development.

At the state level, financial support came from departments concerned with Arts, Youth and Community, Leisure, Sport and Tourism, and Co-operative Development, as well as, for a few stations, assistance in the form of cheap rented or free premises.

The income from commercial sponsorship is increasing, having nearly doubled from 14 per cent of total income in 1982 to 27 per cent in 1985 in the stations covered by the PBF's survey. Six of the 23 stations who answered the question expected to get over half their income from sponsorship in 1985, two of them forecasting over 85 per cent from this cource. The majority of stations wanted to see ABT regulations on sponsorship loosened, and most foresaw closure if sponsorship were abolished. In view of these attitudes, it is perhaps ominous that the ABT regulations do not appear to restrict advertising to local businesses.

Income from listener subscription, fund-raising and local support, though slightly down as the sponsorship trend increased, was 42 per cent in 1985, and apparently healthily based on fund-raising strategies that are similar to those used in North American stations.

Staff and Volunteers

The PBF survey estimated the value of volunteer work to stations as $50m per year. Few stations however pay a volunteer co-ordinator. The report notes that among the skills acquired by young people in the voluntary work they do in public radio, increased self-confidence is important in helping them seek regular employment subsequently. However few stations organise formal training courses; most training is *ad hoc* and little of it on the technical side.

A significant by-product of public radio was revealed by another survey, conducted in 1986 of 14 of the larger and established stations into the number of paid staff and volunteers who had gained subsequent employment in other media. Between 1982 and 1986, 304 people had successfully moved on in this way, nearly half to the ABC and about a third to commercial radio.[30]

Programming

Of the 33 public radio stations surveyed by the PBF, between 16 and 20 reported that the main community groups involved were: cultural/arts, ethnic, youth and student, and health and welfare groups. 14 stations named 'political activist', aboriginal and religious groups. Music programming predominates with three quarters of the surveyed stations scheduling music for over 60 per cent of the time.

Summary

Government commitment to public radio is now firmly established, but the increasing dependence on commercial sponsorship represents competition for the commercial sector and a pressure towards conformity among stations whose original aim was to be alternative. There is a danger that unless this tendency is checked public radio could become the means for stealthy deregulation of the commercial sector.

The commitment of higher (tertiary) education to this form of radio is impressive. About the success of ethnic broadcasting under the present arrangements it is hard to draw conclusions. It maybe that the Special Broadcasting Service will be subsumed in ABC's responsibilities.

Chapter 8

The Listener as Accomplice: Italy and France[1]

The Background

The shock of *radios libres* (free radio) hit Europe at about the time community radio in North America became established – the mid-1970s – and it occurred in the same climate of radical protest. The world was smaller now, thanks to television whose audiences in the late Sixties had seen police beating students in Paris and Chicago, and Russian tanks rolling into Prague. By now, protest had turned to participation and media was a prime field for power-sharing.

But 'free' in Europe signalled a revolt against state-dominated broadcasting systems, whereas in North America, land of the free market, the political success of community radio, out of all proportion to its numerical size, was assisted by a move in the reverse direction: federally-supported public broadcasting had been introduced or strengthened to check the commercial sector or make good its deficiencies.

On the economic and cultural plane, Europe had been the target for American commercial pressures since the beginning of the century. The domination of Hollywood was a fact of life before the First World War; Radio Luxembourg between the wars introduced British listeners to the music Reith's BBC refused to play; from the end of the Second World War, American aid – and American military presence – in Europe prepared the way for the giant American advertising industry to knock on the doors of Europe's economy.

European public broadcasting systems proceeded to contain or defuse the commercial pressure within relatively controlled environments. ITV in Britain had been designed to avoid, under a regulatory authority, the 'excesses' of American sponsored television. Germany, Italy and France each strictly limited the proportion of advertising allowed to supplement licence revenue, while the French *radios periphériques*, run by Paris-based commercial companies in which the government had majority shareholdings, effectively absorbed the demand for national advertising on radio. The Scandinavian countries succeeded in excluding commercial broadcasting altogether. Even the consequences of North Sea piracy were contained within the British duopoly in a solution which also responded to a parallel contemporary pressure – the demand for decentralisation in government and state institutions. The controlled devolution of the BBC was imitated by Swedish broadcasting. In Germany, the post-war plan of regionalised broadcasting remained in place, while the Dutch reforms of the mid-1960s had designed the 'pillarised' system where access at national level was guaranteed to recognised interest groups.

Politically and economically, then, the beginning of the 1970s found European broadcasting systems relatively intact even if within some citadels mid-Atlantic accents could be heard and dissident mutterings about democracy. It was however in the countries with a tradition of centralisation and undisguised political control of broadcasting that the status quo was most vulnerable. If the experience of *radios libres* in Italy and France is emphasised in this chapter, it is not least because, filtered through chauvinist barriers of language and culture, it has on the whole reached English-speaking observers in the form of myth and stereotype. The same is true in reverse: discussion of non-commercial, autonomous local radio in Latin countries has on the whole proceeded in ignorance of Anglo-Saxon models. One interesting transmission path can be traced from Frantz Fanon's notice of radio in Algeria ('Suddenly radio has become just as necessary as arms for the people in the struggle against French colonialism'[2]) which was taken up by Quebec activists,[3] whose model of *médias communautaires* was, in turn, influential in Italy and France.

Video was at first the medium in which the Quebec connection was expressed in Europe. The technology signals the arrival of another force – that of the Japanese electronics industry. For a time, the Sony and JVC portapaks became the passion of activists and intellectuals and, allied to cable, briefly absorbed the attention of a number of national and municipal authorities interested in participatory development schemes. The increasing availability of light-weight electronic hardware was an important pre-condition of the arrival of *radios libres*.

Italian Explosion

On 23 November 1974, 'Radio Bologna per l'Accesso Pubblico' began a few weeks of illegal transmission as a publicity campaign aimed at 'hastening the reform of the information system and demonstrating the possibility of decentralisation and free access at a very moderate cost'.[4] Run by a co-operative of workers, students and communications experts, the station's reach, with a 20km radius, was local, but its effect was national and sensational. Coming from the heartland of regional support for the Italian Communist Party (PCI), the broadcast was an explicit criticism of RAI, the Italian state broadcasting organisation, and an appeal to Parliament and public opinion for reform.

Italian broadcasting had been heading for this crisis for some years. Since the war RAI had been dominated by the right-wing Christian Democrat party. Its broadcasting cultivated a metropolitan excellence which had little appeal in the regions. Its news coverage was blatantly biased and failed to represent either the strong regional support for the PCI or the young ultra-left, disillusioned with the PCI's policy of 'historic compromise' and increasingly turning to autonomous groupings. As the Socialists and Communists gained ground in Parliament, the Christian Democrats came under pressure to share the control of national broadcasting. The proposed carve-up did little to placate grass-roots political opinion and what nobody had foreseen was the legal and constitutional loophole at local level.

The Bologna initiative was non-commercial and intended to pressurise the authorities into decentralisation. It took its cue from the incident of Telebiella, earlier in the year, when the authorities closed down a small commercial cable TV station which was relaying foreign programmes without a permit. Telebiella took the Italian government to court, and its appeal led eventually to the

European Court (where its case, though unsuccessful, has perhaps been insufficiently studied as a precedent for challenging government broadcasting monopoly).[5] On the way, the Italian Constitutional Court criticised the broadcasting monopoly in terms which gave encouragement to the Bologna access group.

Scores, then hundreds of stations followed the Bologna example. At first the authorities attempted to close the stations down, but legal appeals were upheld and control was quickly lost. Finally, in July 1976, the Constitutional Court declared that RAI's monopoly was constitutionally invalid at local level and even more stations flooded the airwaves. By June 1978, an official survey counted 2275 radio stations, giving Italy a world record in numbers of radio stations per head of population (1 per 24 747) and one station per 132 square km (compared to the USA's one per 1170 square km).[6]

From the beginning of the explosion most of the stations were commercial, extensions of the music, electronics and publishing industries. Most were supportive of, some directly linked to the political right which was content to see the monopoly thus outflanked if it could not control it at the centre. A complete lack of regulation meant that groups would set up on the FM band wherever there was a space. Ever-increasing transmitter power and round-the-clock occupation of channels (sometimes by tone-signals in default of programming) was necessary to prevent counter-occupation. Such conditions favoured those with strong financial backing, and all-music formats, syndicated programming and networking made their inevitable appearance. Private television quickly followed. Most such broadcasting simply reproduced the traditional relationships between broadcasters and listeners.

Socialist Radio

The reaction of the left, whose Bologna initiative led the way, produced more interesting results. The PCI's attitude was at first equivocal. On the one hand it saw the spread of local radio as a distraction from the long-overdue reform of RAI. On the other hand, much as it disliked some of the far left stations, it saw the importance of protecting the non-commercial sector and bringing it into some relationship with RAI from which both would benefit.

Its proposals at this stage included the setting up of a National Broadcasting Committee which would define service areas, draw up a frequency plan, award licences and compile a list of authorised stations. But other more pressing preoccupations, and the shifting electoral positions of the parties have prevented any such regularisation of local radio.

In Bologna three years after the first appearance of free radio, three stations illustrated the range of 'democratic' (i.e. left) radio which were linked at that period in a national organisation, FRED (Federation of Democratic Radio Broadcasters).

Radio Quartiere was run entirely by volunteers and, as its name suggested, was intended to serve the district, a working-class area. Its 20-watt, FM transmitter had a radius of approximately 2km. Start-up costs (US $5000 at the time) and two years' running costs were met by ARCI (Italian Association for Culture and Recreation). The station's 45 hours per week was overseen by a production committee elected by a 70-strong general assembly. Programmes included slots for tram-drivers, squatters, national servicemen, women, district committees, high school students, trades unions, sports clubs and Greek students. There were regular programmes on the cinema, on science fiction, on drugs; live studio and phone-in debates, and comedy sketches. Music included jazz, soul, pop, Italian regional, Eritrean and Greek music.

Through questionnaires distributed among high schools in the district, Radio Quartiere had ascertained that its weekly reach among high school students was 13 per cent. Typically they listened to two or three music stations for most of the day, switching to Radio Quartiere or Radio Città (see below) for news, especially when something important happened in the city. Three quarters of listening was to free radio, with RAI claiming only a quarter.[7]

Radio Città was on an altogether different scale. Its 400-watt transmitter (FM) reached across the city of Bologna (population $\frac{1}{2}$m) to an audience estimated at 15 000 regular listeners. In May 1977, there were 13 full-time staff and 20 volunteers regularly involved. The station was legally a co-operative, but an assembly, meeting fortnightly, took operational decisions. Community media models from Quebec had influenced this structure, but American-style listener subscription had been rejected. Instead, revenue totalling approximately US $6000 per month came from advertising; from the operation of a news and advertising agency serving a left clientele; from sales of audio equipment, records and cassettes; and from fund-raising concerts and film shows.

News and information were an important part of the schedule which also included regular space for trades unions, the women's movement, education for medical students, safety at work; there were regular programmes for and by prisoners, naturists, craft-workers, strip artists, the police; music (jazz, rock, Greek) and sport filled out the schedule, with Sunday being an open day for free access.[8]

Radio Alice

Bologna's most famous station at this time was Radio Alice. 'Mao-Dadaist', its name proclaiming a debt to Lewis Carroll, Radio Alice denied 'reality' and rejected the idea of schedules. 'We have to break the logic of the mirror. Information is not just the repetition or the display of what is going on in reality, but it is a means of transforming reality.'[9] Franco 'Bifo' Berardi, a member of the A/traverso collective which founded Radio Alice, talking four years after the closure of the station, said

> Radio Alice started with people who came from the experience of *Potere Operaio*, a leftist revolutionary group, and people involved in the movement of *autonomia*. We did not see radio as solely a political means but also as a possibility of organising the experience of homogeneous communities – feminists, gays, workers. We did not conceive of the radio as a political organis-ation that had to state or decide who could speak and who couldn't. We considered the station as a point of intersection of different experiences – each experience being different from the others.[10]

Umberto Eco, who at the University of Bologna was a first-hand witness of this period, described Radio Alice's programming:

> *Radio Alice* is made up of literary citations, classical music, political songs, non-structured dialogues, free-wheeling lan-guage, and direct reporting of such varied events as strikes, squatting, demonstrations and fêtes. The result is that a typical

broadcast is made up of five minutes of highly politicized talk about an ongoing strike followed by a conversation with a pseudo-drug addict who speaks of his personal problems, very 'American' music, and dialogues that must be qualified as being 'Alician . . . which celebrate nonsense and the nonsensical.'[11]

Bifo's claim (in the Relay article cited above) that Alice developed a language that 'opened up the possibility of a close connection between politics and artistic language and direct forms of speech' is confirmed by Eco:

> What is significant is that the language they use is received and adopted by young, sub-proletarian masses who have no particular personal culture and who identify with this kind of language. In other words, the new generation is speaking a language (formerly used only by the avant-garde) . . . without knowing its history . . . The result is that one can no longer tell whether it is someone connected to the radio who is speaking (those who know it all) or whether it is someone from outside who is speaking (those who know nothing). Syntax, semantics, phonetics and ideas are all the same.[12]

This relationship with listeners was encouraged by Radio Alice's use, in common with other left stations, of the telephone reporter. This allowed up-to-the-second reporting of demonstrations, strikes and the reaction of the authorities. There is no doubt that, at this troubled period in Italian politics, the intention was to organise political action. Recalling the occupation of a school by students whose phone call to Radio Alice encouraged many calls from other schools, Bifo comments 'This shows the possibility not only of circulating information about the strike, but also for extending the strike [which] . . . could be immediately diffused, immediately organised in other situations.'[13]

These methods caused Radio Alice's downfall. On 11 March 1977, student uprisings in Bologna were opposed, on orders of the Communist Mayor, Zangheri, with violent police force, supported by armoured cars. In a use of words revealing in the context of our discussion, Zangheri urged the police 'This is war! These people must be eliminated. By their own actions they have *cut themselves off from the community*' (emphasis added).[14] A well-known cartoonist, whose office gave a view of the fighting, phoned a commentary to the station which was explicitly supportive of the student demonstrators.

City officials and police judged that Radio Alice was inciting listeners to riot and shortly afterwards, in a broadcast which circulated as a classic among free radios, the audience heard the police battering down the station door and an announcer describing their armed entrance before the microphone was silenced. Even in those last moments the speaker characteristically 'fictionalised' the situation by comparing the armed police to those in the film *The Last Days of Katherina Blum*. A recording of the cartoonist's commentary was used in evidence against the station.

Milan, May 1977

Two months later in Milan, a brief eruption of street violence was reported very differently by free radio. The fate of Radio Alice cautioned other tactics. In Rome, Radio Città Futura, when it felt itself under threat, had appealed to its listeners to come to the station, and the presence in their number of senior politicians prevented a police storming. In Milan, in both Radio Canale 96 and Radio Popolare a more stable structure than Alice's and a less anarchic policy on information would in any case have led to different results.

What happened on the afternoon of 14 May was that a demonstration had turned violent; a bus was burned, barricades set up, a policeman shot dead, a student badly injured in fighting between rival factions. During these events, RC96 did not interrupt its scheduled programme of music by Joan Baez. In the newsroom telephone calls brought reports of the incidents which were carefully and sympathetically evaluated for later use in the news bulletin.[15]

That night from midnight to two in the morning, Radio Popolare included some of RC96's news in its analysis which sought to discover what had happened and why, and in links with Radio Città Futura in Rome, how the news had been reported by mainstream media. The phone lines were then opened for discussion. Having listened to this particular phone-in, Francesco Cavalli-Sforza, a media analyst living in Milan, commented

'An interpretation of what happened takes shape from the contributions of the different people involved. Each person is asked for their political analysis . . . So, things happen during the day on the streets and are discussed at night on the radio. That's very important. Everyone is in contact through the operation of the radio, and each station is able to be in touch with the other and to make links between stations. The whole thing is absolutely not as anarchic and out of control as the press and government would have us believe. It is the kind of control that comes from an action being discussed by tens of thousands of people over the air. Each person who telephones has something to say. They don't telephone simply to give their personal opinion, but they make their call a political intervention and in this way add something to the debate.[16]

The programme is a good illustration of Radio Popolare's policy as John Downing found it three years later in 1980.[17] RP had developed a way to engage different sections of the left in mutual communication of a kind that its wider listenership could overhear and understand. One of the means of achieving this was its network of volunteer correspondents in schools, factories, union branches, etc. Other stations have used this system, but never maintained it with such consistency over time. It is backed up by a relationship with listeners which has shared journalistic skills to the extent of making the audience an increasingly active partner in information production.

In more light-hearted moments listeners have agreed to their homes being searched while RP reporters gave a running commentary. On other occasions, listeners have been encouraged to role play with each other in linked phone-ins. In the same spirit, RP has often provided a sound commentary to accompany TV programmes, satirical, subversive or complementary, inviting listeners to switch on the TV with the sound down.[18]

Summary

At the level of structure, the chaotic results of a failure to regulate have up till now instilled caution in other governments. The massive flight of audiences from RAI to private radio and television has weakened the case of the public service to receive public funds. With a few notable exceptions the law of the market place has worked against diversity of ownership, original and innovative radio forms, local culture and democratic control. The effects on RAI, however, have not been all bad – in style and language, and in degree of accessibility – the *radios libres* have had an influence.

The remarkable degree to which some stations broke down the traditional barriers between sender and receiver was a symptom and a product of a historical phase of unusual intensity, even for Italian culture and politics. That stations like Radio Popolare have been able to develop this relationship over a long period may perhaps be because, in a commercial market, by now highly diversified in format, a unique service is being offered to a community bound by similar cultural and political interests. In this respect, Italian non-commercial free radio has perhaps reached the same point as US community radio.

FRANCE

If, as Enzensberger has remarked,[19] in May 1968 the Paris students did not take over the radio stations, it was perhaps because they had sympathetic coverage from at least two of them, the *périphériques* RTL and Europe-1, whose detailed reporting of police movements earned them the title of *radio-barricades* from the Minister of the Interior. The subsequent purge from French broadcasting (ORTF) of staff sympathetic to the left was the price exacted by the de Gaulle/Pompidou government, and the splitting of ORTF into seven parts carried out by Giscard d'Estaing after his election to the Presidency in 1974 further isolated radical dissent.

But protest in France in the early 1970s was channelled mainly through the print media. It was typical that the 'spirit of '68' lived on most strongly in *Libération*, an addition to a strong left section of the press which was founded in 1973. Few intellectuals or political activists on the left considered radio as an organising tool. A number of factors combined to change their indifference and bring the medium to the attention of the opposition. One was the example of the successful exploitation of radio by the Italian left – at least in the early stages of the 'explosion'. Another was the Ecology Party's need for publicity which coincided with a libertarian belief in decentralised, self-managed radio by a few *soixante-huitardes*. As the latter's technical skills were spread to groups in the regions, free radio came to symbolise opposition to the centralised tradition of French broadcasting and the cultural and linguistic domination of Paris. Finally, as the economic policies of the Giscard administration began to provoke political and trade union unrest, some astonishingly inept uses of repressive force created soldiarity on the left and won over the uncommitted.

A key figure was Antoine Lefébure who had, interestingly, learned technical skills from the South London pirate Radio Jackie, and spent time as a volunteer with KPFA in Berkeley.[20] On his return to France Lefébure started a magazine, *Interférences*. In its second issue, March 1975, he expounded the possibilities of independent local radio which might demand a licence as an exception (*dérogation*) to the monopoly. 'In the event of refusal, it is possible that private transmitters would multiply, proving that people don't allow themselves to be reduced to silence so easily.'[21]

Radio Vert

By 1977, Lefébure had entered a 'marriage of convenience' with the Ecology Party.[22] He was not interested in 'party radio' as such, but the philosophy of the Ecologists was sympathetic to the idea of decentralised radio and the polls indicated they might achieve some success in the municipal elections in March. A publicity stunt of brilliant ingenuity brought the plan to the attention of the nation. On 20 March, during a studio discussion programme on TF1 with election candidates, Brice Lalonde of the Ecologists produced a radio set broadcasting, he said, the launch of *Radio Vert*. In fact the signal was coming from a transmitter concealed in a bag carried by Lefébure who was standing nearby in the studio. This way they reached a nationwide TV audience and the stunt launched a lengthy press debate which included inevitable comparisons with Italy and the case of Radio Alice, closed down a week before.

On 13 May Radio Vert made a second broadcast and again nationwide publicity was achieved by a filmed report of the event in Antenne 2's main evening news. The government was furious, and the technical division of French broadcasting, TDF, was ordered to jam any further broadcasts. Radio Vert's next two transmissions were rendered inaudible by army helicopters carrying TDF equipment. But up and down the country radical groups began to obtain transmitters and started to broadcast. In July, Radio Fil Bleu in Montpelier was duly jammed, even though its organisers were supporters of the government. They took TDF to court in a test of the monopoly's power to prevent the free expression of opinion. In September, Lefébure and his colleagues formed ALO (Association pour la Libération des Ondes). By January 1978 twenty groups possessed their own transmitter and on February 15 organised simultaneous broadcasting in a day of action in Paris.

The government was successful in the parliamentary elections of March 1978 and, after a pause while the outcome of the Radio Fil Bleu case was awaited, rushed through a bill which closed all loopholes and greatly increased the penalties for illegal broadcasting. At the same time ALO published its own 'bill' which set out its proposals for the legal introduction of local radio. These were a deliberate attempt to avoid the 'capitalist anarchy' of Italy, and included the prohibition of networks, a restriction on transmitter power and the limitation of advertising to five minutes in the hour.

ALO's willingness to entertain the idea of advertising drew severe criticism from groups further to the left who formed in June 1978 the FNRLNC (*Fédération Nationale des Radios Libres Non-Commerciales*). A number of its member stations were backed by Socialist- and Communist-controlled local councils.

Radio 93

Radio 93 provides a good example of the FNRLNC philosophy at this period. As its organisers explained,[23] radio should be the means of expression for a particular group which already had its own identity. If the group disappears, so does the radio. This implies a certain style of working – live transmission in a public place with address and phone number publicised; no fixed schedules, but themes, often suggested by those who pass by or telephone in.

From July 1977, Radio 93 operated in Seine-St. Denis, a suburb to the north of Paris, a working-class area with a large immigrant population. At first the group broadcast irregularly, moving to different locations to avoid jamming and arrest, but as support gathered and funds came in, they installed themselves on the first floor of a bookshop, increased their transmitter power and went public. The collective saw it as their job to put the equipment at the disposal of any who asked, and broadcast debate was very often followed by action. During this period more than half a dozen collectives were formed by residents around issues that concerned this marginalised neighbourhood.

Finally, on 29 April 1978, the police carried out a violent raid. Other free radios rallied to Radio 93's support, lending equipment and broadcasting an appeal for a demonstration of solidarity. The next day Radio 93 opened its microphone to a large crowd of well-wishers. The presence on this occasion of well-known intellectuals like Gilles Deleuze and Félix Guattari, well publicised next day in the left press, was an indication that the cause of free radio was winning influential support.

In Paris that year an exotic variety of stations could be heard defying the government and dodging the jamming – *Noctiluque/ Nid de Coucou, Onz'débrouille, Les Radioteuses, Radio Flip, Radio Ivre, Radio Bakelite, Fil Qui Chante, Oxygène, Abbesses Echo*, etc. The titles expressed rejection of tradition and a search for new forms, as well as a political act which was risky considering the violence of the police and their support in high places. Frequently the TDF jammers turned a blind eye to the transmissions. Members themselves of the socialist trade union, CFDT, their refusal to take action was often motivated by a respect for the protests of colleagues.[24]

Trade Union Radio

This was the case when French broadcasting went on strike in February 1979 and a group of ten free radios transmitted a cassette made by the strikers. Subsequently the CFDT branch in the broadcasting studios, after taking lessons from free radio practitioners, organised Radio Franche, which put out a daily broadcast for several days without being jammed.

Radio SOS Emploi in Longwy, Lorraine, went unjammed as well. A local initiative which began in December 1978, it was supported by the CFDT as part of its campaign to oppose the government plan to make 20 000 steel-workers redundant. A group of workers learned from Radio Vert Fessenheim, the Strasbourg radio, the techniques of transmission and production and maintained a daily 45-minute programme for 9 months. As so often happens, the presence of an outlet attracted a rich variety of programme material from local people that was not directly connected to the original issue the station was set up to address. So poems and plays, music and local history were transmitted as well as information about the strike. Its organisers claimed Radio SOS Emploi was, in contrast to the stations up till then launched by 'intellectuals', the 'first working-class radio in France'.

Radio Lorraine Coeur d'Acier started three months later in the same town of Longwy. Backed by a budget from the central funds of the Communist trade union CGT, installed in the town hall and with its transmitter fixed to the church spire, the station was opened ceremonially (and with video coverage) by the mayor herself. RLCA broadcast from 8 a.m. to 10 p.m., stopping between 7 and 7.45 so as not to disturb the transmissions of SOS Emploi going out on a neighbouring wavelength. Its 300-watt transmitter was bought in Italy and CGT headquarters sent two professional journalists from Paris to organise it.

The government took this challenge more seriously. After its helicopters were prevented by an injunction from flying over Longwy, it ordered CRS police from Paris to support the TDF takeover of a nearby TV relay transmitter from which jamming began on 17 May. SOS Emploi, still spared from jamming, appealed in support of its sister station for listeners to gather at the relay transmitter in protest. Within the hour 1500 responded. Retaliating to police baton charges and tear-gas, some of the younger workers smashed shops and offices in the town in a night of violence in which 25 people were injured, 15 of them police. By the autumn, however, negotiations and redundancy pay offers for steel workers in the region had taken the heat out of the situation, and the stations ceased transmissions at the end of the year. Before their closedown, a team of sociology students from the University of Nancy carried out a survey which showed that *RCLA* was reaching a regular 22 per cent of the local population despite the jamming, and that the figure before the jamming had been 45 per cent.[25]

Radio Riposte

By now, thanks to assiduous lobbying by ALO, some significant
foothills of the Socialist Party had been won over, if not to ALO's
position, at least to agreeing that the issue of free radio and the
monopoly should be put on the agenda. It remained to convince
François Mitterrand, and he was finally persuaded to put himself
on the line by taking part in an illegal broadcast. Radio Riposte was
given wide-scale advance publicity. Duly condemned by the government, the broadcast from the Socialist Party headquarters on
the night of 28 June 1979, was, after a few minutes, duly jammed.
The police arrived, as did the TV cameras. Almost, it seemed,
without realising the consequences, the Socialist Party was committed to ending the monopoly.

Socialist Government

After the Socialist election victory on 10 May 1981, the story of
free radio took a new twist. To begin with, the jamming continued
just as if no one had told the TDF of the change of government.
Despite it, old pirates and new arrivals began in increasing numbers to occupy every available space on the FM band – in the
regions and especially in Paris where every kind of sound began to
be heard in an exotic mix of musical styles, political tendencies,
languages and radiophonic experiment. By the end of the year it
was possible to hear 113 stations in Paris alone.

Meanwhile the new government began to plan parliamentary
legislation to reform communications and set up a Consultative
Commission (on which the main free radio associations were
represented) to settle the technical and administrative criteria for
licensing private local radio (RLP), as well as adjudicate between
the flood of licence applications. The Prime Minister, Mauroy, was
implacably opposed to advertising; his idea of free radio was based
on the non-profit associations and militant groups which had
battled to keep a 'space for liberty' in the period of opposition. At
first President Mitterrand supported his stand. Pending completion
of the Consultative Commission's work, an amnesty was granted
only to those stations which undertook not to carry advertising nor
set up networks, to limit transmission power and to be constituted

as non-profit associations. To help the smaller stations, the government announced it would make available starting-up grants from a fund 'for the encouragement of local expression in broadcasting' taken from TV and *périphérique* advertising revenue.

The High Authority

The Consultative Commission's task was relatively easy in the provinces where there were few contenders for the frequencies; the problem was Paris. By July 1982, 155 groups were applying for 15 frequencies and lobbying was intense. That month the new communications law created the High Authority to whom the final decision passed. The Authority ('the most visible sign of the break with the past', Mitterrand) was to be responsible for all broadcast licence awards. Its President, Michèle Cotta, extracted more frequencies from the TDF, but its final list of 22 licences included a number of strange forced combinations sharing frequencies in uneasy alliances. Still, prizes went to the strongest lobbies across the political spectrum: the free radio associations, the press, the right-wing Mayor of Paris, Jacques Chirac, the Roman Catholic Archbishop, the Jewish community. Fréquence Gaie was there after a successful protest at its earlier exclusion, and Radio Libre Paris representing fifteen different ethnic groups. NRJ was chosen as a music station and some of the old originals – Radio Ivre, Gilda and Radio Vert.

Thereafter a long and difficult task began of forcing the closedown of unlicensed stations and enforcing the regulations. Some paid heed to warnings and went off the air voluntarily. A series of police raids in August disposed of others. The Authority was in a difficulty because its only weapon was the ultimate one of revoking the licence. A compromise on transmission power was agreed, leading to a new higher limit of 1.5kW.

Advertising

More serious were the infringements over advertising. Many stations were stretching the rules about on-air mention of goods and services, or receiving payment for covering sponsored events.

Some were blatantly running advertising jingles. By now some 1300 stations had been licensed, and twice the number of applications remained to be dealt with. The size of the market was beginning to attract the attention of the big advertising firms. The first of a series of audience surveys demonstrated that RLPs were gaining significantly at the expense of the *périphériques*. A number of key decisions by advertising agencies and production agencies focused the attention of business on the remarkable effectiveness of the new medium in selling to the 15–34 age group. National and regional press groups had not been debarred from participation and were also keen to see their advertising outlets extended.

Finally, at a press conference on 4 April 1984, Mitterrand announced that he was willing to permit advertising and ordered the government to prepare the necessary legislation. So began a process of commercialisation which was to accelerate and change the landscape of French broadcasting. It was not to stop at radio, either, though the rapid development of plans for private cable and satellite networks, and the retaliatory privatisation of TF1 after the election of the Chirac government in 1986, fall outside our story.

By the end of 1985, 1600 RLPs had been licensed. A survey carried out by IFOP in August that year showed that in the Paris area among 15–34 year-olds, RLPs had taken 62.5 per cent of the audience; that the share of the *périphériques* had dropped to 25 per cent and Radio France to 12.5 per cent. In the provinces, the same order prevailed. In every city surveyed, over the whole age-range, RLPs took the major share of the audience from lunchtime onwards, and also, in what had been the *périphériques'* prime slot, the 6 a.m. to 9 a.m. band.

The advertising boom has not been at the expense of the regional press. It has been partly due to an expansion of the market, partly at the expense of the poster business, rather more at the expense of the *périphériques*. A year after the go- ahead for advertising, *Le Monde* estimated that in a total of 2 billion francs spent on advertising, local radio's share had grown from virtually nothing to 400m francs.[26]

The CNCL

A further twist in the *folle histoire* of French FM occurred when the Chirac government changed the regulatory structure after its election success in 1985. Abolishing the High Authority, it created a 13-member Comité Nationale de Communication et Liberté (CNCL) which brought back the overtly political control its predecessor was meant to avoid. According to one observer,[27] it did so literally with a vengeance after the main state TV channel, TF1, had been responsible in 1986 for mobilising public opinion against the government's proposals for higher education. The CNCL thereupon appointed five hard-line Gaullists to run the state radio and TV channels. Having attended to the franchises for the remaining commercial TV channels, the CNCL, between April and June 1987, turned its attention to the RLP licences. In the Paris area its decisions caused the disappearance of almost every station of left sympathies. Amidst allegations of corruption in the CNCL, President Mitterrand openly expressed his criticism of the Committee, and after the defeat of Chirac and the Right in the 1988 elections, the succeeding Socialist-led government announced its intention to replace the CNCL with a new body. The 'Superior Council for Audio-Visual Affairs' will be established with constitutional safeguards to prevent its being dismantled by succeeding governments. In its last months, the CNCL, with its decisions in the Rhone-Alpes region, completed the national reallocation of licences. Though networks were favoured, a number of smaller *radios associatives* and community radios were reinstated in a pattern of judgements which reflected the political change at the centre.

NRJ and the Networks

What are the characteristics of French local radio today? In any reckoning an explanation of NRJ's success must come first. It was the first to dominate the Paris region and to win a substantial listener share in many of the regions. NRJ's presence outside Paris is the result of its now much imitated franchising arrangement which links regional stations to the main Paris station. Franchised stations take the name and adopt the format of the mother-station, receiving a play- list, advice, technical assistance and training. In return, NRJ handles the advertising, taking a percentage of the local revenue and all of the regional and national takings. Franchising was an ingenious way round the rules which at the time insisted on 80 per cent of production coming from the individual station. Like British ILR stations, NRJ had found that local demand for multinational product, supplied locally, counted as local. The whole arrangement gave NRJ a network – sought after and lucrative, with rates that soon exceeded those of the *périphériques*.

Behind all this was NRJ's founder, Jean-Paul Baudecroux. He was brought up in his parents' business which created *Le Baiser*, the enormously successful range of cosmetics that epitomised French chic in the 1950s. The background clearly gave Baudecroux a sense of style and a headstart in understanding the processes needed to market it. To this was added experience of American methods acquired with the sales division of Revlon. Marketing has been the key to NRJ's success. Its strategy has been to associate the radio with other consumer products not necessarily connected with media, an association underpinned by reciprocal agreements, often by ownership.[28] To consume NRJ – and the metaphor was actively invoked by the campaign which pictured a hamburger entitled 'Super Big Radio' – is to adopt a lifestyle which the station proposes for its listeners for each segment of the day, 'relieving them of the trouble of making the complex consumer choices necessary to be 'in'. In short what NRJ sells is a badge of conformity to a group.'[29] Its young audience was mobilised to good effect when the station was threatened with suspension in December 1984. NRJ's advertising agency planned the huge demonstration which underlined the station's popularity and its good connections with the Socialist Party: the President himself had intervened to prevent a police raid.

As for its programming, what NRJ gave 'les kids' was non-stop hits with a quality of sound superior to any other station, a minimum of chat between records, but some news. 'Music and News' as a format is not a French invention, but the competitive demands of a swiftly expanding medium forced on French local radio broadcasters the realisation that local audiences had to be held, even at those points where habit had long encouraged them to switch to Europe-1 or France Inter for the traditional bulletins. The formula arrived at contained sufficient news to make listeners feel they had done their duty in keeping up with events, but was sufficiently anodyne not to disturb the mood.

NRJ's network success encouraged rivals to compete for the same, or target different, audiences. A range of differentiated formats developed in a process familiar in contemporary American radio.

The Hersant group established Fun, Nostalgie grew national from a Lyon base, Pacific FM, Skyrock and Kiss Fm are others.

Music and News in the network recipe has forced many stations to look again at the cost effectiveness of their commitment to information. Even stations linked to the press and staffed with experienced journalists such as Radio Nuée Bleue in Strasbourg, with the loss of their audience to newly arrived NRJ competition, decided to re-target their efforts towards a primarily music format, different from NRJ's, but like it in having a minimal news presence.

Other RLPs

NRJ and its competitors have affected virtually all the other RLPs. How can they be categorised? In terms of legal status and funding sources there are three types: (1) straight commercial stations and networks (2) stations with mixed funding, allowed to have limited advertising, retaining their association status, but disqualified from receiving government funding (3) non- profit associations, receiving no advertising, which qualify for the 'local expression' fund. There are also (4) the decentralised stations of Radio France.

Commercial Stations

The commercial stations are allowed up to 100 per cent of revenue from advertising, but not more than 10 per cent from any one client. Many are subsidiaries of *périphériques* (e.g. Radio 95.2 in Paris, created by Europe-1), of regional and national press groups which moved into local radio in different ways, either risking involvement in the early (non- profit) days, or buying in to stations with an established identity.

Many of these have been christened '*neo- périphériques*', reproducing as they do a traditional style. Such stations are, musically, generalist; they maintain regular news bulletins produced by a team of journalists; quizzes and games keep the tone happy and optimistic. Alouette-FM in the Vendée, far exceeding the authorised transmission power with its 10kW, covers five *départements*, has a staff of 35, over a hundred volunteers, two mobile units and seven relay studios. Originally a non-profit station connected to an association responsible for an annual *son et lumière* event, it went commercial in 1985. Its annual budget is 5mF. With a vigorous and successful policy of community involvement, organised through networks of the centre-right, (its founder went on to be Secretary of State for Culture in the Chirac government), Alouette-FM is another illustration, admittedly in an area unserved by NRJ and the *périphériques*, of the success of RLP in satisfying the previous deficiencies of French broadcasting, especially in the matter of regional information.

'Mixed' Stations

Most RLPs have opted for mixed funding status which brings in the revenue to pay for staff while still allowing the connections with the local community which association status facilitates.

Radio G in the north Paris suburbs, till it lost its licence in the 1987 reallocation, was an example of a station that managed to find a stability in matching resources to aims. It employed 20 staff, 13 of them full-time. A quarter of its 1.6mF budget came from the municipal council of Gennevilliers, its home town, and the rest from central government grants, membership, donations, etc. It covered a lively area of some ten townships including Nanterre, and, interestingly, the same Seine-St. Denis where Radio 93 used to operate (see p. 149).

Radio G was strong on news, employed four full-time journalists to cover local affairs and to edit national and international news received through its subscription to *Agence France Presse*. 6 a.m. to 9 a.m. was an important news time, and between 6.30 p.m. and 8 p.m. when listeners phoned in with their comments on the news or with their own information. The station was in existence long enough for people to seek it out with programme ideas and found that local history is particularly important. Volunteers produced 40 per cent of its programming – classical music, guitar, the cinema, and slots for ethnic communities – Portugese, Spanish, Creole, Arabic, the last for 20 hours per week.[30]

Non-profit Stations

The non-profit community stations are the smallest group. The European Institute for the Media study of the Acquitaine region found examples there 'poor but enthusiastic', relying on young volunteer staff but still not finding that the 'local expression' fund covers all their expenses.

The former Radio Vert Fessenheim, now Radio Dreyekland, makes an interesting contrast, as a regional station, with Alouette-FM. RVF was one of the more unusual of the pre-1981 pirates. It was originally set up in 1977 to support the anti-nuclear campaign opposed to the building of a reactor south of Strasbourg, at a time when neither the regional press nor regional radio and TV were paying any attention to the issue. RVF's mobilising capacity soon led to other topics being aired (redundancies, strikes, conditions for foreign workers, women's issues, the problems of national service conscripts) and the team was duplicated by other groups on both sides of the Rhine and down to the Swiss border in a region whose common characteristic was the neglect of its language and culture by the centres of power in Bonn and Paris. Transmitters multiplied and by 1980, thirteen groups were regularly involved in the transmissions. At the height of the pre-1981 political tension, RVF was closely involved in the region's struggles – and closely pursued by the authorities.[31]

When the opportunity came to submit licence applications to the Socialist government, RVF adopted a new name which signified its regional identity and the three corners of the countries which met there – Radio Régionale Libre Dreyekland. Five licence applications were submitted from an amalgam of the former groups, but the law of July 1982 was not able to respond adequately: only one was granted, for the standard 500-watt power. Unlike Alouette-FM, Radio Dreyekland chose not to flout the law and currently maintains a bare presence on the frequency with only one staff person (paid by the 'local expression' fund) whose time is mainly spent trying to extend the base of support. The irony is that on the German side of the Rhine Dreyekland is still illegal and in a situation where all attempts at free radio are severely repressed, its clandestine operations attract devoted support. The contrast underlines the point made by Mattelart and Piemme[32] in their discussion of the problems that face an alternative medium once legalisation allows it to be permanent.

Radio France: the Decentralised stations

Prior to the Socialist reform of July 1982, FR3, the regional wing of French broadcasting, had been responsible for some limited programme origination in regional centres. Radio France also, in the last years of the Giscard administration, launched three experiments. The one in Laval, Radio Mayenne, opening in June 1980, proved to be the most successful. Broadcasting on FM only, it employed a staff of 26 with some dozen freelancers, and attempted to reflect local life in a style distinctly different from the Paris-based France-Inter. After three months, ownership of FM receivers had risen by 15 per cent and the station had won a daily share of 29 per cent. Only the younger listeners, dismissing it as 'a bit Radio Tractor', gave signs of the need RLPs were soon to meet. This need was recognised in Paris at least by the creation of the all-music station Radio 7 the same year.

After the Socialist reform, Radio France was authorised to set up thirteen local stations and the scale chosen was, like that of Radio Mayenne, departmental. Their installation depends on a favourable vote in the Department's General Council which then bears the capital cost. Thereafter Radio France meets the F8m annual running costs. At the current exchange rate this is slightly more expensive than a contemporary BBC local radio station. A team of similar size to Radio Mayenne is divided equally between journalists, producer/presenters and engineers, and one observer has noted that, in contrast to the RLPs, job hierarchisation and demarcation, is characteristic.[33] The programme schedule is divided between news and community service information; discrete programmes on sport, the countryside and for children; and evening music with chat, phone-ins and discussion.

Radio Style

Such are the four types of local radio. The CNET study by Chantal de Gournay categorises the stations in its sample in terms of stylistic approach, and has some interesting comments to make about 'innovatory broadcasters'. At the time of her survey these were attempting to make a complete break with traditional commercial radio style. The pretended relationship between presenter and public was suppressed, as was any reference to a schedule which would allow listeners to establish daily or weekly 'dates' with a particular programme or presenter. Record requests and dedications were abandoned, though the charts still determined the playlist without being referred to openly. Outside broadcast and dramatic on-the-spot reports were disappearing, replaced by news that was 'deliberately made neutral, undramatic, with no particular headlining or emphasis'. Stations no longer felt the need to legitimate themselves by giving access to speakers or invited guests. Quiz shows and competitions were disappearing as a means of colonising audiences.

Anglo-Saxon commercial radio watchers, schooled to cynicism, may detect in these trends a sheer lack of cash – radio on the cheap. The programme directors interviewed by de Gournay, however, invoked the need to offer a format distinctly different from the false spontaneity or jocular tone of the *périphériques*. The innovatory formats ideally presuppose an audience listening on personal stereos who use the station as a soundtrack for living and are content with the total absence of the human factor. The crucial consideration is that it should be a uniform, unvarying format. Originality is less important than loyalty to an audience with a specialised musical taste, quick to protest at any departure from the format. To achieve such an effect is not necessarily cheap.

Comment

From a historical perspective, French local radio provides a clear illustration of two issues. First, the problem experienced by what Collin calls 'radio of political and social intervention'[34] when it becomes legalised. It is clear that much of this radio is ephemeral and its objectives short-term. Some such stations die, others survive the transition to 'peacetime', but need funding at least to match the voluntary effort for which there must always be room in *associative radio*.

The second issue relates to the peculiar historical conjuncture in which free radio became institutionalised in France. Politically, a very centralised monopoly was due to be broken. Economically, a system which, unlike Britain, had not experienced privatisation at regional and local level, provided rich incentives – and pickings – for the advertising industry. Culturally, the meaning of this radical breakthrough had a 'generational' significance more akin to the era of North Sea piracy than ITV's appearance in Britain of the 1950s. The development of audio technology (particularly in the form of personal stereos) reinforced the desire of a young generation to withdraw from the traditions, symbols and institutions of its parents and become accomplices of the transnational forces promising stylistic links across national boundaries.

Where is community radio in all this? Examples in the Anglo-Saxon tradition certainly flourish, and to better effect than they are given credit for by studies such as that by the European Institute for the Media whose yardstick is a professional one, or by de Gournay who seems insufficiently aware of North American experience. But perhaps more important is to recognise, as de Gournay does, that what was originally a political initiative has been overtaken by different dynamic. French local radio has to be seen in relationship to a sophisticated consumer environment in which sound plays multiple roles: it is both a link in a chain of products *and* assists in the construction of a 'discipline of leisure' *and* for a post-modern generation which has rejected the text, it provides the context for living.

Chapter 9

Third World Radio: Development and Struggle

The previous two chapters have traced the emergence in Western industrialised countries of a kind of radio that challenges the relationship established since broadcasting began between producers and audiences. It has been called community radio in North America and northern Europe, public radio in Australia, free radio in the Latin countries of Europe. Although in these last we have seen that what began as a radical opposition to monopoly opened the door to expansion financed by private capital, there remains a core of oppositional theory and practice that aims in the last analysis to redistribute power: to claim for groups that are socially and politically marginalised or oppressed the right to a fairer share of resources so as to take control of their own lives. Communication media are both part of the resources claimed and an essential factor in the struggle against domination. The distortions, silences and failures of mass media are what provoke oppositional media.

In this chapter we look at examples in Third World countries of producer/audience relationships that differ from the mainstream broadcasting tradition. But first we want to stress the point that on a global level the less well-off countries of the world are in the same position *vis-à-vis* rich countries as are the marginalised and oppressed communities within Western societies to the dominant sections of society. The point needs elaboration in order to contextualise the examples which follow.

163

Historical Background

In the 'First' World's 'discovery' and colonial exploitation of the
countries now called Third World[1] communications were of the
essence. The need to finance economic and political expansion by
trade led to the development of the sea routes that first brought
Europeans to the African and American continents. The subsequent formalisation of colonial and economic relationships with
metropolitan powers established a pattern which followed the
same routes in which, typically, communications were quicker and
more efficient between a colonial capital and its European government than between neighbouring colonies.[2] Often the colonies
were artificial units, composed of scores, even hundreds of different language communities, set in opposition to each other by the
imposition over each of different European languages and cultures.

What all the colonies had in common was an economic exploitation which changed existing economies to ones dependent on a
primary product or raw material being extracted and shipped to
Europe to feed the factories of the industrial revolution. Nor
should we ignore the significant trade in human beings which
transported Africans westwards across the Atlantic and stored up
inescapable social pressures which are now being experienced in
contemporary European and American societies.

Political independence, occurring for many countries in the
1960s, did not bring escape from this economic trap. The Cold
War was by then extending into new forms of rivalry: aid programmes to Third World countries and the space race. The latter's
military programme had its civil counterpart in the development of
satellite communication systems. In both economic aid and communications development, Western- (and American-) dominated
international agencies gave the imprimatur to a situation which
favoured the rich and powerful nations. They provided the capital,
technology and expertise deemed necessary to bring Third World
economies into the modern market place. The same organisations
which had dominated news provision from the second half of the
nineteenth century, and entertainment from the early twentieth
century, had by now moved into satellite-based distribution, with
an ideological updating of the claim for the 'freedom of the press'.
An appeal to the 'free flow of communications' justified a continued imbalance in which news and entertainment produced by

and about a few rich nations was exported to the many poorer ones.[3] Indeed, the period was marked by the emergence on to the world scene of multinational corporations whose capital bases extend far beyond the size or the control of any single government.[4] When, in the forum of UNESCO, Third World countries made proposals which attempted to remedy this imbalance, in a package known as the New World Information Order, Western governments detected the influence of Moscow, while the response of Western media to the MacBride Report dwelt on the threats to journalistic freedom implied by the demand for social responsibility in journalism.

If Cold War politics and multinational capital have secured a domination of communication channels and traffic, they have yet to redress the disparity between rich and poor countries in the matter of communications hardware and infrastructures. In Africa, for example, in 1979, there were 35m radio receivers, an average of 77 per thousand inhabitants, with variations from 8 per thousand in Ethiopia to 275 per thousand in South Africa. In that year 41.8 per cent of the world's radio sets were in North America, 29.5 per cent in Europe, 14.1 per cent in Asia, 9.2 per cent in Latin America and 1.9 per cent in Africa.[5]

Western Broadcasting Models

The above very generalised historical summary serves to underline the point that in relation to communications resources and communications flow, Third World countries suffer the same marginalised position as do the groups which in Western countries campaign for more equitable broadcasting. The picture must now be qualified by reference to the two dominant models of broadcasting, the American commercial and the European public service monopoly models which have influenced post-colonial broadcasting systems differently.

In Latin American countries, European capital investment which succeeded formal political independence was displaced by American capital from the late nineteenth century onwards. The models of broadcasting introduced in the 1920s were consequently overwhelmingly commercial. State ownership in the region is insignificant though each country has at least one government-owned station. Recent figures (including the Caribbean with Latin

America) show 320 radio receivers per thousand inhabitants and a total of 4500 transmitters of which only a little over 600 belong to non-commercial stations.[6] A similar commercial dominance is found in other areas of American influence such as the Pacific and Asian regions.

Most African countries inherited either the British or French broadcasting systems. The latter were from the first more closely state-controlled; the British ex-colonies soon abandoned the notional BBC-like autonomy of broadcasting from the state. Typically, a government values broadcasting as an instrument to forge national identity. Broadcasters are part of the civil service. English or French is the official language, the only common denominator in countries where most people otherwise speak only their mother tongue. Television, symbol of modernity, comes to dominate the system in terms of budget and prestige. Staff are trained in Europe and absorb an ideology, practice and expectations that are at odds with the needs of a newly developing country.[7] Imported equipment is designed for systems where the division of labour, maintenance skills, supply of spares and levels of infrastructure ensure a functioning which cannot be guaranteed in the Third World. Programming is supplied with the hardware on terms which make it difficult to refuse, at costs far below those incurred by local production. A dependence sets in, for the broadcasters who can fill time with inexpensive product, and for audiences who are conditioned to expensive production values as well as the lifestyles they portray.[8] Television transmission is all too often confined to the cities, for reasons both of the expense involved in extending transmission and electrical power over difficult terrain and of the cost of domestic receivers. There it provides one more incentive for the flight of landless people exchanging rural for urban poverty.

In African countries, the problem is how to make broadcasting work in the development process for economies where the impact of Western capital is relatively recent. In regions such as Latin America, the entrenched position of an urban elite, often supporting harshly oppressive regimes, has led development specialists to reject mass media altogether as a development tool. Mass media are seen as 'intent on goals of profitability, implanting habits of consumption and strengthening an ideology of domination'.[9]

This exceedingly gloomy picture is lightened by some strands of radio broadcasting which began earlier than (and quite separately from) those described in the previous two chapters. More recently, however, the strands have come together, suggested by the following proposition: the traditional relationship between broadcasters and audiences has provoked significant opposition in industrialised countries in the form of, let us call it, 'community radio'. The same relationship imposed as a result of the colonial or neo-colonial legacy on Third World countries has been found wanting (except where profit or the maintenance of political power is the aim). Question: What has the approach of western 'community radio' to offer in a Third World context? And, looked at from the other direction, what can industrialised countries learn in turn from the modifications to their broadcasting systems which have been developed in the Third World use of radio? We will return to these questions after sketching some of the examples of 'modifications'.

Farm Forums

One type is known as the 'farm forum'. Its first appearance was in Canada during the Second World War. A few months before the outbreak of war, the Canadian Association for Adult Education (CAAE) proposed to the Canadian Broadcasting Corporation (CBC) that the two organisations should undertake a joint project involving listening groups. This was an idea which appealed to the CBC General Manager, Gladstone Murray, who as a senior BBC administrator under Reith, had been interested in the BBC's adult education listening groups (see Chapter 4).[10] Murray provided funds and the CBC, CAAE and the Canadian Federation of Agriculture combined to organise groups of farmers who met in each others' homes to listen to broadcasts, study a pamphlet and discuss particular problems with a view to co-operative action in solving them. A statement of aims for the series in 1940 remarked

> We should not tell people what they ought to do, but rather it is important to let them find out for themselves what needs to be done. An attempt should be made to make them realise that they must assume responsibility and take action themselves towards a solution of the problems facing them.[11]

The Canadian farm forums lasted for over twenty years, and in 1949 some of the regional stations of All India Radio adopted the idea. A lack of radio receivers hampered the first experiments, but a later project in the Bombay area, supported by UNESCO, was better resourced and achieved measurable improvements in agricultural practice. By 1977, there were 22 500 registered forums, though by this time the Satellite Instructional Television Experiment (SITE) had eclipsed the radio activity in prestige. (SITE has since given way to a permanent programme which uses satellite technology and terrestial relay transmitters to reach 70 per cent of the Indian population with television broadcasts from Delhi.[12]

Radio forums were taken up by Ghana, where the Rural Broadcasting Unit had been making educational programmes since 1961. In 1964, with UNESCO and Canadian aid, 40 villages were involved in an experiment that showed increased take-up where discussions, use of study guides, visual aids and dramatisation followed the broadcasts. The system was adopted on a regular and more widespread basis and by 1973 some 400 groups were involved. Similar schemes followed in Zambia, Malawi and Nigeria.

Radio Clubs

In francophone Africa somewhat similar arrangements centred on 'radio clubs' which went further in a participatory direction by involving club members in sending back their view of problems, in recording discussions and even making programmes. A famous example of listener feedback was organised by Senegal's Radio Educative Rurale (RER).[13] Drought and low prices for groundnuts in the late 1960s caused severe hardship among farmers in the Wolof region. Radio Disoo (Wolof for haggling) broadcast interviews and comments from farmers as well as advice from government officials. Listening clubs were invited, through their literate members, to write directly to the President who was personally committed to measures for improvement and prepared to take action on criticisms of government policy and officials. Using the local language, giving voice to the farmers, and backed by concrete action at the highest level these programmes provided clear evidence of the effectiveness of listener feedback. Over the years the hours of Radio Disoo were extended and programmes were also broadcast in the other language regions of Senegal.

Radio Campaigns

Tanzania's broadcasting system is remarkable for having refused television (except in Zanzibar). Radio was a key instrument in mass campaigns between 1969 and 1975 involving broadcasts (in Swahili, the language used by Radio Tanzania's national service), study groups and the co-operation of the ruling party, TANU, a number of different ministries and the University of Dar es Salaam's Institute of Adult Education. Campaigns were run to explain elections ('The Choice is Yours'), to celebrate the tenth anniversary of independence and the nation's history ('A Time for Rejoicing'), on preventive health measures ('Man is Health') and on food habits and nutritional values ('Food is Life'). It is estimated that 2m people were involved in the 'Man is Health' campaign, and the kind of improved practices urged in the campaign created visible and conveniently measurable results – the elimination of rubbish and stagnant water near dwellings and the building of latrines were among the most striking. One commentator, assessing the effects of this campaign, observed

> Rural people never before called to think creatively need help getting started. Villagers may have grown accustomed to leaving major decisions about the most fundamental economic relationships within their community to others . . . It takes time for people to rediscover they have power and creativity, and that they can initiate positive alternatives to their present options or lack of options.[14]

Agricultural extension methods and a reliance on experts or book knowledge often fail whereas group discussion with 'complete and equal participation of all members' (the campaign's stated objective) evidently worked.

More recently, Radio Tanzania has turned from campaigns to a policy of trying to increase the amount of programming originated in rural areas by dispatching teams of producers on month-long trips to regions. The expense of such operations limits their number and more economical is the plan to station producers and journalists at relay transmitters.[15]

Radio Mauritania, with similar aims, operated a Regions sans Frontières mobile unit between 1975 and 1977. The ownership of radio receivers in the remote Saharan villages is high and the unit's mobile transmitter enabled it to make local broadcasts assembled from research done by journalists in co-operation with local people. Music, poetry, stories, history and debates on current affairs were thus included in the programmes. A regular schedule of visits allowed all the areas of the country to be visited, and feedback and material to be gathered for use to the national service.[16]

African Audiences

To summarise, we must first note the special nature of the listening experience in Africa. The lack of receivers means that group listening is the norm, and an oral culture which favours debate makes the forum/discussion approach especially suited in the region. The broadcasts are supported by printed and audio-visual materials and crucial is an efficient organisational infrastructure with trained staff which can give groups encouragement. (Exactly the same points could be made about school broadcasting in Western countries which, by the late 1960s, had been a thriving genre for forty years. By this time the Open University was started in Britain and cross-fertilisation between distance teaching in Western and Third World countries was to increase.)

To continue with Africa, an inter-ministerial group which at government level can cut across departmental responsibilities and rivalries has been usually found essential. Finally, the African experience demonstrates the economies that national mass campaigns achieve, as well as the value of decentralised operations which are very effective in mobilising local support for development schemes and have a vital role to play in the rehabilitation of local languages. However, neither a narrowly-focused mass campaign nor local production are the same as the original forum idea. Their development is an implicit criticism of the forum approach which certainly has its defects: in India studies showed that often groups became cosy clubs dominated by a local elite which inhibited discussion of social and political change; generally, programmes made in cities by broadcasting organisations not equipped, trained or motivated to do production in the field often came over as boring and failed to elicit input and feedback.

Local Radio: Homa Bay, Kenya

On the other hand, locally-controlled radio production can create troublesome pressure from the periphery on the centre, and has rarely been allowed by African governments. Almost the only example was in Kenya, where Homa Bay Community Radio (HBCR), 450 miles west of Nairobi on the shores of Lake Victoria, transmitted a few hours of local programming a week between 1982 and 1984. This small FM station was part of a UNESCO Regional initiative which hoped to learn from it principles of training broadcasters for such localised development operations. It coincided with the government's scheme for decentralising development planning, and a further aim was realised by the completion of the station at a very low cost with parts entirely manufactured in Africa. Voice of Kenya staff were seconded from Nairobi, but it was found that they had to unlearn many of their professional habits and attitudes. As the organiser, John Nkingyangi, put it

> While the acquisition of technical and production skills is necessary, it is not a sufficient requirement for the generation of programmes that might transform radio into a tool for development. Producers need also to develop analytical skills to enable them first to interpret and then to translate the prevailing social reality in their country into relevant radio programmes.[17]

The 'prevailing social reality' in the South Nyanza region of Kenya where HBCR operated is one of poverty with chronic drought and traditions of crop cultivation and livestocking that impoverished the soil and failed to provide a nutritionally adequate diet. The presence of the HBCR team raised issues about the size of families (in the conditions, regarded as a measure of wealth) versus family planning, in which the producers tried to help the women's voice, traditionally subservient to the men's, to emerge. Cultural, religious and educational strands of programming were developed, all in Luo, the local language, with news both locally produced and relayed in Swahili from Nairobi. The HBCR team's approach here was sociological and anthropological rather than journalistic. Nkingyangi's comment on the problem of changing attitudes is reminiscent of Hall's on the Tanzanian campaigns and indeed could have been said by any community radio worker in a Western city:

> People in rural areas are used to a different type of news – reports of past doings of high officials, announcements. People are not used to the idea that they themselves can make news. News is conceived of as the activity of certain members of society and not others . . . We are also trying to get people away from the notion simply of 'events' and reportage towards a different type of news that is interpretive. Why does such and such happen? – to report that is more important than to catalogue happenings.[18]

The Kenyan government closed the experiment in 1984 and Nkingyangi's final comment is an apt postscript:

> While appropriate radio programming can inspire more participation in community activities, it cannot actually make people participate. While radio can also provide the knowledge and information to whittle away the ignorance that is the cause of many diseases, it cannot change the primary social conditions that are manifested through poverty.[19]

A more recent attempt to devolve broadcasting decision-making is reported from Liberia where, in September 1986, the government opened three new rural broadcasting stations as part of a policy to decentralise rural development. Supported by the centrally-based Liberian Rural Communications Network the three stations transmit programming, 70 per cent of it locally produced, in the major local languages as well as English. Listening groups and audience feedback were planned as part of the service.[20]

Radio Schools: ACPO

According to Young *et al*. (1980) the Canadian farm forum was also what inspired the Columbian Father Salcedo to develop his radio school idea. It began in 1947 with an old transmitter and a few receivers distributed to neighbouring peasants in the mountainous region of Sutatenza. Salcedo used the system to announce parish notices, hold prayers with the peasants and start a little informal literacy training. From such small beginnings grew an important radio genre and the most powerful educational station in the region, Radio Sutatenza. In Columbia itself, an organisation called Cultural Popular Action (ACPO) has developed out of the original radio station. A private, Catholic-funded, non-profit operation, its various divisions administer other Columbian radio schools, a multi-media publishing house, a weekly newspaper and a number of training centres for peasants. Its staff number 1000, its enrolled listeners 250 000 and the general audience for its associated stations some eight million.

Non-formal education for the campesino (peasant) is what ACPO offers in courses which include health, literacy, agriculture, ethics and religion.[21] The six basic characteristics of radio school operation are:

1. A central team of administrators who design courses and train campesino leaders as assistant field teachers.
2. A multi-media approach in which the broadcast is a component alongside printed texts, cassettes, audio-visual materials and often a newspaper.
3. The assistant field teacher, drawn from the community, who can follow printed guides, enrol students, handle administration and attend regular meetings with the regional supervisor.
4. An independent radio station which has a complete programme schedule, in addition to the radio school classes, reaching a wide general audience with a broadly educational service, including local music, drama and news.
5. The goal of encouraging the formation of, and working with, agencies at local level such as co-operatives, women's organisations, self-help projects for building, transport, agriculture, etc.
6. The co-operation by the radio school organisation with existing development agencies in the field so as to reach remote communities without duplication of effort.[22]

Other Radio School Approaches

Radio school systems began to multiply in neighbouring countries and by 1972 formed themselves into the Latin American Association for Radiophonic Education (ALER).[23] By 1983 there were 42 affiliated systems in 17 out of the 21 Latin American countries.

The member systems do not all share ACPO's 'motivation toward community, family and individual self-improvement, and individual upward mobility within the given political and economic structures'.[24] This particular orientation was largely conditioned by the political situation at the time ACPO was formed. A violent ten-year war (known to Columbians as La Violencia) began in 1948 whose main victims were the campesinos. ACPO felt bound to avoid encouragement to action that could bring lethal retaliation.

However, in Bolivia, Brazil and Central America, there was a tradition of more aggressive agrarian action, in which the writings of the Brazilian educator, Paulo Freire, were influential. In his Pedagogy of the Oppressed, Freire develops the notion of 'conscientization', a method which begins from the peasant's own experience of the reality around her/him and rejects what Freire calls the 'banking' concept of education in which knowledge manufactured by experts in far-off cities is stored in books and transferred to minds unable and unmotivated to decode its relevance. Drawing on such traditions, other radio schools have helped their listeners to understand the underlying structural reasons for their poverty, suggesting that a fairer redistribution of resources would be a step towards a solution. It was natural that this approach should encourage a participation in the management of the radio school itself and a network less hierarchical than ACPO's, more equal and horizontal. Under the slogan 'a voice for the voiceless', radio school broadcasters transformed the notion of broadcasting professionalism to embrace a role as facilitators of campesino organisations and opinion, rather than as mediators of cultural messages from distant political or educational centres.

Use of Church Radio

A variant of the radio school organisation is illustrated by the case of Radio S. Gabriel whose transmissions cover La Paz, Bolivia's capital and the surrounding area. Here an approach which is less formally structured has been given a space within this Catholic-owned station. An organisation called CIPCA (Centre for the Research and Promotion of Campesino Affairs) arranged in the late 1970s to supply a daily three hours of programming in the Aymara language, one of the two main non-Spanish languages spoken in Bolivia. Of the other nineteen stations broadcasting in La Paz, four use Aymara to target this language community.

CIPCA's team of eight included five campesino-reporters who used portable equipment to record in peasants' homes and whose presence encouraged visits by their comrades to the studio. Songs, poems, stories, radio novellas ('soaps'), advice and information programmes on legal, technical and agricultural matters, and local history as a result filled three programme slots – early in the morning, at midday and in the early evening. Popular leaflets illustrated by cartoons (a technique common among radio schools) supported and publicised the programmes. An American visitor in 1978 commented

> Many of the programmes border on being political but stop just a step short of being explicit so as not to incur intervention by the government. One of their main tactics for getting peasants to realise their condition is by simply asking questions. Thus the radio itself makes no condemnation of the status quo.[26]

In Peru, a somewhat similar arrangement found space in the schedules of a church station in the Arequipa region of the interior. *Inquietudes* (the Spanish word is best translated as 'motivating concerns') was the outcome of a British Council-funded project which was careful to share with the inhabitants of the 'new town' developments around Arequipa, all the stages of planning, training, production and audience feedback. Young volunteers were trained in discussion and investigation techniques and in radio production. Weekly magazine programmes with an important musical element were transmitted by the Dominican-owned Radio San Martin for two years between 1984 and 1986. When the slot was withdrawn, the project built its own studio and made an agreement with a commercial station, Radio Hispana. The influence of the programmes on development projects has been noticeable: 'communities hearing about the work of others will initiate construction of their own community kitchens, libraries, youth clubs or sports facilities'.[27]

Miners' Radio, Bolivia

This kind of broadcasting involves a continual tightrope act in relation to the authorities. The protection of the Roman Catholic Church, whose regional leaders have an honourable record of opposition to oppressive regimes, is clearly indispensable to survival.

Not all such radio activity is undertaken under the Church's umbrella, however. Indeed, the early stages of the Bolivian miners' use of radio were marked by bitter clashes in the town of Siglo XX (Twentieth Century) with the Catholic station Radio Pio XII, originally set up to combat communism. By 1964, the Catholic broadcasting staff were replaced by others more sympathetic to the miners' cause and eventually became so identified with it that they were bombed by the government. The Bolivian miners, though only about 9 per cent of the population, are powerful politically and economically, producing more than two-thirds of foreign exchange by their efforts. Their use of radio began as a result of local decisions, taken in the early 1950s, to set up three stations, including one in Siglo XX, 'The Miner's Voice'. The battles with the Catholic Radio Pio XII helped to strengthen the mining radios and by 1965 there were 30. Their status has no official recognition; at best, they are tolerated when the administration cannot afford to alienate the miners. At other times they are repressed, closed down, even occupied. Ownership is collective, funding by monthly subscription from union members. They are staffed by volunteer miners, students, teachers and women in the mining communities. In 1978 a hunger strike by some of the miners' wives led the stations to try and win support from the campesinos whom governments had long tried to divide from the miners by a calculated policy. A succession of contacts built up mutual trust and resulted in regular arrangements for programme participation, news slots in Quechua and Aymara and the sale of campesino produce. The stations eke out a precarious existence with insufficient funding, out-of-date equipment and well-resourced competition from commercial neighbours.[28]

Oppositional radio in Latin America shares the hazardous existence of all groups who struggle for human rights and basic freedoms. Bombing, assassination and torture can be the penalties which serve as grim indications of how seriously governments feel threatened by such broadcasting.

Mexico

In Mexico, for example, in April 1983, the attempts of XEUAG, the Radio of the Autonomous University of Guerrera, to gain official recognition culminated in demonstrations in Mexico City, and a two-week hunger strike by the University Rector, two local

MPs and fifty supporters on the doorstep of the Ministry of Communications. For several years the authorities had prevaricated, avoiding meetings and refusing to answer letters, and finally saying no frequencies were available despite a technical survey by the university demonstrating the availability of seven. Finally, in May 1982, the University decided to go ahead, built a transmitter and started broadcasts. Jamming, harassment and the arrest and torture of the station's chief engineer followed. After the April 1983 demonstration, the government waited for the protest to die down. Then in July, police and para-military groups attacked the University, destroyed the radio station, killed a student and caused the 'disappearance' of sixty others.[29]

Sometimes illegality one day turns to heroic revolt and freedom the next. Two cases in 1986 concern the ending of dictatorships in Haiti and the Philippines.

Haiti

In Haiti, Radio Soleil, Catholic-owned, had seen its Belgian director, Father Hugo Triest, expelled in the crackdown on media by Duvalier Junior after Reagan's election in 1980 seemed to hold out promise of support for the dictatorship. The new excesses of the regime were attacked by the Haitian press in exile in the States and as foreign media began to notice what was going on, Radio Soleil's broadcasting became more daring. Its network of provincial reporters detailed the pattern of oppression and the station publicised the bishops' call for reform and the existence of a growing number of Church-organised local committees which were to be a crucial base for the final uprising. In 1985 the station successfully organised a boycott of the July referendum held to endorse Duvalier's life presidency, and by on-the-spot reports exposed the government's claim of a 99 per cent vote in its favour. In December the government managed to close down an increasingly vociferous Radio Soleil but by then Washington's support was being withdrawn.[30]

Philippines

In Manila, another Catholic station, Radio Veritas, in addition to serving a domestic audience, broadcasts in thirteen languages across South East Asia and can be heard in Japan, Vietnam and

Sri Lanka. On the day that Ninoy Aquino was assassinated at Manila Airport, out of 300 Philippine radio stations, five TV stations and eight newspapers, only Radio Veritas reported the event. The silence of the media was a measure of the grip of the Marcos regime.[31] The Archbishop of Manila, in order to protect Radio Veritas, agreed with Marcos who was putting pressure on the station, to remain neutral in the pre-election period. Cory Aquino at this time therefore was refused airtime on Veritas as well as on all Marcos-controlled media. The circulation of cassettes and mass attendance at her rallies ensured that her message reached the people, and at a crucial moment in the polling itself, Radio Veritas broke silence and denounced the fraud taking place. Broadcasting 24 hours a day, the station became the focus of resistance, receiving and broadcasting telephoned reports from NAMFREL (The National Movement for Free and Honest Elections) from all over the country. Its transmission of the Archbishop's appeal on 22 February for people to come out in the streets and oppose the Army's move to crush the rebel military camp was a turning point. Though the memorable non-violent demonstration which resulted stopped Marcos's troops, Radio Veritas was stormed and destroyed two days later and had to continue broadcasting from another station.[32]

El Salvador

Returning to Latin America we should note a remarkable example of broadcasting from the 'illegal' side of the line in the radio stations operated by the FMLN in El Salvador. Radio Venceremos is one of three clandestine stations used by the FMLN since January 1981 to support the guerilla war against the government.[33] It is based in the liberated zone in Morazan province, 30 miles from the capital, moving constantly under fire, learning to operate literally underground as aerial bombing has intensified. A US Navy vessel anchored in the Gulf of Fonseca jams the station with regular transmissions of music on high power. Till funds were available to build a more powerful transmitter, Radio Venceremos had to change its frequency from time to time while broadcasting. An intensely loyal audience, listener feedback showed, continued to follow the programmes through the frequency changes.

Speaking under an assumed name at AMARC-1, Daniel Solis, a station worker, said

Truth is the axis of our work. At the beginning there was a triumphalist tendency which led to exaggeration. Now we don't announce details of enemy prisoners taken, for example, till we've checked the facts ourselves. We know from talking to prisoners that we are listened to in secret by Government troops and junior officers because we tell them more than their superiors or the state radio. The US Embassy are regular listeners too. More and more they cite Radio Venceremos in order to deny our reports and give 'the true picture'.[34]

At this period the station's credibility was being confirmed nightly for the citizens of San Salvador who from their rooftops could see and hear the bombing in Morazan, reported by the radio as it happened. Using captured US Army short-wave the station kept in touch with its two sister stations in other parts of the war zone, rebroadcasting their reports on its wavelength.

Besides news there is a systematic attempt to express popular culture in songs, poetry and performance by popular theatre groups. One village band that used to play at weddings and festivals, now writes songs linked to the war and life in the province. Talks and documentaries help make sense of the fighting's political context, and interviews with visiting trades unionists and reports from the foreign press convey international support for the FMLN struggle.

Programmes for women by women connect the different liberated zones explaining the connection between the political and women's own struggle and suggesting how to organise for that. Said Solis,

For us, it is not only a problem of where to find a place where we can resist the army for a number of hours and then evacuate all the equipment afterwards. It isn't enough to give different information. It is also a question of trying to design a new style of communication which would correspond to the needs of a war and the mobilisation of a people.[35]

Nicaragua

In tragic contrast, the legal broadcasting of CORADEP in Nicaragua is subjected to the same type of harassment as the FMLN stations in El Salvador. A study by the University of Ohio's School of Telecommunications documents how, increasingly since the successful Sandinista revolution of 1979, powerful, US-financed radio stations on Nicaragua's borders have attempted to drown Nicaraguan stations with propaganda, music and advertising. The most powerful culprits are HRN ('The Voice of Honduras'), Radio Impacto from Costa Rica and the Voice of America itself which has circumvented Costa Rican neutrality by using the transmitters of a conservative Costa Rican company set up for the purpose. Three clandestine stations broadcast as Contra mouthpieces on Honduran and Costa Rican soil, while smaller stations like Radio Valle are heard in north-east Nicaragua and contribute, in the opinion of the Ohio study, 'to an impression in the mind of the average Nicaraguan that life may be better in the exterior'.[36]

In Nicaragua itself, aside from two national radio channels, there are 32 privately-owned local stations, many of them Church-owned, and 18 local stations belonging to the Corporation of Radio Broadcasting and Public Education (CORADEP). It is these last which are the government's main defence in the radio war and in support of its attempts to implement a social policy deemed so threatening by the Reagan administration. The stations themselves are in a poor state, left over from the Somoza regime, and with deteriorating, out-dated equipment which cannot be replaced because of the US trade embargo. Everything from tapes to microphones is in short supply.

The eighteen CORADEP stations schedule different programming for the four types of region they serve – rural areas (10), urban areas (2), suburban (2) and four multi-ethnic stations serving Miskito, Suma and Ramos-speakers, as well as the Spanish-speaking Pacific coast population, and English-speaking Caribbean coast population. As explained by CORADEP's Programme Director a common approach to programme planning has developed as a result of a policy of dialogue with listeners in each region. Teams consisting of specialists in anthropology, social psychology, communications and education conduct meetings with representatives of different sections of the community, including campesinos, workers, women and young people. These meetings ascertain listening habits and preferences, as well as needs unmet by existing programming.

What people ask first is that radio be their means of communication. They have asked that through radio they should make clear their own suggestions, their complaints, their protests and say what they wish their own community to be in terms of government administration. For this we have created a series called 'Opinion', as a result of which many government officials have felt it necessary to use the radio. Speaking over the air they respond to the avalanche of questions that the people ask. It has led to some officials being fired who were unable to fulfil their duties.

Another example of the dialogue is that people in rural areas have demanded their station be the means of expression, rescuing their own cultural values. In response we have created programmes featuring campesino music festivals which include material that nobody has ever heard before, handed down through the oral tradition. To-day we are distributing that music throughout the country through copying and transmission on the CORADEP network.[37]

Other programming consists of community service messages between families, people at work, relating to visits, meetings, transport, etc. An American journalist acting as a correspondent for the Pacifica News service in Nicaragua commented that 'you really get a sense when you listen that the radio station is open to that kind of communication. You could walk into the station and give a message so that some important life crisis be handled using the mass media.' The Managua station networks a national news and current affairs programme, and until recently produced a daily humorous drama and musical entertainment serial which included comments on topical issues, called the Six O'Clock Train, which was enormously popular but very expensive to produce.[38]

Summary

In this chapter we have looked at the way, in two quite different contexts, Africa and Latin America, radio has adapted Western models to suit development programmes. We have also seen examples of radio supporting revolutionary change. Radio forums, campaigns and schools stand in the tradition of educational broadcasting, presupposing reception in groups, study of support publications, discussion and action, all co-ordinated by local group leaders. As in industrialised countries such broadcasting is a means to an end – the education and development of the listener – but recognises the autonomy of the listener/subject, who, as Julius Nyerere said, cannot *'be* developed' but can only develop him/herself. In Africa, the values put across by such broadcasting are those which the state approves, and scope for local initiatives is strictly limited. In Latin America, such radio – most of it provided under the protection of the Church – treads a narrow line between marginality and dissent. Even – and perhaps especially – in conditions of armed struggle, although news is obviously paramount, what is striking is that radio is using poetry, music and drama to assert *now* its difference from the hitherto dominant form of commercial broadcasting: the struggle is cultural as well as political.

Conclusion

What has this kind of radio to do with the community radio tolerated at the margins of media systems in Western countries? And what can one learn from the other? These were the questions we posed at the beginning of the chapter. They are not academic and have been asked with some urgency in international forums such as UNESCO and the three gatherings of community radio broadcasters known as AMARC (Association Mondiale des Artisans des Radios Communautaires) which have taken place in Montreal, Vancouver and Managua since 1983.

An early contribution to UNESCO's strand of debate and experiment was Frances Berrigan's 1977 study *Access: Some Western Models of Community Media*.[39] In that year UNESCO held a seminar in Belgrade entitled *Access, Participation and Self-Management in Communications*[40] for which Josiane Jouët wrote the background paper.[41] Following Berrigan, Jouët proposed definitions of access, participation and self-management which have been widely used since. In this scheme, *access* is related to two levels, that of choice and of feedback. The latter implies interaction between producers and receivers through regular feedback systems, participation by the audience during programme transmissions and the 'right to comment and criticise'. *Participation* is seen as applying at the levels of production, decision-making and planning. The first level describes the kind of 'Open Door' facility offered by many broadcasting and cable organisations; the second extends to the 'management, administration and financing of communication organisations' and thus includes the kind of local and community radio covered in this book; at the planning level, participation is seen as involving a 'right of the public to contribute to the formulation of national, regional and local communication plans'. Here examples would be the involvement of French free radio organisations in the Consultative Commission or that of the American NFCB in FCC policy-making. *Self-management*, included in the title of the seminar because of its importance in Yugoslav economic and social policy, was taken to be equivalent to full public participation. Lekovic and Bjelica[42] have filled out the principles underlying self-management of media in the Yugoslav system:

Information is an integral part of the socio-political system . . . Working people and citizens, and their organisations and associations, are not just receivers and above all beneficiaries; they are increasingly active subjects which give information and influence the entire system . . . from the development to the content of programmes and information . . . Hence in the area of information, it is impossible to establish a basic line between those who supply and those who receive services.[43]

Jouët's paper was endorsed by a second UNESCO meeting organised by CIESPAL in Quito in 1978. Here the Latin American participants added a gloss critical of mass media which was cited earlier in the chapter. Further UNESCO studies, with the Intermediate Technology Group in 1979,[44] and on urban community media in 1984[45] gathered examples of initiatives each of which incorporated, as Salter noted of Vancouver Co-op Radio, an analysis of society, a commentary on media's role in it and a prescription for programming and organisational structure. Similar studies were commissioned by the Council of Europe.[46] By this time the MacBride Report[47] had offered a historical and global analysis which was useful in contextualising the record of small-scale media against the background of proposals for a New World Information Order.

A number of projects in Third World countries, part-funded by

UNESCO and other international agencies, have tried to put these ideas into practice, but all have suffered from a marginality *vis-à-vis* the main media or governmental bases of power, or from a duration too brief to make an impact.

The problem is that the problem is *both* local *and* global, structural and connecting First and Third Worlds. Local interventions in support of indigenous cultural production fail unless the imbalance in the world cultural market is also addressed. As the importance to national economies of the information sector grows, governments are delivered into the hands of multinational corporations which dominate the market: either they abdicate policy in favour of the free market, as in Britain under Thatcher, or they form alliances with multinational capital as the French have done. In either case, the flagship of public service broadcasting – television – is forced into a competitive international stance which consumes the bulk of available finance and in its programming tends to marginalise important social groups.

It is arguable, and there were many who so argued at the world community radio conference, AMARC 1 and 2, that the battle-lines of cultural resistance must be re-drawn at local level and that governments concerned with cultural sovereignty would do well to redefine public service so as to admit the claims of small autonomous units to receive a share of public funding.

There is, then, a continuity between community radio in industrialised countries and radio which supports the struggle of Third World countries to achieve a fairer distribution of resources. Participants at AMARC 2 were in no doubt of that.

Spanish-speaking communities in the USA and Canada involved in community radio are concerned *both* to encourage their communities to take advantage of the rights and benefits to which they are entitled *and* to support the struggle of their comrades in Central America. This they can do not only by giving a platform to recently arrived exiles, but by the celebration of a culture most effectively expressed in music which does not have to follow market imperatives.

Black community radio groups in London, thwarted by the Thatcher government of licences to broadcast, received messages of solidarity from American black community radio programmers. The latter also made connections at AMARC 2 with the government-sponsored representatives of countries such as Burkina Faso,

Benin and Senegal where, as we have seen, rural radio is working to assist economies distorted by First World policies.

Radio in support of development in Third World countries has much in common with a significant strand of community radio in North America and Australia – that provided for their communities by native Americans in Alaska and the South Western USA, by native Canadians in the north, and by aboriginal Australians. In all such areas a traditional economy, culture and language have been all but destroyed and local radio has an important part to play in rediscovering the past and making sense of a present which, if it cannot turn back history, can at least assert historical rights and claims.

Rosalie Bertell, the veteran anti-nuclear campaigner, addressing AMARC 2, described community radio as potentially an 'alarm-system for survival' for a world in which mainstream media were often too complicit with government to reveal the truth. The Chernobyl disaster with its chain of effects that led to contaminated milk being sold to Third World countries symbolises the inextricable links which bind the two parts of the world together.

Chapter 10

New Definitions, New Structures

Radio could be the most wonderful public communication system imaginable, a gigantic system of channels – could be, that is, if it were capable not only of transmitting but of receiving, of making listeners hear but also speak, not of isolating them but connecting them. (Brecht, 1930[1])

When Brecht in 1930 discussed the two-way, democratic possibilities of radio as a means of public communication, he described his proposals as 'utopian', by which he meant that they could not be achieved in the social system prevailing at the time. And, his own experiments excepted, radio was then barely emerging from its first, imitative phase in which it acted as a substitute for the theatre, the concert hall and the press. Over half a century later we can trace more clearly the successive stages in which radio developed an identity in relation to other media and realised a specific radiophonic potential. But the elaboration of an aural aesthetic has not, in mainstream broadcasting, changed the relations between producers and listeners, nor could it, as Brecht emphasised, without changed social relations. It was a tragic irony that his call for radio 'to transform the reports of our rulers into answers to the questions of the ruled' was followed within a few years in Germany by a regime which proceeded to demonstrate the most organised use of radio for propaganda yet seen.

Contemporary capitalism furnishes far more sophisticated examples of radio's use to try and affect behaviour. With the growth of technology to reproduce sound and the emphasis on individual reception, radio nowadays takes its place as a link in a chain of domestic products nearer to the hi-fi and music areas of cultural consumption than the television set. It is the latter which has taken over radio's early role as the organiser of domestic routines and the chief mediator of the attentions of the state and of capital at the hearth.

But, to turn from the receiving end of the communication process to the senders, for how much longer will the structures of state-linked public service broadcasting organisations survive the assaults of multinational competition and policies under which, in Garnham's words, 'the state's ideological functions . . . are progressively transferred to the market with the active collaboration of the state'?[2] In this scenario, national cultural institutions are transformed into junior partners of multinational enterprises and their audiences fragmented and reassembled in trans-national aggregations which answer to market 'demand'. Nor, if we are to believe one commentator's predictions for deregulation, based on an analysis of the American experience of the process, is there a place for the local in all this. The backyard dish connecting the individual to the satellite symbolises the economies of scale, the distance-shrinking reach of new technologies and the tendency for intermediary levels to disappear between the individual household and the national supplier. All these trends work against localism in communications.[3] In the USA the profitability of local advertising depends on a canny balance of cheap local news supplied by local official sources and syndicated material into which local interest can be seamlessly inserted. The tendency was noted as long ago as 1981 in the case of British local radio,[4] and, as we have seen, is evident in French local radio's response to the commercial success of the NRJ network.[5]

This book is itself an attempt at the enterprise to which we believe all media needs to be dedicated. It tries to bring together examples of the diverse uses of radio, uses which connect audiences. We do not believe that radio can create communities where none exist, and we hope that the analysis of local radio in the UK has demonstrated that. The essentially idealist notion that it could do this may be found in various public statements made both at its inception and later, and they should be treated with suspicion.

We think that our examples demonstrate clearly that at the most general level what radio (and by extension other media) are best at is reflecting common interests. It cannot create them and, as Nkingyangi said, it cannot actually make people participate. Our analysis of the notion of community and the examples from throughout the world show that very often small-scale radio springs from opposition to prevailing forms. This is so even when the political stance of the stations and the groups supporting them differs markedly. For instance, nobody would want to claim that there was much in common between the offshore pirates which broadcast to the UK in the 1960s and the instances from Latin America and Italy, except their opposition to prevailing forms. The differential support for Radio Dreyekland on either side of the Franco-German border is a neat example of the different ways in which the same content can be perceived by audiences in different contexts.

It is noticeable that the pressure for new radio forms comes from two different directions – those seeking to set up commercial stations and those who wish to use radio for community development. In many places the 'new' form of radio has been locally based, but that is not the ground on which either side has most to gain. As Mattelart and others have persuasively argued, localism serves to fragment opposition to the prevailing order. It may form an ideological smokescreen, but it does not necessarily make sense in either commercial or community terms. The difference is that (as with NRJ in France and IR in the UK) commercial concerns can to a greater or lesser extent ignore or circumvent regulations designed to ensure local origination, whilst the community lobby does not. The result has been that the restrictions of localism apply at an ideological rather than at a commercial level. A commitment to serve the whole audience in the public service tradition leads to fragmentation in programming and audience terms and is probably economically difficult, but as we have seen most Western community radio thinking remains firmly rooted in the public service tradition. For financial and ideological reasons then community activists work within the limitations of localism, whilst commercial companies form regional or national links which economise on sales and programming while they continue to lobby for changes in the structure to give them more commercial freedom.

So commercial interests are better at making the connections than the community radio lobby. Not only do they use the network to defray costs, they connect with other commercial arenas. NRJ's promotion of 'lifestyle' is not new – the offshore pirates capitalised on similar audience needs – and both recognised the cultural and commercial possibilities of a medium which appeals to young people seeking a form of identity. We have seen that radio can express identity and interest: this is what it must do in its community form. This means that it should look up from the local to recognise identity of interests both nationally and perhaps internationally. The problems of ethnic groups in London will in many respects be the same as those in Birmingham or those in Paris, and the position of mineworkers and steelworkers will be similar within western industrialised nations, and may not be that different from those in Bolivia. Unless these connections are made community radio will, we believe, be outmanoevred by commercial radio which will use networking to save money and provide a bland backdrop to their advertising messages.

It is at this point that our discussion must move from descriptive analysis to prescriptive proposals, from 'is' to 'ought'. We have found wanting the claims of British broadcasters to serve local publics. What is missing is, quite simply, democracy – a redistribution of power between producers and audience. All too often 'community' in its public-relations version is, as Raymond Williams noted, 'a mere front for irresponsible networks which have their real centres elsewhere'.[6]

Nor up till now have been able look to the Soviet bloc for examples of democratic control of media. Although there, as Downing observes, public control of media has officially won the day, in fact oppositional media survive, if at all, in conditions of repression.[7] Whether this will change in the new political climate in the Soviet Union remains to be seen.

So is community radio, as described in earlier chapters, a model we can use? The remainder of this concluding chapter attempts an answer to the question.

First, let us admit that we are considering a type of democratic, non-profit-oriented communication in a world where resources, including communication resources, are unevenly distributed. It is an old debate on the left whether superstructural struggle is justified in advance of radical change in basic relations of production. Our answer to this is an unequivocal 'yes'. The hegemonic role of communications media by definition provides an arena for dominated but protesting ideologies to challenge the system.[8] The social democratic tradition of tolerance for opposition has hitherto allowed space for this. What is not yet clear is whether a reliance on market forces is a more effective weapon against dissent than totalitarian repression.

The Italian example illustrates the result of breaking a state monopoly without having in place a regulatory framework to control concentrations of ownership and the importation of foreign software. With some honourable exceptions, like Radio Popolare, the original left-inspired local initiatives have worked in favour of the policy of the major electronics corporations. Siliato has argued that the movement of such firms towards experiment with highly localised ventures is designed to sidetrack awareness of the national and international stakes. Energy can be focused on local issues and apparent solutions identified, whereas, more and more, local problems have their origins in the international system of power.[9]

The Socialist French government, before the 'internationalisation' of television overtook in magnitude the issue of radio, had not found a satisfactory answer to protect and foster the non-profit sector. Pressure from an advertising industry for whom the local dimension was an untapped seam coincided with a young generation's appetite for rock music in a revised repeat of the North Sea pirate phenomenon. The social significance of the phenomenon and the sophistication of the innovatory music formats that resulted may be intriguing but do not alter the fact that original intentions were overtaken by the logic of the marketing and industrial dynamic.

The evidence from North America and Australia is more encouraging, even if the number of community radio stations are marginal compared to mainstream commercial broadcasting. It is not a case of community radio stations providing worthy but boring programming. As Lewis Hill long ago remarked of KPFA Pacifica, the programming is 'as much a product *of* the audience as a service to it'[10] and the musical tastes which community and public radio have satisfied have been an important part of the success, to the extent, as we have seen, of having been imitated by the commercial sector.

The point brings us unavoidably to the discussion of 'needs' and 'wants'. Reith's aphorism that 'few people know what they want and very few what they need' justified the unaccountable paternalism of the BBC in his time – and long after. His present-day successors, like their commercial competitors, point to the felt needs expressed in ratings or diagnosed by audience research to justify a programme policy which marginalises important sections of opinion. But 'real' needs are not reflected by felt needs. If a service is lacking in range and diversity, its users often have low standards of felt needs.[11] Market demand can only be regarded as socially just if other conditions and resources are fairly distributed – which they patently are not. What the autonomous, non-profit, locally and democratically controlled radio station allows is for needs to be explored and articulated by interest groups themselves.

The analysis of Chapter 5, however, should warn community radio advocates of an acceptance of the local as the sole defining principle of the kind of radio they want. The communities of interest for whom community radio might provide a vehicle, perhaps the *only* available broadcast vehicle, 'an alarm system for survival' (Rosalie Bertell) are, like the aggregated markets of the multinationals, dispersed over many localities. Downing, in the concluding summary of his book *Radical Media*, points out that political atomisation is found no less in western than in Soviet models of domination, and, drawing on the discussion in *Beyond the Fragments*[12] suggests that the solution in western countries is for the separated constituencies to develop a 'lateral debate' between each other.[13]

We have seen that the promotion of lateral communication is very much the aim which stations like KPFA and Vancouver Co-op Radio set themselves. A community radio station that is working well is more than the sum of its separate programme-making groups, and attempts to structure its programming and publicity to enable listeners to make connections between the separate elements, providing the means for an analysis which mainstream media rarely offer and which can break through the isolation of separate constituencies. So a discussion about male competition in a sexual politics slot can make sense of militarism, providing insights for an anti-nuclear constituency. A local campaign against chemical pollution can be contextualised by reference to the workings of multinational capital, while those attracted

by Latin American music will learn something about the struggle
for human rights in Central America, and so on. Even in the most
difficult conditions imaginable for broadcasting, those that Radio
Venceremos endures in El Salvador, we have seen how programmes for women connect the political and military struggle
with that for women's own liberation.

In late-1980s Britain, the tabloid press invokes such labels as
'rent-a-crowd' and 'loony left' to deride such connections, while
mainstream broadcasters routinely fail to make them. As a BBC
producer long ago remarked, to the extent that they fail, they
support the system with propaganda instead of assisting change by
critical debate.[14]

For the coming together of different constituencies will not be
smooth, and the sector of broadcasting inhabited by the ideal type
of community radio station we are considering will be a space for
controversy and contradiction, not the 'mirror for accepted
opinions' which all too often is what public service has become.[15]
Mattelart and Piemme foresee, in the conclusion of their analysis
of the failures of traditional forms of public service broadcasting,
the need for a new definition of public service – 'one which will
integrate old and new technologies, the national and local dimension'. And the key, they continue, to this new definition 'should be
the relationship (of broadcasting) with active groups' – groups and
alliances which will form in response to new and shifting social
relations, in turn responding to the changed economic realities of
an era in which information is of central importance.[16]

Perhaps cut off from acquaintance with some of the evidence we
have presented here, Mattelart and Piemme ask how it is possible
'to imagine a permanent radio as an alternative to the process of
multinationalisation being experienced by broadcasting companies?'
Let us conclude by attempting an answer which draws on the
lessons and experience we have summarised, using Britain as an
example.

British Radio in the Late 1980s[17]

First we need to bring the story of British radio more up to date. In
Chapter 6 we had reached the point where the Thatcher government had cancelled its community radio experiment in 1986,

announcing that it preferred to wait till the forthcoming Green Paper had spelled out the context in which community radio would operate.

In the Green Paper of 1987[18] respectful references to public service broadcasting sat side by side with radical proposals to deregulate radio. Instead of the one national commercial channel expected by the industry, the government proposed three, which would use two frequencies taken from the BBC and one in the additional VHF spectrum made available under international re-allocation in the early 1990s. Several hundred small stations were proposed and no distinction was made between commercially-oriented stations and genuine non-profit community stations. Indeed the concept of community radio was barely discussed, while public funding for radio in this commercial sector was denied. BBC local radio was to continue to provide public service at local level, but commercial stations were to be freed from all such obligations and overseen with a lighter regulatory touch by either the IBA, the Cable Authority or a new Radio Authority. The Green Paper urged an end to simulcasting and, in an ominous phrase, left the BBC free to 'judge the size of its commitment to local radio alongside the other claims on its resources'.[19] These resources were to be confined to a proposal of the Peacock Committee already implemented: the linking of the licence fee to the Retail Price Index. The Green Paper specifically rejected the Peacock proposal that the BBC should take advertising.

The IBA's response to the Green Paper[20], with its local radio empire at stake, represented its most forceful argument yet to be a joint provider of a public service different from but complementary to the BBC's. It commented that the proposed programme requirements and ownership controls were 'much tougher than may appear at first sight' and that, the government need to choose between a relatively expensive regulatory system . . . or allowing radio operators greater freedom than the Green Paper suggests'.[21] The Authority argued that its experience and infrastructure gave it the best claim to be the new regulator.

Over the preceding eighteen months, the IBA had indeed shown that it was capable of loosening some of the quite stringent controls which, ILR stations had been complaining, were contributing significantly to the poor financial showing of the system. Mergers and takeovers had been allowed in order to maintain ILR presence in some regions, while relaxation of rules on sponsorship and the syndication of programme material – including the Network Chart Show, intended to directly challenge BBC Radio 1's highly popular Top 40 programme – had begun to make ILR more attractive to national advertisers. The 'L' for Local was dropped from the acronym and IR's economic fortunes improved to the point where, in the year ending September 1987, advertising revenues went up by a record 26 per cent to £94m. In 1988, the increase was maintained with revenues of £119.4m. Though still a low percentage of total media advertising expenditure compared to countries where commercial radio had preceded television, this improvement gave the majority of the industry confidence to welcome the enlargement of the market proposed in the Green Paper.

The BBC's response to the Green Paper was affected by the experience of perhaps the most bruising year in the entire history of the Corporation. It began in January 1987 with the summary dismissal by the Governors, chaired by the recently appointed Marmaduke Hussey, of the Director-General, Alastair Milne. Milne was thought to have mishandled a number of incidents which had brought the BBC damaging publicity, such as the clash with the government over the Real Lives affair[22] and the Panorama libel case,[23] and was neither popular with politicians nor experienced in matters of finance which increasingly was becoming a major function of the DG post. The Managing Director of Radio, Brian Wenham, on failing to get the vacant top job, resigned. The successful appointee, Michael Checkland, came from the financial side of the BBC and his lack of programme experience was offset by bringing in from ITV John Birt as Deputy Director-General with a brief to create a combined directorate of news and current affairs across both television and radio. Sweeping changes resulted, and in the shake-up, Michael Grade, due to succeed as Managing Director of Television, left to become Chief Executive of Channel 4. Another change which affected local radio directly was the regrouping of regional television and local radio responsibilities under regional managers answering to a Managing Director of Regional Broadcasting. Although this was designed to create more regional autonomy, it removed the link with the centre local radio had enjoyed through the Controller, Local Radio, a post that was now abolished.

The BBC's public image and internal morale was further weakened by two acts of judicial intervention by the government. Police raided BBC offices in Glasgow to confiscate the videotape of a programme dealing with the spy satellite, Zircon, in the series *Secret Society*, and the government obtained an injunction banning a Radio 4 series, *My Country Right or Wrong*, which reviewed the role of the security services, even though the programmes had been already cleared through the vetting system of the 'D' Notice Committee.[24]

Battered by these misfortunes, the BBC, in planning a response to the Green Paper, must have felt it wiser not to take the government on in another area. Its five year plan[25], announced in October 1987, included some pre-emptive moves clearly designed to ease the way for the government scheme. Simulcasting and 'splitting' (see Chapter 2) were to end, the two medium-wave frequencies of Radios 1 and 3 were to be vacated on the presumption that they would be suitable for the national commercial networks, and the four networks were to be relocated on VHF. A major campaign would be launched to encourage VHF listening, while an assortment of the specialist services unpopular under existing arrangements with large sections of the audience because they interrupt the main programme flow – Open University, continuing education, schools repeats, sport, children's and Open College – would be brought together on Radio 2's old medium-wave frequency. Radio 4's long-wave frequency was to be considered as the site for special events – parliamentary coverage, party conferences, state occasions or running news stories. Thus by ending simulcasting, the BBC was proposing six networks in place of the previous 4. Of the main networks, Radio 1 and 2 were to have a wider editorial brief, including drama, documentary and specialist music.[26] Meanwhile, both Radio 3 and Radio 4 were making attempts under new controllers to 'liven up their image' in a search for younger listeners. Local radio, however, fared less well. Though the seven new stations were to go ahead, making 39 English stations in all, local radio as a whole was to suffer 10 per cent cuts in less than two years, and the London, Birmingham and Manchester stations were put on a three-year notice to show 'evidence of increased and sustained demand for their services.'[27]

The responses of the two halves of the broadcasting 'duopoly' have to be seen against the background of Mrs Thatcher's third

general election victory in June 1987 which left her with a majority
of 100 in the House of Commons. This gave her the time-scale and
the majority to carry through quite sweeping changes if she
wished, and from what was happening in education and the health
service it was clear that she and her colleagues had little time for
existing 'public service' institutions. It was also becoming increasingly clear that the key to the government's intentions for broadcasting lay in the Peacock Committee's vision of the future.
Though the Committee finally stopped short of recommending
that BBC TV should carry advertisements and though the government rejected its suggestion of 'privatising' Radios 1 and 2, the
index-linking of the licence fee had been accepted, as well as the
principle of access for independent producers to the three main
TV channels up to a proportion of 25 per cent of the output of
each. (Peacock had advocated a 40 per cent target.) Independents
had been the only group encouraged when the Prime Minister
summoned broadcasters to 10 Downing Street for a seminar which
capped the 1987 round of broadcasting conferences. Her remark
that ITV was now 'the last bastion of restrictive practices' was
taken as heralding the switch of the offensive from a humbled BBC
to the old-style commercial sector.

In the months that followed, Mrs Thatcher's hand was seen in
the announcement of the intention to remove radio from the IBA,
the plan to auction ITV franchises, the investigation of the industry by the Monopolies and Mergers Commission, and above all – a
measure which struck at the heart of the principle of relative
autonomy for both broadcasting authorities – in the creation of the
Broadcasting Standards Council under Sir William Rees-Mogg.

Peacock, whose vision of the future seemed rapidly to be being
overtaken by events, had foreseen a staged progression towards
deregulation in which, though the BBC should remain in place, it
might not be the sole purveyor of public service (Channel 4 had
already proved the viability of public service outside the BBC).
The existence of some public service programming was necessry,
Peacock thought, because on its own the market would provide an
inadequate supply of 'medium-appeal and minority programmes,
which most people want to see or hear some of the time'. There
was also a need for demanding programmes which people may not
themselves want to watch, but which they feel ought to be broadcast, and for which they are prepared to pay, as taxpayers and

voters.[28] Overall, though, the market should determine the supply of services with subscription and advertising the main means of finance, and TV franchises and radio frequencies being put out to competitive tender. An even more radical proposal appeared in a report, published after Peacock and commissioned by the Department of Trade and Industry (DTI), suggesting that spectrum management itself should be delegated to commercial frequency planning organisations (FPOs) who would

> have responsibility for determining the use of frequency bands for the country as a whole . . . Any technically feasible application which does not contravene international regulations would be permitted.[29]

The proposal was typical of a climate in which the DTI and the Home Office seemed openly in competition to control the direction of communications development. Suggestions made by independent consultants or by Ministers in off-the-cuff remarks would become reified as policy, at least for a time, while in a series of anticipatory moves the radio industry prepared itself for the promised deregulation.

Other contributions to the deregulatory climate were, first, the government's firm wish to see an end to the copyright restrictions which inhibited a music-based expansion of radio. This aspect of industry practice also was referred to the Monopolies and Mergers Commission. Second, the widespread flouting of those regulations – and the law, despite DTI raids and prosecutions[30] – by a growing number of pirates.[31] Third, the launch of a number of services transcending the existing franchise boundaries. One example was the plan of the Irish broadcasting authority (RTE) to launch, in the autumn of 1988, a commercial pop music channel, broadcasting in daytime from a powerful long-wave transmitter, which would be heard by up to 25m listeners on the UK mainland.[32] Others took the form of satellite-delivered services to stations for retransmission. Virgin's Radio Radio, Radio Nova International, Murdoch's Sky service and Radio Luxembourg's nighttime service were the forerunners.

The government plans for radio were announced on 19 January 1988. They followed the lines of the earlier Green Paper, but contained three surprises. Leapfrogging Peacock's first stage, the government proposed to auction the national commercial channels to the highest bidder; the IBA was to lose its commercial radio empire to a new Radio Authority; and the three national channels would each be required to provide 'a diverse programme service calculated to appeal to a variety of tastes and interests and not limited to a single format'.[33]

Reaction at the time among broadcasters dubbed this requirement variously as 'old-fashioned', 'quirky' and 'unrealistic'. It was one of the points on which the House of Commons Home Affairs Committee raised questions and eventually pronounced itself satisfied with the Home Office Minister's response. Diverse programming could still be consistent, it seemed, with an approach 'weighted in favour of particular interest groups'. The Radio Authority, using a two-tiered selection process, 'would not base its decisions on purely financial grounds'. The Committee accepted that an Authority solely concerned with radio was the best solution, but urged that it should be funded and staffed to enable it to be an effective regulator.[34] The government's response was on the whole reassuring, but failed to satisfy anxieties about the BBC's ability to meet the new competition. Worst of all, from a radio industry point of view, it became clear by mid-1988 that complexities in drafting legislation for television were going to delay implementation of radio plans until late 1990. This news was particularly disappointing for the community radio lobby which had to be content with the crumbs of 'special event' licences to allay the impatience of its followers (but see note 51, p. 229).

An added irony was that government decisions about radio were reached in advance of the findings of research the Home Office itself had commissioned.[35] The Broadcasting Research Unit's report, *The Listener Speaks*, revealed surprisingly strong support for speech programming, a widespread dislike of advertisements, a suspicion that more radio might mean less quality and mixed feelings about community radio. For most respondents small neighbourhood radio was less welcome than a larger scale service, but ethnic groups, especially the Afro-Caribbean community, were keen to be involved in operating stations of their own.

The Future for Public Service

In the phoney war of deregulation, what were the prospects for public service? The BBC, the institution that pioneered public service broadcasting, was now being buffeted by the contradictory push-pull of free market ideology and the Thatcherite penchant for state intervention – 'the two halves of the modern Tory mind', as a former BBC Managing Director Radio put it.[36] Financially, the BBC had its hands tied behind its back while it was compelled to face competition at national as well as local radio level. This struggle was subordinate to the demands of television, where the growing reach of satellite, cable and video was intensifying the competition for a BBC already having to behave like a commercial conglomerate.

Interpreting government intentions for the BBC has never been a straightforward business. The policy 'print-out' at any one time is the sum of contending forces – hawkish DTI, conservative Home Office, Mrs Thatcher's dominant role in the Cabinet and the state of Tory backbench pressure. The logic of this kind of intervention and control risks leading to a state system without autonomy on the continental model. Such a government would need the BBC for decorative purposes, like Big Ben or Buckingham Palace; its quality product would be a useful earner of foreign exchange; at times of national triumph or emergency it could be on hand to respond and rejoice appropriately. What would not be relished would be the kind of critical independence that had become a habit in the era of political consensus.

For BBC local radio the outlook is even more dismal. It is hard to see how the stations can continue to fulfil their basic news function in supplying BBC regional stations and networks,[37] let alone retain listeners against an expanding commercial sector free to develop any specialist format the market will bear. Nor is it a happy prospect from the point of view of the kind of community radio we have been describing in earlier chapters. The plans for 'setting radio free' are those of a government which cancelled its previous cautious experiment for fear of the electoral consequences of allowing 'unbalanced programming'. Now a much larger number of stations will be allowed to operate, with a minimum of regulation, in a largely commercial sector: the marketplace will ensure 'balance', and public money will only go to the sort of project 'intended to provide a specific benefit to the community'. Stations will not be allowed to 'set up as political platforms'.[38]

We have already seen that the economic and territorial logic of Britain's commercial radio system as originally constituted tends towards regional – rather than local-sized stations, and that cuts have forced a similar shift on the BBC. The government's latest proposals will put pressure on an enlarged commercial sector to increase radio's share of advertising from the 2 1/2 per cent in 1987 to at least 5 per cent; some calculations put the figure at 10 per cent necessary to break even when three national channels are running. The very small station may get by on a level of advertising demand not yet or wholly met by IR or the local or free press, but for the middle range there will be even greater pressures than at present to be absorbed into regional units.

As for the non-profit-oriented community radio stations, recent European radio experience suggests that without some regulation large fish will swallow smaller and that they tend to be driven out by commercially oriented ones. The result will be to banish diversity and originality and to concede yet more ground to multinational ownership and software.

The French, without any substantial experience of local public service radio, devised a 'fund for the encouragement of local expression in radio', designed to protect the non-profit type of local radio. On the face of it, the trend in Britain is against even this kind of protection, yet there are amidst the disintegration of the old order, some precedents and instruments that might provide the space within which to build up a new kind of public service.

Again, surprisingly, the Peacock Report suggests an answer. Peacock argued that in the progression towards deregulation the 'ability of the existing system to finance [public service] programmes could wither away without any alternative source of provision of finance having been developed'[39] and 'rather than engage in a fruitless battle to maintain regulation . . . it would be better for parliament to take more positive action to make finance available for public service broadcasting'.[40] The means to do this, the Committee suggested, was a Public service Broadcasting Council (PSBC). The PSBC would act as a conduit for public funding and give the BBC first priority, but avoid concentrating its support on a single channel. Peacock saw no objection in principle to the PSBC getting its finance from a continuing licence fee but suggested it would be 'more securely funded if it could be financed from within broadcasting', for example, by the proceeds from the auction of franchises.[41]

A similar suggestion was made from a quite different quarter over a decade ago by the Community Communications Group

(COMCOM), in its Comments on Annan. Supporting Annan's recommendation for a Local Broadcasting Authority, but rejecting the Committee's proposal that a local radio should be mainly funded by advertising, COMCOM argued that if non-commercial broadcasting ceased to be the *exclusive* domain of the BBC, the licence fee should cease to be its *exclusive* property.[42] COMCOM also argued for a proportion of cross-subsidy from ITV profits on a principle which the financing of C4 has subsequently recognised.

A nationally networked publishing house, funded by subscriptions from the ITV companies, C4, is statutorily required to provide for minority interests. Its presence has encouraged the creation of some hundreds of independent production companies, some of them, by agreement with the broadcasting union, ACTT, very small groups recognised as suppliers although part publicly-funded and not wholly professionally staffed. C4 has had a healthy effect on the television broadcasting ecology, and has admirably succeeded in a policy which Peacock describes for its PSBC as 'positive patronage of creative broadcasting'.[43]

As yet there is no equivalent in radio but the Institute for Contemporary Arts (ICA) suggested in a response to the Green Paper that the argument for such a 'national radio station . . gained considerably in strength' in the light of the Green Paper proposal for three national networks. Its 1985 bid for a 'community of interest' licence in the cancelled experiment had shown, the ICA said 'that there exists a wide constituency of radio producers for whom the current radio structure offers inadequate – if any – outlets. At the same time there remains little room for experiment and innovation and few opportunities for new voices to be heard'.[44]

At the time of writing, it remains to be seen what kind of format will be developed by the contenders for the national networks. Though the government was far from giving any C4-type hints, the idea of a Channel 4 for radio began to surface in a number of forms since the first drafting of the suggestions we set out below.[45] There was also a growing awareness of the possibilities of non-national programme-sharing with, possibly, distribution by satellite.

We have already argued in previous chapters that what makes economic and social sense in contemporary British radio is the *local* provision of *specialist* programming by outlets *some* of whose programming is originated *nationally*. (This is not for a moment to

suggest that national networks of news, music and quality programming are not also a part of a public service.) But a terrestrially-
transmitted national network is not necessary for programme
distribution. Commercial systems tend towards national syndication. If they are to compete, so must non-profit systems.

Here is where the BBC comes in. In our view, a project to
redefine public service radio must draw on the infrastructural
resources and the creative talent *within* the BBC, while at the
same time finding ways to nurture local talent and dissenting
opinion outside the Corporation without co-opting or stifling it.

As we have seen BBC managers have occasionally suggested
that the BBC should 'act as a midwife' to a lowest tier of community
radio, supplying engineering advice and training skills. As they
stand suggestions of this kind make the same mistake as the
original local radio design by limiting the proposed new 'free
zones' to a local level. But if we think in terms of the kind of
nationwide communities of interest which C4 has exploited, then
perhaps the BBC local radio system can make an alliance with
community radio that goes beyond local ad hoc arrangements.

In its 1982 pamphlet *BBC Radio for the Nineties*, the BBC
sketched out plans for *five* services: Radios 1 to 4, 'plus in effect
Radio 5' (Radio 5 has since acquired another meaning, see note
51, p. 229):

> a system of some 40 English Local Radio stations and National
> Regional Radio, primarily broadcasting locally-oriented pro-
> grammes, news and information, but also carrying, outside the
> hours available for local programming, a distinctive service of
> common programming, containing, say, elements of popular
> drama, light music, continuing education, and programmes of
> minority ethnic interest.[46]

At the time *BBC Radio for the Nineties* irritated by its imperialist
pretensions to lay claim to *all* available frequency space and
programme supply obligations – except those assumed by the IBA
for its stations. Where it showed insight was in its linking of local
programming with, effectively, supra-local communities of interest.

The presence of 'minority ethnic interest' programming in any
plan connected with the BBC might depend on the extent to which
the BBC's big metropolitan stations, in the three-year probation-

ary period, manage to convince the relevant communities that their concern is matched by better budgets and slots than previously.

There will certainly be licence bids by minority ethnic groups – Black, Asian, Greek and Turkish radio projects (and pirates) are among the known potential applicants – not all of them offering a music-only format. The pirates CDR in London and PCRL in Birmingham, scheduled a significant proportion of speech and features, and the Brixton-based Afro-Caribbean Radio Project, out of studios originally funded by the GLC, planned to provide 50:50 music and speech, and expected to find similar black stations willing to exchange programming.[47]

The case for black stations was forcefully put by a DJ then working in DBC, the black pirate station which broadcast from Notting Hill between 1981 and 1984:

National black music radio is what's needed. We maintain that this is one of the ways that the recommendations of the Scarman Report could be carried out. Half of what he said would be catered for by just having black stations. Straight away you've got business, money going back into the black community, you've got a livelihood, the kids can say 'Yeh, at last we've got something'.[48]

What is needed to create the space in which community radio can flourish is something like a cross between Channel 4 and the BBC's old Radio 5 idea. Radio 10 might be a better title – allowing for six BBC channels and commercial networks. Radio 10 would be – a radio publishing house which provides a distinctive service of the kind of material community radio stations could use, the British equivalent of Pacifica's programme services. Radio 10 should not be a junior member of the BBC, but a cousin, related by entitlement to a share of the licence fee, but also receiving, perhaps via a PSBC, cross-subsidy from commercial radio and TV profits. Numerous schemes to support community radio have been debated in the Brtish community radio movement since the late 1970s and submitted to the Home Office. Common to all is the emphasis on self-regulation, adherence to a code stressing non-profit aims and democratic control of stations,[49] a willingness to accept finance from a variety of sources, public and private (though with advertising strictly limited to local) and a franchising and co-ordinating role for some form of agency or trust which would also channel and dispense pump-priming funds.[50]

Our 'Radio 10' suggestion adds a national dimension to programme production and supply in the community radio sector. 'Radio 10', part-publicly financed, part earning revenue from sales at home and abroad, could be linked to an agency or trust which is part of, or funded by a Peacock-style PSBC.

What would be important to British broadcasting is a public service/community radio presence that was defined both locally and nationally, affecting mainstream practice and institutions from below *and* from the margins. The alliances (communities of interest) that, with Mattelart and Piemme, we see as being significant in a redefined public service will thus be both rooted in localities *and* have access to each other across local boundaries. Such an infusion of innovation and dissent is necessary in a democratic society – and, in a Europe whose frontiers are disappearing under the satellite gaze, across the Continent as well. For as transnational pressure forces the old national broadcasting systems and monopolies to jettison some of their public service obligations under the necessity of competition, the mantle could well be picked up by a cross-border alliance of those who have formerly called themselves free or community broadcasters.[51]

Appendix A

Historical Narratives

1. The technology – 1896 to the present (see Chapter 2)

By the 1890s, the electric telegraph and the telephone were the two main devices which exploited the scientific principles of electricity and magnetism. But, confined to wire, they were inadequate for the expanding imperial ambitions of the advanced industrialised nations. Naval fleets, the prime military weapon of the period, needed a means of communication between ships out of sight beyond the horizon.

Wireless telegraphy met this need. Working from the theoretical principles outlined by James Clerk Maxwell (1867), a number of experimenters in different countries, notably the German Hertz in 1886–9, had succeeded in transmitting signals over short distances. It was Marconi who drew on this work and improved it to the point where, beginning in Britain (1896), his commercial company made deals with most western governments. His success in transmitting across the Atlantic (1901) encouraged the commercial application of wireless telegraphy. Its use at sea, using Morse code, greatly increased after the device saved lives in the Titanic disaster (1912). Marconi concentrated on point-to-point long-distance transmission, while the American Fessenden began to develop voice signals from 1906. The same year, another American, De Forest, patented the 'Audion' vacuum tube or valve, essential for effective voice and music transmission and reception. By the outbreak of the First World War in Europe (1914), thousands of amateurs on each side of the Atlantic were transmitting and receiving broadcasts, while the big corporations began buying up patents and financing research.

When broadcasting was developed as entertainment after the war, the wavelengths that continued to be used were medium and long. Broadcasts were received on sets constructed at home from bought parts, including crystals, or on manufactured sets using valves. By the mid-1920s, increasing interference on crowded airwaves stimulated broadcasting regulation within countries and at the international level.

Meanwhile *short waves* (also known as HF – High Frequency) were found to facilitate long-distance transmission and so reduce the cost of high-powered transmitting equipment. By 1924 international exchanges were being conducted on short wave by both amateurs and broadcasters.

Subsequently short wave became the major means of overseas broadcasting.

Apart from improving transmission technology, the main improvements in this period concerned microphone and receiver sensitivity and studio acoustics. The first cumbersome car radios were marketed in the USA in 1931.

FM (frequency modulation) was demonstrated by the American Armstrong to RCA in 1933. Potentially it offered vastly increased quality of reception as well as an escape from the overcrowded medium wave. But disputes between Armstrong and RCA, and between RCA and the FCC, as well as the latters's hesitations over the frequency assignments for television in the same area of the spectrum, delayed FM's development. The Second World War halted station use of FM but spurred technical improvement.

After the war, the American industry's optimism about FM led to 900 station licences being issued by 1947, 20 FM channels having been reserved by the FCC in 1945 for non-commercial use. Then followed the television boom, loss of revenue for radio and consequent setback for FM. However, by the late 1950s, the rapid growth of the hi-fi market and increased consumer sophistication in home sound encouraged the renewal of interest in FM and, increasingly, the broadcasting of stereo music.

By this time reception had been revolutionised by the transistor. Invented in Bell Laboratories in 1947, the transistor used less power and created less heat than the valve, was far smaller, cheaper and more durable. 'Trannies' first came on the market in 1953 and doubled the annual sale of portable radios in America to 3.1m by 1956. By 1965 the annual figure was over 12m.

In Britain, where traditionally broadcasters have used the term VHF rather than FM, the BBC's Engineering Division was recommending its development in 1946. After the 1952 Stockholm agreement on the use of VHF in Europe, the BBC developed VHF as a complement to its national networks on long and medium wave. When BBC local radio started in 1968 the stations at first broadcast on VHF only. 'Simulcasting' on medium wave was added in 1970 to allow BBC local radio to reach wider audiences in anticipation of commercial competition. ILR stations, too, introduced from 1973 onwards, simulcast on medium wave and VHF until the IBA was permitted to encourage frequency splitting from 1986. Some of the last radio franchises offered by the IBA were for VHF only, and the 1987 Green Paper, with the plans for radio announced in January 1988, proposed the end of simulcasting.

In America, splitting was ordered by the FCC in 1964: AM-FM licencees serving populations of over 100 000 had to broadcast original programming on FM at least half their transmission time. This move allowed FM to grow in response to other factors (described in Chapter 3).

At the reception end, the increase in car radios – by 1979 95 per cent of American cars were fitted with radio; in 1987 in Britain 63 per cent of listening was in cars – became important as a factor influencing programming policies. In recent years, the arrival of the Compact Disc (CD) player has increased the capabilities of high quality music production and reception. Use of sub-carrier frequencies allowed the BBC to introduce its Radio Data System (RDS) in 1988, allowing automatic tuning, station identification and possibilities for pre-set listening by programme type. Digital transmission when introduced will minimise loss of quality, and increasingly distribution of programmes to station networks or between broadcasting organisations is being effected via satellite. The year 1988–9 saw the launch of three satellite-delivered programme services, aimed at supplying stations (rather than listeners), those of Radio Radio, Radio Nova International, and Murdoch's Sky service.

2. US Radio, 1899 to 1967 (see Chapter 3)

Marconi's arrival in the USA in 1899 and the formation of the Marconi Company's American subsidiary the same year stimulated research and experimentation among individuals, some of whom started commercial enterprises. The US Navy at first negotiated with Marconi, but refused to accept the stiff terms the Company demanded and broke off to commission its own research. The Department of Agriculture, interested in weather information, gave Fessenden his first commission; De Forest formed his own company. In 1912, Congress passed the first licensing law and nearly a thousand licences were issued, many to colleges and universities. In 1917, the University of Wisconsin's 9XM began regular weather bulletins in Morse code. By now the giant corporations had begun to move to acquire patents – American Telephone and Telegraph Company (AT&T), General Electric and Westinghouse.

War led to government takeover, as provided for in the 1912 Act, and by its end in 1918, the Navy was in a dominant position. Pressure from three directions prevented a Navy-sponsored government monopoly: the desire and need of the corporations, after wartime expansion, to create a domestic market for their wireless equipment; the fear of the foreign-(British) owned Marconi Company gaining overall control of the industry; the action of amateurs in building transmitters and getting into broadcasting. The Radio Corporation of America (RCA) was formed in 1919 – with General Electric, AT&T and United Fruit the major shareholders – and bought out American Marconi. Meanwhile the removal of the wartime ban on broadcasting resulted in a myriad of amateur experimentation. A Westinghouse employee, Conrad, was responsible for bringing his company into the picture with broadcasts by their station KDKA of the results in the Presidential Elections in November 1920. Detroit News's 8MK also broadcast the election results. Westinghouse in particular received wide publicity. The result was a huge demand for receivers as well as a stake in RCA for Westinghouse. David Sarnoff's appointment as General Manager of RCA in 1921 encouraged the drive towards broadcasting and the manufacture of sets, while a flood of licence applications overwhelmed the Secretary for Commerce, Herbert Hoover. The free for all in the airwaves at this time was noted by other countries, especially Britain, as a warning of the need for tight regulation. It was not until 1927 that both regulatory principles and a prototype set of networks were arrived at.

Radio survived the Depression, the three main networks settled in their patterns, a fourth, Mutual, was added in the mid-1930s and though some high quality programmes were produced, the majority of the output was bland, unadventurous and formulaic. For this, blame must be laid on the system of sponsorship, networking and a dependence on audience ratings. FCC pressure succeeded in checking the worst monopolistic tendencies in the 1942 network shake-up. The networks emerged from the Second World War with the wealth and prestige enabling them to launch and develop television, and by the early 1950s, the consequent fall in radio advertising revenues caused a crisis. The necessary adaptation was assisted by increasingly sophisticated market research techniques and the growth of the consumer power of young people. FM provided a space for innovatory rock music formats, as well as for non-commercial use in colleges and universities – a grassroots development which was officially recognised by the creation of National Public Radio, following the Public Broadcasting Act of 1967.

3. British Radio, 1918 to the Present (see Chapters 4, 5 & 6)

After the end of the First World War in 1918, the British government retained control of wireless, its main concern being the renewal of a scheme, planned before the war with the Marconi Company under contract, to create long distance links between London and the Empire. The wireless equipment manufacturers were given restricted scope to experiment and finally pressure from amateurs forced the government to consider broadcasting. The influence of the military and the example of frequency chaos in the USA were the chief factors determining the outcome – the assignment of a few frequencies to a consortium of manufacturers.

While questions of finance and relationship to government were considered by the Sykes and Crawford Committees, John Reith, the Managing Director of the British Broadcasting Company, created a national network out of the original local stations and, taking an active part in policy formation, persuaded manufacturers, politicians and Post Office to his view of broadcasting as a public service, to be financed by a licence fee. Reith's handling of the BBC during the General Strike of 1926 confirmed his position and that of the Corporation created the following year under Royal Charter and with a ten-year licence. The BBC was henceforth allowed to broadcast news and eventually tackle controversial matters.

The range of programmes developed under Reith inclined to the serious, especially on Sundays. But a diet, on the National Service, of sport, Royal occasions, plays, music, talks and educational programmes proved popular and ensured a steady increase in purchase of licences. There was, after all, no alternative except the Regional Service and, from the early 1930s, competition from the commercial stations across the Channel. The following for these stations indicated an unsatisfied appetite for dance music and variety which Reith only grudgingly included in the BBC schedules. 'Better to overestimate the mentality of the public' was his principle and audience research was only started a year before his departure in 1938. That year saw the first of the BBC's foreign services, the Arabic, financed by the Foreign Office; the Empire Service had begun in 1932.

At the outbreak of war in 1939, the Regional Service was closed down. The Forces Programme was introduced alongside the renamed Home Service and the BBC's reputation was enhanced by its news at home – as well as the services directed to Nazi-occupied Europe – and its morale-boosting entertainment and discussion programmes.

After the war, the Forces became the Light Programme and in 1946 the Third Programme was created, scheduling music, arts and speech of a highbrow character. Confirmed in its monopoly by the first of the post-war Reports, that of the Beveridge Committee (1951), the BBC lost it when the Conservatives introduced commercial television (ITV) in 1954. Its energies absorbed in television competition, BBC radio lost touch with its young listeners, although this period saw a flowering of features and drama.

The Pilkington Report (1962) recommended that the BBC should be allowed to go ahead with its plan for local radio, but the government instead chose to concentrate on the development of BBC 2 (TV). As a lobby for commercial radio built up, the North Sea pirates (from 1964) proved the popularity of the pop and rock music the BBC had been denying its listeners, and that advertisers were keen to support this kind of programming. A Labour government closed down the pirates with the Marine Offences Act (1967) and at the same time authorised the BBC to start Radio 1, devoted to pop music, and an eight-station local radio experiment. The BBC's plan *Broadcasting in the Seventies* confirmed the 'generic' division of programming between Radios 1, 2, 3 and 4.

In 1970, the Conservatives came back to power and introduced commercial local radio (ILR), to be supervised, from 1973, by the Independent Broadcasting Authority (IBA). The IBA was to run ILR in the same way as it did ITV, owning and leasing the transmitters to the franchise holders who obtained their revenue from 'spot' advertising (rather than sponsorship on the American model) and whose programming was expected to include elements of public service. The Conservative plan for 60 ILR stations was pegged to 19 by Labour on its return in 1974 and all local radio development was frozen while awaiting the Annan Committee's Report.

Published in 1977, this recommended a Local Broadcasting Authority to take over all ILR and BBC local radio stations. This was successfully opposed by the IBA/BBC duopoly, and a cautious even-handed expansion of local radio began. The return of the Conservatives under Mrs Thatcher in 1979 held back the BBC and favoured ILR stations which were soon to predominate in a 2:1 ratio. Other preoccupations diverted attention from radio (cable and satellite plans). ILR went through a bad period financially, while BBC local radio suffered budget cuts.

A growing lobby for non-profit community radio found itself overtaken on the one hand by the Conservative espousal of a small-business entrepreneurial approach that co-opted community as a concept, and on the other hand by the pressure exerted by the increased activity of land-based piracy. A 21-licence community radio experiment announced in July 1985 was cancelled a year later after 286 applications had signalled widespread interest in small-scale radio. The pretext for the cancellation was the need to place such a departure in an overall context of radio development to be covered by a forthcoming Green Paper. This was published in 1987 and proposed an expansion of commercial local radio under a lighter regulatory touch – probably under a new authority – and the development of three national commercial channels with frequencies taken from the BBC.

Though by this time the Corporation had successfully weathered the immediate dangers posed by the setting up in 1985 of the Peacock Committee to investigate whether certain services such as Radio 1 should be financed by advertising (the Committee's Report in 1986 did not so recommend), the BBC had suffered a number of traumatic encounters with the government which stemmed from the latter's determination to bring the Corporation under control. The BBC's response to the Green Paper showed the suitably chastened compliance of an organisation that did not wish to give occasion for further dispute.

In January 1988, the Government confirmed its intention to implement the proposals of its radio Green Paper (with the expanded sector of commercial radio being taken from the IBA and placed under a new Radio Authority). But the complexities of planning for change in television delayed the approval of legislation affecting radio until 1990. Meanwhile, with improved finances, Independent Radio began to anticipate the new era with mergers resulting in regionalisation, with syndication and programme sharing, and by introducing new services on split frequencies. (For the November White Paper see p. 229.)

4. British Radio 1946–88: A Brief Chronology

1946 Labour government in power. BBC adds Third Programme to Light Programme and Home Service.
      BBC Engineering recommends development of VHF.
1949 Government sets up Beveridge Committee on Future of Broadcasting.
1951 Conservatives win election. BBC evidence to Beveridge proposes national VHF plan.
      Beveridge Report recommends BBC retain monopoly, but is critical of its centralisation; recommends experiment in local radio by BBC 'or entirely independent bodies'.

1952 Stockholm agreement on use of VHF Band II in Europe
1954 Conservatives' ITA Act introduces commercial television under the Independent Television Authority. BBC's Frank Gillard visits USA to study small-scale local radio.
1955 Conservatives win second successive election. BBC inaugurates VHF complement to its national networks.
1959 Conservatives win third successive election. Conservative backbench MPs press for commercial local radio.
1960 BBC local radio experiments on VHF. Pye Ltd's 'Plan for Local Broadcasting' proposes 100 commercial radio stations. Government sets up Pilkington Committee on Future of Broadcasting.
1962 Pilkington Report critical of ITV, supports BBC plan for 250 local stations. Government response to Pilkington strengthens ITA, authorises start of BBC-2, rejects local radio proposal.
1964 *March* Radio Caroline begins North Sea piracy. Local Radio Association formed to lobby for commercial local radio. *June* Richard Hoggart and Stuart Hall call in Peace News for non-commercial development of local radio, independent of BBC. (Hoggart & Hall, 1964)
October Labour wins election.
1965 Advertisers spend £2m on North Sea pirates.
Possibilities for Local Radio published as Paper No. 1 by Birmingham Centre for Contemporary Cultural Studies. (Powell, 1965).
1966 Labour government prepares action against North Sea pirates. BBC's *Local Radio in the Public Interest* published. Conservative Broadcasting Committee Chairman, Paul Bryan talks to pirates. White Paper announces BBC Radio 1 and experiments in BBC local radio.
1967 Marine Offences Act becomes law. *October* Radio 1 begins and 8 BBC local radio stations on VHF only in two-year experiment.
1969 BBC's *Broadcasting in the Seventies* proposes abolition of BBC Regions and redeployment of frequencies for Radios 1, 2, 3 and 4, plus 40 local radio stations. Government approves BBC plans, sets up Annan Committee on Future of Broadcasting.
1970 Conservatives win election, committed to commercial local radio. Annan Committee disbanded. BBC local radio plans frozen: 8 in existence plus 12 being planned can go ahead. John Thompson seconded to Minpostel to plan commercial local radio. Pressure from commercial lobbyists for national commercial radio.
1971 Conservative White Paper proposes 60 ILR stations under Independent Broadcasting Authority. Lobbyists settle for local but VHF *plus* MF, the latter to compensate for nighttime loss of reach.
1972 BBC closes Radio Durham. Sound Broadcasting Act authorises IBA to develop franchise award system for ILR.
1973 Crawford Committee recommends better service for rural areas. BBC opens Radio Carlisle. *October* LBC and Capital open. IBA announces location of further 25 ILR stations.
1974 Labour wins election, reappoints Annan Committee, transfers

broadcasting to Home Office, freezes all local radio development till Annan reports. IBA completes development of 19 out of planned 27 ILR stations. *Score*: BBC 20, IBA 19.

1975   BBC evidence to Annan proposes 45 local stations in England plus 30 in national regions. BBC 'mini-local' experiment in Barrow.

1976   BBC Whitehaven experiment. Home Office announces willingness to license six cable radio stations.

1977   Annan Report proposes transfer of local radio to Local Broadcasting Authority (LBA). Home Secretary invites comments on Annan. BBC and IBA oppose LBA, IBA suggests neighbourhood radio and government funding to help start up non-profit franchises. COMCOM founded, gives LBA qualified support in *Comments on Annan*. BBC Radio Wales uses RTE mobile VHF van for Welsh local Broadcasting experiment. BBC Radio Orkney and Radio Shetland set up.

1978   Parliamentary Select Committee on Nationalised Industries (SCNI) reports on IBA. Labour White Paper acknowledges existence of Home Office Local Radio Working Party (HOLRWP), suggests IBA award at least one non-profit ILR franchise. HOLRWP Report No. 1 authorises 18 more local radio stations, nine each to BBC and IBA. *Score* BBC 29, IBA 28.

1979   *March* Broadcasting Rights and Information Project founded. *April* CBC wins Cardiff franchise with community-based bid. *May* Thatcher election victory. HOLRWP Report No. 2 awards one more station to BBC, 15 to IBA. *Score* BBC 30, IBA 43. IBA rejects community-based bids in Aberdeen, Peterborough and Leeds.

1980   COMCOM Local Radio Working Party and Association of Community Broadcasting Stations (ACBS – representing cable radio) talk to HOLRWP. 'On Air in 81' campaign. *December* HOLRWP Report No. 3 awards 10 more stations to BBC, 25 to IBA (*Score* BBC 40, IBA 68); devotes 14 pages to discussion of community radio. BBC local radio stations 'go county'. IBA rejects community-based bid in Bristol.

1981   Local Radio Workshop monitors London's local radio. LBC closes London's newsdesk. 'Open Letter' to Home Secretary from community radio coalition. RELAY magazine No. 1 in autumn. IBA rejects Great Western Radio bid for Swindon. Broadcasting Act requires 8-year 'break-points' in ILR franchises. Citizens' Band legalised.

1982   John Whitney, Capital Radio's Managing Director, leaves Capital to become IBA Director-General. LBC wins franchise reaward. IBA rejects Gwent Broadcasting's community-based bid. Greater London Council's London Radio Forum.

1983   Capital wins franchise reaward. Thatcher re-elected. CRA formed. AMARC 1 in Montreal. Sheffield Peace Radio at CND Annual Conference.

1984   80 pirates broadcasting (*Sunday Times*). Telecommunications Act gives increased powers against pirates to DTI.

1985 *January* Government announces intention to allow community radio. *July* Brittan announces terms of experiment. *September* Brittan replaced by Hurd as Home Secretary. HO Advisory Panel appointed. *November* 286 applications received for community radio licences.

1986 *January* Panel recommendations to Home Office *June* Government cancels experiment. *July* Peacock Report published. Duke Hussey appointed BBC Chairman.

1987 Hussey replaces Milne with Checkland as DG. brings in Birt as Deputy. Hatch replaces Wenham as Radio MD. Green, Controller R4, announces plans to popularise channel. Government tries to suppress Spycatcher, confiscates Zircon programme, bans *My Country Right or Wrong*. Green Paper *Radio Choices and Opportunities* proposes 3 national commercial and 'hundreds' of local stations under 'lighter regulatory touch'. In response, BBC proposes major network changes. IR ad. revenue leaps to record £94m. IBA changes arrangements for financing IRN. Grade replaces Isaacs at C4.

1988 R3 Controller Drummond announces plans to 'widen appeal'. Douglas Hurd, Home Secretary, announces plans to deregulate radio, under a new Radio Authority, along lines proposed in Green Paper, but with national channels 'auctioned' to highest bidder. IBA and BBC resist government pressure to ban programmes over Gibraltar shooting of IRA team. Sir William Rees-Mogg appointed to Chair Broadcasting Standards Council. Radio Radio and Radio Nova International launch satellite-delivered services. *November* A White Paper, mainly concerned with television, confirmed the previously announced plans for radio (see p. 229).

Appendix B
CRA Code of Practice

Community Radio Stations:

1. Serve geographically recognisable communities or communities of interest.
2. Enable the development, well-being and enjoyment of their listeners through meeting their information, communication or cultural needs; encourage their participation in these processes through providing them with access to training, production and transmitting facilities; and to stimulate innovation in radio programming and technology. In particular to seek out and involve those sections of the community who are socially disadvantaged or who are under-represented in existing broadcasting services.
3. Take positive action to ensure that management, programming and employment policies encourage non-sexist, non-racist attitudes and representations. For example, by including such pledges in their constitutions and secondary rules and by instituting relevant training and awareness programmes.
4. Reflect the plurality and diversity of views within the listening community and provide a 'right to reply' to any person or organisation subject to serious misrepresentation.
5. Draw their programming from mostly local/regional rather than national sources.
6. Have their general management and programme policy made by a broadly based Council of Management, including the producers.
7. Are legally constituted as non-profit-making trusts, cooperatives[1] or non-profit maximising limited companies.
8. Are financed from more than one source, including public and private loans, shares, limited advertising (of a suitable nature), listener subscriptions, public grants atc.
9. Have ownership solely representative of their locality or community of interest.
10. Recognise the right of paid radio workers to be unionised and encourage the use of volunteers.

    1. Legally co-operatives are not prevented from making profits. However, there is a legal limit on the return on any share capital, and such shares can only belong to listeners or workers, and carry one vote regardless of shareholding. Any surpluses thus generated are reinvested, distributed as bonuses to listeners or workers, or used to support other co-operative enterprises or local charitable activities.

Notes and References

1 Founding myths

1. Plato (1965) p. 161.
2. Barthes (1984) p. 142.
3. Ibid., p. 151.
4. Windlesham (1980) p. 145.
5. E.g. Paul Lazarsfeld *Radio and the Printed Page* (1940), *The People Look at Radio* (with H. Field, 1946), *Radio Listening in America* (1948).
6. Murdock (1981).
7. In cultural studies, the single published exception of which we are aware was, interestingly, the first paper in the occasional series from the University of Birmingham's Centre for Contemporary Cultural Studies, a powerful argument for non-commercial small-scale radio: Rachel Powell *Possibilities for Local Radio* (Powell, 1965).
8. Drakakis (1981); Lewis, P. (1981) op.cit.; Rodger (1982).
9. Briggs (1961, 1965, 1970 and 1979).
10. Scannell & Cardiff (1982) summarises and refers to the two authors' longer articles.
11. Radio chapters in Curran & Seaton (1988).
12. Briggs (1985).
13. Hall (1980).
14. R. Williams *The Long Revolution*, Pelican reprint, 1984, p. 69.
15. Ibid.
16. Milan Kundera, *The Book of Laughter and Forgetting*, Penguin, 1983.
17. For an introduction and analysis of Habermas, see John B. Thompson *Studies in the Theory of Ideology*, Polity Press, 1984.
18. Broadcasting Act, 1981, quoted in Peacock (1986).
19. See note 18 above.
20. Peacock (1986) op.cit., para. 32.
21. Heller (1978).
22. Peacock, ibid.
23. Pilkington (1962); Annan (1977).
24. Broadcasting Research Unit (1985a) undated but published in 1985/6 as a submission to the Peacock Report.
25. Broadcasting Research Unit, op.cit., pp. 7–8. Authorship of the commentaries in the pamphlet is not attributed, but this passage is clearly by Nicholas Garnham whose longer article on *The Media and the Public Sphere* appears in *Intermedia* January 1986, Vol. 14, No. 1.
26. See Appendix 1 for the British Community Radio Association's Code of Practice, and, for fuller discussion of community media definitions,

Chapters 1 and 2 in Lewis, P.M. (1984a).
27. Cardiff (1980); Scannell (1981).

2 The Making of Radio

1. Quoted p. 65 in Marconi (1962).
2. See Williams (1974) ch. 1 for a concise account of this period of experimentation.
3. Roberts (1970).
4. Quoted in Codding (1952).
5. Winston (1986).
6. For a simple diagrammatic explanation of radio transmission, see Lewis, P.M. & Pearlman (1986) p. 26–31.
7. International Institute of Communications (1979).
8. In January 1988, the BBC decided henceforth to refer in publicity and on-air announcements to FM only.
9. Briggs (1961), footnote p. 49.
10. The service to mankind argument was dusted off to be used against the citizens' band lobby in the UK in the 1970s.
11. Briggs (1961) p. 55.
12. Ibid., p. 51.
13. Quoted in Archer, (1938) p. 157.
14. Quoted in ibid., p. 158.
15. Curran (1979) p. 173.
16. Reith (1949) p. 91.
17. Briggs (1979) p. 248.
18. Ibid., p. 242.
19. Fornatale & Mills (1980).
20. Allan (1951) p. 174.
21. Beveridge (1951).
22. Curran (1979) contains an interesting discussion of the BBC's frequency policy in the period, on which we have drawn in this section.
23. *Neighbour Shall Speak Unto Neighbour*, programme produced by BBC Local Radio Services, November 1987.
24. Hill (1974) ch. 20. In fact Chataway wanted to launch commercial radio as a national network, using a frequency taken from the BBC, but he was over-ruled by the Cabinet: Terence Kelly *Crown Prince of Radio* in Broadcast, 13 May 1988.
25. Curran (1979) op. cit., p. 172.
26. Ibid., p. 171.
27. David Hatch, BBC Managing Director of Radio, speaking at Voice of the Listener conference, London, 3 November 1987.
28. *TV and Radio 1987*, Yearbook of Independent Broadcasting, IBA, p. 144.
29. SCNI Report (1978).

3 Free for All: The American Model

1. Quoted in Archer, (1938) p. 181.
2. Ibid, pp. 112–3.
3. Quoted in ibid, p. 201.
4. Quoted in Siepmann (1950) p. 6.
5. Quoted in ibid, p. 10.
6. Radio Broadcast, May 1922, quoted in Barnouw (1966) p. 107.
7. Radio Broadcast Magazine quoted in Siepmann (1950) p. 10.
8. Rothafel & Yates (1925) p. 148.
9. E.g. in April 1924 to the Chicago Chamber of Commerce, quoted in full in Rothafel & Yates, op. cit.
10. Ibid. See also Barnouw (1966) p. 157.
11. Ibid., p. 156.
12. Ibid., pp. 210 and 229.
13. Hearings on Jurisdiction of Radio Commission, quoted in Siepmann op. cit., p. 11.
14. Reith (1949) p. 147.
15. Hearings of House Interstate Commerce Commission, quoted in Siepmann, p. 12.
16. Communications Act of 1934, Section 303.
17. Ibid., Section 307.
18. Report of the FCC to Congress, 1935, quoted in Siepmann, p. 22.
19. Barnouw (1966) p. 281.
20. Ibid., pp. 206–9, 239.
21. Lazarsfeld (1940) pp. 6–8, 332.
22. In this section we have followed John Witherspoon's useful account, *A History of Public Broadcasting*, serialised in 1987 in successive issues of Current, obtainable from 2311, 18th St NW, Washington DC, 20009 USA.
23. Frith (1983) p. 120.
24. Fornatale & Mills, p. 119 f.
25. Briggs (1970) p. 645.
26. Barnouw (1977) p. 95.

4 They Know They Can Trust Us: The Public Service Model

1. Briggs (1961) p. 68.
2. Quoted in ibid., p. 106.
3. Reith (1949) p. 89.
4. Pegg (1983) p. 17.
5. Eckersley (1941) p. 70.
6. Reith *The Facade of Public Corporations*, *The Times*, 28 March 1966, quoted in Heller (1978) p. 8.
7. Reith (1949) p. 92.
8. Heller, op. cit., pp. 4–8.

9. Reith, op. cit., p. 99.
10. Eckersley, p. 48.
11. Briggs (1961) pp. 236–9.
12. Matheson (1933) p. 47.
13. Foucault (1979) p. 149.
14. Anderson (1983) p. 39.
15. Scannell (1986) p. 28.
16. Lewis (1924) p. 64.
17. Briggs (1961) p. 245.
18. *The Position of Women in the BBC: a note based on papers held at the BBC Written Archive Centre*, WAC, 2 July 1985, citing Reith memorandum of 30 April 1926.
19. Cheris Kramarae *Resistance to Women's Public Speaking*, English version of article in S. Trömel-Plötz (ed.) *Gewalt durch Sprache*, Frankfurt, Fisher Taschenbuch Verlag, 1984, pp. 203–28.
20. Matheson, op. cit., pp. 188–90.
21. Briggs (1965) p. 195.
22. Lewis (1924) p. 100.
23. Scannell (1981); Frith (1983).
24. Lewis (1924) p. 51.
25. Matheson, op. cit., pp. 156–7.
26. Smith (1974) p. 75.
27. Pegg p. 141.
28. Pickles (1949) p. 94.
29. Kumar (1977).
30. Cardiff (1980).
31. *Sunday Dispatch*, 22 July 1945, quoted in Kramarae, op. cit.
32. Maine (1939) p. 68.
33. BBC WAC R34/323 14.2.28.
34. John Hilton's talk '*On Giving a Talk*' is a witty, and still relevant, guide to the art (Hilton 1938); and see Cardiff, op.cit.
35. Victoria Glendinning *Vita: The Life of Vita Sackville-West*, Weidenfeld & Nicholson, 1983.
36. Briggs (1961) p. 256.
37. Grace Wyndham Goldie, *The Listener*, March 1939, cited in Scannell & Cardiff (1982).
38. Scannell & Cardiff ibid.
39. Scannell (1986).
40. Anderson (1983).
41. Edward Bond *Restoration*, Methuen, 1982. p. 57.
42. Filson Young in *The Saturday Review*, cited in S. Briggs (1981) p. 30.
43. See quotation at head of Chapter 10.
44. BBC WAC R34/323, 14.1.26.
45. Lewis (1924) p. 114.
46. Scannell (1986) p. 19.
47. BBC WAC R44/23/2 March 1924 and Briggs (1965) p. 263.
48. Cited in Briggs, S. (1981) p. 156.
49. Pegg (1983).

50. For an account of the internal BBC debate about audience research at this time, see Briggs (1965) pp. 253–80.
51. Reith (1924) p. 37.
52. Burns (1977) p. 42.
53. Matheson (1933) p. 52.
54. Fielden, L., *The Natural Bent*, Deutsch, 1960.

5 Catering for Calibans: The BBC's Response to Competition

1. Scannell & Cardiff (1982).
2. Briggs (1970) pp. 93–4.
3. Dimbleby (1977).
4. Briggs (1970) p. 123.
5. Nevett (1982).
6. Ironside to Tallents, Controller of Public Relations, quoted in Cardiff & Scannell (1981).
7. From *Listening by the BEF*, A.P. Ryan, January 1940 in Cardiff & Scannell (1981) op. cit.
8. Nicolls BBC Year Book 1943, quoted in Briggs (1970) p. 140.
9. P. Fleming *Invasion 1940*, quoted in Briggs (1970) op. cit., p. 287.
10. Ibid., p. 566.
11. Maconachie, quoted in ibid., p. 212.
12. Ibid p. 601.
13. See Cardiff & Scannell (1981) for a discussion of these issues.
14. Memorandum August 1944 quoted in Briggs (1970) pp. 567–8.
15. Quoted ibid., pp. 577–8.
16. WAC R27/245/1–2 quoted in Scannell (1981).
17. Quoted in Smith (1974) p. 83.
18. Grisewood (1968) p. 162f.
19. Siepmann op. cit., p. 140.
20. Hoggart (1984) p. 248.
21. Abrams p. 10.
22. Ibid., p. 13.
23. Frith (1983a) p. 228.
24. De Gournay (1986) p. 8.
25. Ibid.
26. Laing (1969) p. 76.
27. Frith (1983a).
28. Ibid., p. 217.
29. Ibid., p. 213.
30. M. Herr *Dispatches*.
31. Baron (1975).

6 Serving Neighbourhood and Nation: British Local Radio

1. Karel Jacubowicz *Mass (?) Communication (?)*, paper presented at International Association of Mass Communication Research 1984 Prague Conference.

2. Crisell (1986) in his historical chapter, dwells mainly on the BBC and somewhat uncritically groups ILR, community radio and pirates in one perspective; Local Radio Workshop (1983) is good on the origins of commercial radio and the compaign around the 1981 Broadcasting bill and for the rest is, as the title indicates, confined to an analysis of Capital Radio; Partridge (1982) describes the community radio campaign up till 1982, but curiously omits reference to Cardiff Broadcasting. CBC's story is touched on but not fully told in Baehr & Ryan (1984). Between 1981 and 1988 when it ceased publication, *Relay* magazine was perhaps the best single source though in no way a complete record.

3. *Serving Neighbourhood and Nation* is the title of a BBC pamphlet on local radio, published in 1977.

4. Booth (1980).

5. T. Burns, *The Meaning of Community in Local Radio*, paper at the 7th Manchester University Broadcasting Symposium, 1976.

6. Burns ibid., Bell & Newby (1971).

7. Coser (1956), Burns.

8. Young & Wilmot (1962).

9. Newby et al (1978).

10. Curran & Seaton (1988) p. 187.

11. Pilkington (1962).

12. Ibid., para. 811.

13. Ibid., para. 842.

14. Frank Gillard, speaking on *Neighbour Shall Speak unto Neighbour*, programme produced by BBC Local Radio Services Unit, November 1987.

15. Smith (1974) p. 151–2.

16. White Paper (1966).

17. See e.g. Sam Richards *Why Doesn't the BBC Close Down the Regions?*, *Guardian*, 5 February 1983.

18. Hugh Herbert *Locals Look to Laurels*, *Guardian*, 12 July 1979; N. Higham *The Unkindest Cuts of All?*, *The Listener*, 14 January 1988; *BBC Local Radio Must Lose 100 Jobs*, Broadcast, 17 June 1988. See also *The Journalist*, February and July/August 1988.

19. BBC (1979).

20. Burns op.cit.

21. See, e.g. IBA (1977).

22. Annan (1977).

23. BBC Wales transmission *Wales and the Welsh*, 24 November 1978; Postgate *et al.* (1979) p. 92. Ten opt-out stations were originally planned in Wales. A. Edwards, 'The Development and Present State of Radio in Wales', unpublished diploma dissertation, Goldsmith's College, 1988.

24. *Daily Telegraph* 24 February 1978, and *Neighbour Shall Speak Unto Neighbour*, op. cit.

25. *Thame Gazette*, Friday 11 January 1980.

26. Broadcast 26 January 1981.

27. T. Kelly, *Inner-city problems for the BBC*, Broadcast 8 January 1988, cites BBC Audience Research figures for the three metropolitan stations in 1987.
28. Broadcast 9 April 1979.
29. Singer, op. cit.
30. Anne Karpf 'Not Airwaving but Drowning', *New Statesman*, 1 March 1985. In October 1988, under notice from top management to improve or face closure, a new Managing Editor carried out a drastic re-organisation and relaunched the station, as Greater London Radio, with a format targetted at 25–45 year-olds.
31. Community Communications Group (1977).
32. SCNI Report (1978).
33. *Broadcast*, 20 November and 18 December, 1978; Local Radio Workshop, *Report 1979*.
34. Local Radio Workshop (1982).
35. Higgins & Moss (1982).
36. A. Wright *Local Radio and Local Democracy; a study in Political Education*, IBA, 1980, p. 81.
37. H. Baehr & M. Ryan *Shut Up and Listen*, Comedia, 1984.
38. A. Karpf, 'Women and Radio', *Women's Studies International Quarterly*, vol. 3 no. 1, 1980, reprinted in H. Baehr (ed.), *Women and Media*, Pergamon Press, 1980; al. Karpf, 'Radio Times: Private Women and Public Men' in K. Davies *et al.*(eds), *Out of Focus*, Women's Press, 1987.
39. IBA Audience Research Department *The Public Impression of ILR*, December 1980.
40. Wright, op. cit.
41. T. von Krogh & C. Novotny, *Why weren't we told?*, paper presented at Swedish Radio's conference *People and Media in Local Communities*, Ronneby, 1981.
42. Booth, op. cit.
43. P. M. Lewis, *Who Needs Community Media?* in COMM, 20 December 1983, European Regional Clearing House for Community Work.
44. For more detailed accounts see Partridge, op. cit.; J. Hind & S. Mosco, *Rebel Radio: The Full Story of British Pirate Radio*, Pluto, 1985, which includes some reference to the community radio lobby in an account devoted to land-based piracy; R. Barbrook, 'Community Radio in Britain' in Radical Science Collective, *Making Waves: the Politics of Communication*, Free Association Books, 1985 and al. *A New Way of Talking: Community Radio in 1980s Britain* in Science as Culture, pilot issue 1987, Free Association Books; P. M. Lewis, *Local Radio In Britain: a background document*, Council of Europe, 1979; al. *Community Radio: the Montreal Conference and After*, Media, Culture, and Society, 1984, 6.
45. Peter M. Lewis, *Community Television and Cable in Britain*, British Film Institute, 1978.
46. Association of Cable Broadcasting Stations, *The Development of Neighbourhood Broadcasting in the UK*, April 1980; R. McCron & J.

Dungey, *Aycliffe Community Radio: a Research Evaluation*, University of Leicester Centre for Mass Communication Research, 1980.

47. Annan, p. 209; Peter M. Lewis, *Small is Viable*, Listener, 18 December 1975.
48. Community Communications Group, op. cit.
49. SCNI Report, op. cit, vol. I, p. 125.
50. Bevan Jones *Community Radio in a Capital City – Sydney, Australia*, GLC Community Radio Research & Development Project, June 1985; Broadcasting Research Unit, *The Audience for Community Radio in London*, April 1985; Wireless Workshop, *New Radio Services in London*, January 1983.
51. In addition to the specific sources cited in this section, this account draws on Cardiff Broadcasting Newsletters, *Have a Hand in What You Hear*, 1979 onwards; Mike Engelhard *The Cardiff Example: an Assessment*, unpublished paper for the Telford Conference, August 1980; Volunteer Centre Media Project *Social Action and Mass Media Case Studies: No. 11*, May 1981; Baehr & Ryan, op. cit; and on personal visits to Cardiff, 1979 to 1983.
52. White Paper (1978) para. 39.
53. *Relay*, No. 4, Winter 1982/3.
54. Simon White, 'The Cardiff Trial', *Relay*, No. 10, Autumn 1985.
55. Penny Philcox, 'Action Desk Success', *Relay*, No. 20, November/December 1987.
56. Volunteer Media Centre Project, op. cit. p. 11.
57. Simon White 'CBC: Public Service in the Market Place', *Relay*, No. 20, November/December 1987.
58. Ibid.
59. IBA (1977) para. 3.22.
60. Partridge (1982) p. 32 footnote 6.
61. *Relay*, No. 1, Autumn 1981, p. 11 'Great Western Radio Derailed'.
62. Jonathan Coe, Fighting Pop, Prattle and Profits, *New Statesman*, 20 February 1981.
63. William Phillips, 'ILR '85: Don't Fence Them In', ADMAP, July/Aug 1985.
64. Broadcast 16 November 1984.
65. Philcox, op. cit.
66. Hutt, op. cit.

7 The Listener as Participant: North America and Australia

1. Milam *Sex and Broadcasting: a handbook on starting a Radio Station for the Community*, p. 19. 'Don't be put off by the title' is how the *Journal of Broadcasting* began its review (Vol. XV, No. 4, Fall 1971). The book is an important record of the beginnings of community radio and has been widely influential. For those exasperated by bureaucratic delays on this side of the Atlantic it is an exhilarating read. A

more recent, authoritative survey of American community radio history was published after this chapter was written – Barlow (1988).
2. Pacifica Radio Leaflet, 1986.
3. Helen Kennedy & Janice Woo, *Organising Your Tape Collection: some pointers from the Pacifica Radio Archive*, Audio-International's *Airwaves*, Vol. 2, No. 5, Sept./Oct. 1982.
4. Hill (1958).
5. Salter (1980).
6. Hill p. 62.
7. For a discussion of some of the issues raised by KPFA's division of labour, see Downing (1984).
8. Philip Maldari speaking at AMARC-2 in Vancouver (see p. 182) and interviewed by Peter Lewis, Bellingham, July 1986.
9. Maldari, op. cit.
10. Milam (1986).
11. Theresa Clifford *Self-Management, Access and Participation in Communications: experiences with radio in the USA*, paper at UNESCO Seminar, Belgrade, 1977.
12. For a fuller account of US community radio at this time, see Lewis (1977); Barlow (1988).
13. Commissioner James H. Quello, paper at Radio Academy Festival, Bristol, July 1985.
14. National Public Radio, *Report of Audience-Building Task Force*, July 1986.
15. David Lepage, interview with Peter Lewis, Vancouver, July 1986, on which the following account is based.
16. Ross Reynolds *Why KBOO Needs to Build an Audience*, KBOO Program Guide, July/August 1986.
17. CRTC hearings, April 1974.
18. CRTC, op. cit.
19. Ibid.
20. Much of this section, and the following one on Programming, is taken from a condensed and revised version of this chapter which first appeared in the supplement to *Relay* No. 20, Nov/Dec 1987. The supplement, *Community Radio Station Profiles from Around the World*, was edited by Caroline Mitchell. Thanks are due to Helene Littman, former Co-op Board member and editor of *Radio Waves*, for updating and adding to the article.
21. McNulty (1979) p. 149.
22. Eugene Beauthien, paper at seminar, *New Developments in Local Programming within the Canadian Broadcasting System*, Concordia University, Montreal, September 1979.
23. AMARC *Interadio*, Vol. 1, No. 2, May 1986.
24. Salter (1980).
25. Shari Dunnett, AMARC-2, Panel 1: Communications for Peace and Justice, July 1986.
26. Jillian and Stewart Fist in Lewis (1984a).
27. Dugdale (1979).

28. Fist & Fist, op. cit.
29. The following account of contemporary public radio draws on Jones (1985), and Woods & Anderson (1986).
30. 1986 Survey by Linda Marson, Victorian Public Broadcasting Association Training Project.

8 The Listener as Accomplice: Italy and France

1. An abbreviated version of this chapter first appeared in a supplement to RELAY 18, July/August 1987, *Community Radio – Past Policies, Current Debates*, edited by Peter M. Lewis. Since then, the Fédération Européenne des Radios Libres (FERL) has begun to take a prominent role in policy making for community radio in relation to European communication strategies. The first number of its magazine *Euradio*, No. 1, 1988, obtainable from FERL, Les Quatres Reines, BP42, F-04300 Forcalquier, France, contained a wide range of articles on free radio in different European countries.
2. Cited in Faenza (1977).
3. Salter, p. 93.
4. *Listen to Radio Bologna per l'Accesso Pubblico* cited in Faenza, op. cit.
5. Court of Justice of the European Communities *Reports of Cases Before the Court, 1974–4*, Judgment of 30 April 1974.
6. Postgate *et al.* (1979) p. 66.
7. Ibid. pp. 68–73.
8. Ibid.
9. Francesco 'Bifo' Berardi, quoted in Collin (1982) p. 97.
10. Quoted in Alan Pond & Carlos Ordonez *Italian Radio Lessons*, Relay 3, Summer 1982.
11. Eco (1978).
12. Eco, op. cit.
13. Pond & Ordonez, op. cit.
14. Guattari (1984) p. 238.
15. Peter M. Lewis 'The Italian Experience: Lessons for Others', *Intermedia*, October 1977, Vol. 5, No. 5.
16. Francesco Cavalli-Sforza, interview with Peter Lewis, Milan, 14 May 1977, cited in Lewis (1984b).
17. Downing (1985) pp. 283–301.
18. Jane Dolman, paper at Community Radio Conference, London, 25 Sept. 1982, reprinted in *Relay*, No. 4, Winter 1982/83.
19. Enzensberger (1976) p. 28.
20. Antoine Lefébure, interview with Peter Lewis, London, 6 Dec. 1978.
21. A. Lefébure 'Bases pour un projet', *Interférences*, No. 2, March 1975, quoted in Collin (1982).
22. This account of French free radio, except where otherwise noted, draws on Cojean & Eskenazi (1986), and Prot (1985).
23. Jean Carroir & Patrick Farbiaz, presentation to British Council Study Tour, Paris, 15 Feb. 1979.

24. Peter M. Lewis, 'Paris Diary', *The Listener*, March 1979.
25. Collin, p. 218.
26. *Le Monde*, 15 June 1985, cited in Crooks & Vittet-Philippe (1986) p. 87.
27. Paul Webster *Bruised Chirac takes his Revenge*, *Guardian*, 19 January 1987.
28. NRJ in 1986 moved into TV with a 20 per cent share of the TV6 channel.
29. De Gournay (1986)
30. Ibid., pp. 58–60, 101–3.
31. Gilles Gay, interview with Peter Lewis, Strasbourg, 29 November 1980; Collin (1979).
32. Mattelart & Piemme (1980). In 1988 Radio Dreyekland, Freiburg, finally obtained a licence, the first in W. Germany.
33. De Gournay, op. cit.
34. Collin, (1982) p. 146f

9 Third World Radio: Development and Struggle

1. While admitting the ethnocentric connotations of 'First/Third' (as of 'discovery'), we follow the usage of the MacBride Report (MacBride, 1980).
2. See Smith (1980) ch. 1.
3. MacBride, op. cit., pp. 123–52.
4. Mattelart (1979).
5. Cited in La France, J.P. *Community-Oriented Radio Broadcasting Throughout the World: A Preliminary Appraisal* ch. 3, Working Document presented to AMARC-1, Montreal, 1983.
6. Luis Ramiro Beltran, Keynote address, AMARC-2, Vancouver, July 1986.
7. Golding (1977).
8. Katz & Wedell (1977).
9. Centro Internacional de Etudios Superiores de Communicacion para America-Latina, Report of Seminar in Participatory Communication, Quito, December 1978.
10. Nicol *et al.* (1954) p. 42. It is interesting that an idea the BBC allowed to die was thus reborn in Canada, copied in India and Ghana, and influenced the Latin American radio school (see, p. 172).
11. Nicol *et al.* (1954)
12. Suzanne Franks, 'Satellite to the Villages', *The Listener*, 16 October 1986.
13. Cassirer (1977).
14. Hall (1978); Young, Peraton, Jenkins & Dodds p. 92.
15. M. Samwilu-Mwaffisi *National Policies towards Broadcasting in Tanzania*, paper at International Television Studies Conference, London, July 1986.
16. Mohamed Bezeid *Grassroots Radio: Breaching the Rural-Urban Barrier*, Ceres 18:2, March/April 1985.

17. John Nkingyangi 'Relevant Radio in Africa', *Relay*, No. 7, Winter 1983.
18. Id. cited in Lewis (1984b).
19. Nkingyangi in *Relay*, op. cit.
20. Florida Kweekeh, 'Radio for Rural Development in Liberia', *Intermedia*, March 1987, Vol. 15, No. 2. 'Liberating Rural Speech', *Interadio*, Vol 1, No 1, Spring 1988 (a new magazine launched by AMARC and available from 337 Carrall St, Vancouver BC, Canada V6B 2J4) reports a radical approach to rural radio from Burkina Faso in a project of which there is no news since the *coup d'état* of October 1987.
21. Beltran, op. cit.
22. Robert A. White, 'The Latin American Association for Radiophonic Education', *Media in Education and Development*, Sept. 1983.
23. ALER's headquarters is at: Carilla Postal 46–39–A, Quito, Ecuador.
24. White, op. cit.
25. A searching and well-documented critique of ACPO, Church and alternative self-organised radio in Latin America was presented at the Barcelona meeting of IAMCR, July 1988, by Alan O'Connor of the Department of Communication, Ohio State University (O'Connor, 1988).
26. Postgate *et al.* (1979) p. 34.
27. Talia Pareja Herrera, 'Community Radio for the Pueblos', *Intermedia*, January 1987, Vol. 15, No. 1.
28. Xavier Correa, 'People's Participation in Popular Radio: Peru and Bolivia', *Ideas and Action*, No. 159, 1984/6.
29. Peter M. Lewis, 'Central America', *Relay*, No. 7, Winter 1983.
30. Joseph Georges, Panel 4 at AMARC-2, Vancouver, July 1986; Greg Chamberlain, 'Haitian Media Contribute to Duvalier's Downfall', *Media Development*, 1986/4.
31. Mina Ramirez *From the Ground Up*, paper at the Annual Conference of the International Institute of Communications Edinburgh, 1986.
32. June Keithley, presentation at AMARC-2, Vancouver, July 1986; Paul Brunner, 'Marcos Ousted: a Modern-Day Exodus', *Media Development*, 1986/4.
33. For a graphic account of a day in the life of another, Radio Farabundo Marti, see 'Guerilla Radio in Action', *Relay* 18, July/August 1987.
34. Cited in Lewis, *Relay*, No. 7, op. cit.
35. Ibid.
36. Howard H. Frederick *Radio War Against Nicaragua*, available from Latin American Studies Program, Ohio University, Burson House, Athens, Oh 45701, USA.
37. Humberto Sanchez, Panel 6, AMARC-2, Vancouver, July 1986.
38. Daniel del Solar, presentation at Annual Conference of National Federation of Community Broadcasters, USA, July 1986.
39. Berrigan (1977).
40. Final Report available from Division of Free Flow of Information, UNESCO, 7 Place de Fontenoy, Paris 75700.

41. Jouët (1977).
42. Lekovic & Bjelica (1976).
43. Ibid.
44. Postgate *et al.* (1979).
45. Lewis (1984a).
46. See Beaud (1980).
47. MacBride (1980).

10 New Definition, New Structures

1. Brecht (1930) in Mattelart & Siegelaub (1983) p. 169
2. Nicholas Garnham *Introduction* in Mattelart, Delacourt & Mattelart (1984)
3. Tunstall (1986) p. 289.
4. Wright (1980).
5. de Gournay, op. cit.
6. Williams (1974).
7. Downing, op. cit. p. 15.
8. Harvey (1979).
9. F. Siliato *L'Antenna dei Padroni* (The Bosses' Aerial) Milan: Mazzotta, 1977, cited in Downing, op. cit. pp. 9–10.
10. L. Hill, op. cit.
11. Harvey (1975) p. 103.
12. Rowbotham, Segal & Wainwright (1979).
13. Downing op. cit. p. 358.
14. E.A. Harding, quoted in Bridson (1971) p. 30.
15. Mattelart & Piemme op. cit.
16. Ibid.
17. An earlier version of this chapter was published (in Spanish) in TELOS 14 (Lewis & Booth, 1988).
18. Green Paper (1987).
19. Ibid para 8.8.
20. IBA (1987).
21. Ibid, paras 47 and 59.
22. In July 1985, Leon Brittan, then Home Secretary, publicly asked for (and obtained) the withdrawal of a programme which aired the views of a Northern Irish Republican politician.
23. The BBC TV current affairs flagship programme, *Panorama*, was sued by a Conservative MP for portraying him as having fascist sympathies. The BBC settled out of court before answering the prosecution's case.
24. Peter Fiddick gave a useful summary of these events in *The Year the Boot went in* and *Who Runs the BBC?*, Guardian 28 December 1987.
25. BBC (1987).
26. David Hatch, BBC Managing Director, Radio, at Voice of the Listener conference, London, 3 November 1987.
27. Geraint Stanley Jones, BBC Managing Director, Regional Broad-

casting, quoted in press release *BBC Governors Approve Local Radio Plans*, BBC, 14 January 1988.

28. Peacock, op. cit., para. 581.
29. CSP International (1987) p. 140.
30. In 1987, the DTI's Radio Investigation Service carried out 332 raids on 51 London pirates, with 59 raids on 31 outside London, *Broadcast*, June 6, 1988.
31. Fifty-nine stations were listed broadcasting on the FM band in London in January 1988 (*Independent*, 28 January) and a London listeners' poll the same month showed the pirate Kiss-FM beating BBC Radio 1 into third place after Capital Radio (*Independent*, 13 January)
32. Broadcast, 22 January 1988.
33. *Hansard*, 19 January 1988, Written Answer No. 150.
34. House of Commons Home Affairs Committee Second Report, *The Government's Plans for Radio Broadcasting*, HMSO 386, April 1988. The Report reprints evidence heard by the Committee, including a thoughtful critique of government plans by the Centre for Communication and Information Studies.
35. Barnett & Morrison (1988).
36. Brian Wenham, 'Mr Hurd's New Recipe for Radio', *Observer*, 24 January 1988.
37. N. Higham 'The Unkindest Cuts of All?', *The Listener*, 14 January 1988.
38. Douglas Hurd, 'A Boring Mishmash? That's Not My Plan', *Guardian*, 1 February 1988.
39. Peacock, op. cit., para. 591.
40. Ibid., para. 682.
41. Ibid., paras. 687–8.
42. Community Communications Group (1977).
43. Peacock, op. cit., para, 691.
44. ICA press release, undated, March 1987.
45. E.g. by Simon Partridge, *What is Community Radio and What Are Its Prospects?*, talk to the Radio Academy Conference, 22 January 1988; by the Labour spokesperson for Arts and the Media, Mark Fisher MP *Jukebox Radio Plan*, Film and Television Technician, March 1988; in the 'Endpiece' of the BRU Report (Barnett & Morrison 1988); by the Commission for Racial Equality, *Broadcast*, 24 June 1988; and by the Institute for Contemporary Arts.
46. BBC (1982).
47. Interview: Peter Lewis with Stan Reid, 22 January 1988.
48. Lepke, cited in Hind & Mosco (1985).
49. See Appendix B for the final form of the CRA's Code of Practice.
50. See, e.g., Community Radio Association (1986) which envisaged a Community and Special Broadcasting Agency (CSBA) presiding over a separate sector of community radio.
51. This book went to press before the publication of the White Paper *Broadcasting in the '90s: Competition, Choice and Quality: the Government's Plans for Broadcasting Legislation*. There is space here

briefly to summarise the points relevant to radio and other associated developments. Only two out of the White Paper's forty-five pages were devoted to radio, and these confirmed the main proposals already announced the previous January, with additions arising from points made in the public debate following that announcement.

On *ownership*, 'no group will be able to control more than one national service and more than six local services. There will be a 20 per cent limit on radio interests in newspapers, and vice versa. The Government will seek flexibility by setting these limits in subordinate legislation.' (8.4)

On *public funding*, 'stations will not generally be able to receive public authority funding, but there will be certain clearly defined exceptions.' (8.5)

On *financing the BBC*, the White Paper demanded a faster move towards subscription than had been expected, and of its radio services said only that 'account will need to be taken in due course of the implications for financing [them].' (3.10)

On Peacock's suggestion of a *Public Service Broadcasting Council* (see our discussion on p. 200), 'it would be premature . . to express a view . . Experience needs to be gained first of the progress and impact of the reforms set out in this White Paper.' (3.19)

The IBA's demise was confirmed in the proposal to set up an Independent Television Commission to replace it and the Cable Authority. The IBA was, however, allowed, 'as a step towards the new radio arrangements' to carry through its proposal to offer twenty 'incremental contracts' within existing ILR areas. Some of these would be 'community-of-interest' stations with coverage of 12km radius, others – 'small geographical/community stations' – would be of 6km radius. Existing ILR contractors and their associates were allowed to apply. The measure, besides going some way to placate the community radio lobby, was clearly aimed also at reducing piracy. The Home Office warned that any pirate convicted after 1 January 1989 would be barred from applying for a franchise for five years. Some 150 bids were expected in the London area alone, many of them from groups representing the kind of minority ethnic communities referred to in p. 203.

Finally, we should note, to avoid confusion in the references to Radio 5 (pp. 202–3), that the BBC is now applying this title to its Sport and Education channel destined to use the old Radio 2 medium wave frequency (see p. 195).

Bibliography

Abrams, M. (1959) *The Teenage Consumer*, London Press Exchange.
Allan, E. & D. (1951) *Good Listening: a Survey of Broadcasting*, Hutchinson.
Anderson, B. (1983) *Imagined Communities*, Verso.
Annan (1977) *Report of the Committee on the Future of Broadcasting*, (Chairman: Lord Annan) HMSO, Cmnd 6753.
Archer, G.L. (1938) *History of Radio to 1926*, The American Historical Society.
Association of Cable Broadcasting Stations (1980) *The Development of Neighbourhood Broadcasting in the UK*, April 1980.
Baehr, H. & Ryan, M. (1984) *Shut Up & Listen: a view from the inside*, Comedia
Barbrook, R. (1985) 'Community Radio in Britain' in Radical Science Collective, *Making Waves: the Politics of Communication*, Free Association Books
Barbrook, R. (1987) 'A New Way of Talking: Community Radio in 1980s Britain' in *Science as Culture*, pilot issue 1987, Free Association Books.
Barlow, W. (1988), 'Community Radio in the US: the struggle for a democratic medium', *Media, Culture and Society*, vol. 10, no. 1.
Barnett, S. & Morrison, D. (1988) *The Listener Speaks: The Radio Audience and the Future of Radio*, Report for the Home Office, Broadcasting Research Unit, April 1988.
Barnouw, E. (1966) *A Tower in Babel: a History of Broadcasting in the United States, Volume 1 – to 1933* Oxford University Press, New York.
Barnouw, E. (1977) *Tube of Plenty: The Evolution of American Television*, Oxford University Press.
Baron, M. (1975) *Radio Onederland: the story of independent radio in the UK*, Dalton.
Barthes, R. (1984) *Mythologies*, Paladin.
BBC (1977) *Serving Neighbourhood and Nation*.
BBC (1979) *Action Stations*.
BBC (1982) *BBC Radio For The Nineties: a Discussion Paper on Radio Programme Strategy*.
Beaud, P. (1980) *Community Media? Local Radio Television and Audio-Visual Animation Experiments in Europe*, Council of Europe.
Bell, C. & Newby, H. (1971) *Community Studies*, Allen & Unwin.
Berrigan, F. (1977) *Access: Some Western Models of Community Media*, UNESCO.
Beveridge (1951) *Report of the Broadcasting Committee*, HMSO, Cmnd 8116.

Booth, J. (1980) *A Different Animal*, IBA Fellowship Report.

Brecht, B. (1930) 'Radio as a Means of Communication: A Talk on the Function of Radio' in Mattelart and Siegelaub (1983).

Bridson, D.G. (1971) *Prospero and Ariel: The Rise and Fall of Radio – a Personal Recollection*, Gollancz.

Briggs, A. (1961) *The History of Broadcasting in the United Kingdom, Volume I – The Birth of Broadcasting* Oxford University Press.

Briggs, A. (1965) *The History of Broadcasting in the United Kingdom: Volume II – The Golden Age of Wireless*, Oxford University Press.

Briggs, A. (1970) *The History of Broadcasting in the United Kingdom: Volume III – The War of Words*, Oxford University Press.

Briggs, A. (1979) *The History of Broadcasting in the United Kingdom: Volume IV – Sound and Vision*, Oxford University Press.

Briggs, A. (1985) *The BBC: The First Fifty Years*, Oxford University Press.

Briggs, S. (1981) *Those Radio Times*, Weidenfeld & Nicolson.

Broadcasting Research Unit (1985a) *The Public Service Idea in British Broadcasting*.

Broadcasting Research Unit (1985b) *The Audience for Community Radio in London*.

Burns, T. (1977) *The BBC: Public Institution, Private World*, Macmillan.

Cardiff, D. (1980) 'The Serious and the Popular: Aspects of the Evolution of Style in the Radio Talk, 1928–1939', *Media, Culture and Society*, 2,1.

Cardiff, D. & Scannell, P. (1981) *Radio in World War II*, Unit 8 in *The Historical Development of Popular Culture in Britain (2)*, Open University.

Cassirer, H. (1977) *Radio in an African Context: a description of Senegal's Pilot Project* in Spain, P. *et al.* (eds) *Radio for Education and Development*, World Bank, 1977, Vol. II, pp. 300–7.

Codding, G.A. (1952) *The International Telecommunication Union*, Arno Press, New York.

Cojean, A. & Eskenazi, F. (1986) *FM: La Folle Histoire des Radios Libres*, Grasset, Paris.

Collin, C. (1979) *Écoutez la Vraie Différence*, La Pensée Sauvage.

Collin, C. (1982) *Ondes de Choc: de l'Usage de la Radio en Temps de Lutte*, l'Harmattan, Paris.

Community Communications Group, *Comments to the Home Secretary on the Recommendations of the Annan Committee on the Future of Broadcasting*, June 1977.

Community Radio Association (1986) *Community Radio: An Open Door to Media Access*.

Coser, L. (1956) *The Functions of Social Conflict*, Routledge.

Crisell, A. (1986) *Understanding Radio*, Methuen.

Crooks, P. & Vittet-Philippe, P. (1986) *Local Radio and Regional Development in Europe*, European Institute for the Media.

CSP International (1987) (for Department of Trade and Industry) *Deregulation of the Radio Spectrum in the UK*, HMSO.

Curran, C. (1979) *A Seamless Robe: Broadcasting Philosophy and Practice*, Collins.

Curran, J. & Seaton, J. (1988) *Power Without Responsibility: the Press and Broadcasting in Britain*, Methuen.

Dimbleby, J. (1977) *Richard Dimbleby – a Biography*, Hodder & Stoughton.

Downing, J. (1984) *Radical Media*, South End Press, USA.

Drakakis, J. (1981) (ed.) *British Radio Drama*, Cambridge University Press.

Dugdale, J. (1979) *Radio Power*, Hyland House, Melbourne.

Eckersley, P. (1941) *The Power Behind the Microphone*, Jonathan Cape.

Eco, U with Grieco, Allen J. (1978) 'Independent Radio In Italy: Cultural and Ideological Diversification', *Cultures*, vol. V no. 1.

Enzensberger, H.M. (1976) 'Constituents of a Theory of Media', in *Raids and Reconstructions: Essays in Politics, Crime and Culture*, Pluto Press.

Faenza, R. (1977) *The Radio Phenomenon in Italy*, Council of Europe.

Fornatale, P. & Mills, J.E. (1980) *Radio in the Television Age*, Overlook Press, New York.

Foucault, M. (1979) *Discipline and Punish*, Vintage Books.

Frith, S. (1983a) *Sound Effects*, Constable.

Frith, S. (1983b) 'The Pleasures of the Hearth' in *Formations of Pleasure*, Routledge & Kegan Paul.

Golding, P. (1977) 'Media Professionalism in the Third World: the transfer of an ideology' in Curran *et al.* (eds) *Mass Communication and Society*, Edward Arnold/OU.

Gournay, C. de (1986) *Le Local par la Bande: enquête sociologique auprès de quinze radios locales*, CNET, Paris.

Green Paper (1987) *Radio Choices and Opportunities: a consultative document*, HMSO, Cmnd 92.

Grisewood, H. (1968) *One Thing at a Time: an autobiography*, Hutchinson.

Guattari, F. (1984) *Molecular Revolution: Psychiatry and Politics*, Penguin.

Hall, B. (1978) *Mtu Ni Afya: Tanzania's Health Campaign*, Clearinghouse on Development Communication, Washington, DC, USA.

Hall, S. (1980) 'Encoding/decoding' in Hall *et al.* (eds) *Culture, Media, Language*, Hutchinson/CCCS.

Harvey, D. (1975) *Social Justice and the City*, Edward Arnold.

Harvey, S. (1979) 'Ideology: The 'Base and Superstructure' Debate' in Photography Workshop (1979) *Photography/Politics: One.*

Heller, C. (1978) *Broadcasting and Accountability*, BFI Television Monograph.

Higgins, C.S. & Moss, P.D. (1982) *Sounds Real: Radio in Everyday Life*, University of Queensland Press.

Hill, C. (1974) *Behind the Screen*, Sidgwick & Jackson.

Hill, L. (1958) *Voluntary Listener-Sponsorship*, Pacifica Foundation.

Hilton, J. (1938) *This and That: the broadcast talks of John Hilton*, Allen & Unwin.

Hind, J. & Mosco, S. (1985) *Rebel Radio: the full story of British pirate radio*, Pluto.

Hoggart, R. (1984) *Uses of Literacy*, Penguin.

Hoggart, R. & Hall, S. (1964) *Local Radio: why it must not be commercial'*, *Peace News*, 14 August.

House of Commons Home Affairs Committee (Second Report) *The Government's Plans for Radio Broadcasting*, HMSO, 386, 1988.

Independent Broadcasting Authority *Independent Broadcasting* No. 12, July 1977, Comments on Annan.

Independent Broadcasting Authority (1980) Audience Research Department *The Public Impression of ILR*.

Independent Broadcasting Authority (1987) *The IBA's View: The Future of UK Independent Radio*.

International Institute of Communications (1979) *Frequency Planning and Local Radio Broadcasting*.

Jones, B. (1985) *Community Radio in a Capital City – Sydney, Australia*, GLC Community Radio Research & Development Project.

Karpf, A. (1980) 'Women and Radio', *Women's Studies International Quarterly*, vol. 3 no. 1, 1980, reprinted in H. Baehr (ed.) *Women and Media*, Pergamon Press, 1980.

Karpf, A. (1987) 'Radio Times: private women and public men' in K. Davies *et al.* (eds) *Out of Focus*, Women's Press.

Katz, E. & Wedell, G. (1977) *Broadcasting in the Third World: Promise and Performance*, Macmillan.

Kumar, K. (1977) 'Holding the Middle Ground: the BBC, the public and the professional broadcaster' in J. Curran *et al.* (eds) *Mass Communication and Society*, Arnold and Open University.

LaFrance, J.-P. (1984) (ed.) *Les Radios Nouvelles dans le Monde*, Documentation Française.

Laing, D. (1969) *The Sound of Our Time*, Sheed & Ward.

Lazarsfeld, P. (1940) *Radio and the Printed Page: an Introduction to the Study of Radio and its Role in the Communication of Ideas*, New York, Duell, Sloan & Pearce.

Lekovic, Z. & Bjelica, M. (1976) *Communication Policies in Yugoslavia*, UNESCO.

Lewis, C.A. (1924) *Broadcasting from Within*, London, George Newnes.

Lewis, P. (1981) (ed.) *Radio Drama*, Longman.

Lewis, P.M. (1977) *Different Keepers: models of structure and finance in community radio*, International Institute of Communications.

Lewis, P.M. (1978) *Community Television and Cable in Britain*, British Film Institute.

Lewis, P.M. (1979) *Local Radio in Britain: a background document*, Council of Europe.

Lewis, P.M. (1984a) (ed.) *Media for People in Cities: a study of community media in the urban context*, UNESCO.

Lewis, P.M. (1984b) 'Community Radio: the Montreal Conference and After', *Media, Culture, and Society*, no. 6.

Lewis, P.M. & Booth, J. 'Profundas Transformaciones en la Radio Británica', *Telos*, no. 14, May 1988, Fundesco, Madrid.

Lewis, P.M. & Pearlman, C. (1986) *Media and Power: From Marconi to Murdoch – A Graphic Guide*, Camden Press.

Local Radio Workshop (1982) *Local Radio in London: an analysis of* programmes broadcast by BBC Radio London, Capital Radio and LBC, based on a monitoring exercise conducted between 27 April and 3 May, 1981, Republished as *Nothing Local About It*, Comedia, 1983.

Local Radio Workshop (1983) *Capital: Local Radio, Private Profit*, Comedia Series No. 15.

MacBride Report, The (1980) *Many Voices, One World*, report by the International Commission for the Study of Communication Problems (Chair: Sean MacBride), UNESCO/Kogan Paul.

McCron, R. & Dungey, J. (1980) *Aycliffe Community Radio: a Research Evaluation*, University of Leicester Centre for Mass Communication Research.

McNulty, J. (1979) *Other Voices in Broadcasting: the Evolution of New Forms of Local Programming in Canada*, Telecommunications Research Group, Simon Fraser University.

Maine, B. (1939) *The BBC and its Audience*, Nelson.

Marconi, D. (1962) *My Father, Marconi*, Frederick Muller.

Matheson, H. (1933) *Broadcasting*, Thornton Butterworth.

Mattelart, A. (1979) *Multinational Corporations and the Control of Culture: the Ideological Apparatuses of Imperialism*, Harvester.

Mattelart, A. & Piemme, J.-M. (1980) 'New Means of Communication: New Questions for the Left, *Media, Culture and Society*, 2, 321–38.

Mattelart, A. & Siegelaub, S (1983) (eds) *Communication and Class Struggle Vol. 2: Liberation, Socialism*, IMMRC, France.

Mattelart, A., Delacourt, X., & Mattelart, M. (1984) *International Image Markets*, Comedia Series 21.

Milam, L.W. (1974) *Sex and Broadcasting: a Handbook on Starting a Radio Station for the Community*, Dildo Press, 3rd Edition (available from MHO & MHO Works, Post Box 33435, San Diego, California, USA).

Milam, L.W. (1986) *The Radio Papers: From KRAB to KCHU*, MHO & MHO Works.

Murdock, G. (1981) 'Organising the Imagination: sociological perspectives in radio drama' in Lewis (1981).

Nevett, T.R. (1982) *Advertising in Britain*, Heinemann.

Newby, H. *et al.* (1978) *Property, Paternalism and Power*, Hutchinson.

Nicol *et al.* (1954) (eds) *Canada's Farm Radio Forum*, UNESCO, Paris.

O'Connor, A. (1988) *People's Radio in Latin America*, paper for Working Group on Community Radio and Television, IAMCR, Barcelona.

Partridge, S. (1981) *Not the BBC/IBA: the case for Community Radio*, Comedia.

Peacock (1986) *Report of the Committee on Financing the BBC*, (Chairman: Professor Sir A. Peacock), HMSO, Cmnd 9824.

Pegg, M. (1983) *Broadcasting and Society: 1918–1939*, Croom Helm.

Pilkington (1962) *Report of the Committee on Broadcasting* (Chairman: Sir H. Pilkington) HMSO, Cmnd 1753.

Pickles, W. (1949) *Between You and Me*, Werner Laurie.

Plato (1965) *The Republic*, transl. H.D.P. Lee, Penguin.

Postgate, R. Lewis, P.M. & Southwood, W.A. (1979) *Low-Cost Communications for Educational and Development Purposes in Third World Countries*, ITDG/UNESCO.

Powell, R. (1965) *Possibilities for Local Radio*, University of Birmingham, Centre for Contemporary Cultural Studies, Paper No. 1.

Prot, R. (1985) *Des Radios Pour Se Parler: Les Radios Locales en France*, La Documentation Française.

Reith, J.C.W. (1924) *Broadcast Over Britain*, Hodder & Stoughton.

Reith, J.C.W. (1949) *Into The Wind*, Hodder & Stoughton.

Relay Magazine, Nos 1–21, 1981–8, available from Off Stage Bookshop, 37 Chalk Farm Road, London NW1 8AJ.

Roberts, K. (1970) *Pavane*, Panther.

Rodger, I. (1982) *Radio Drama*, Macmillan.

Rothafel, S.L. & Yates, R.F. (1925) *Broadcasting Its New Day*, Century, New York, 1925.

Rowbotham, S., Segal, L. & Wainwright, H. (1979) *Beyond the Fragments: Feminism and the Making of Socialism*, Merlin Press.

Salter, L. (1980) *Two Directions on a One-Way Street: Old and New Approaches in Media Analysis in Two Decades*, Studies in Communications, JAI Press, vol. I pp. 85–117.

Scannell, P. (1981) 'Music for the Multitude? The Dilemmas of the BBC's Music Policy, 1923–1946', *Media, Culture and Society*, vol. 3 no. 3.

Scannell, P. & Cardiff, D. (1982) 'Serving the Nation: Public Service Broadcasting before the War' in B. Waites *et al.* (eds) *Popular Culture Past and Present*, Croom Helm & Open University Press.

Scannell, P. (1986) 'Radio Times: the temporal arrangements of broadcasting in the modern world', paper presented to the 1986 International Television Studies Conference, University of London Institute of Education.

SCNI (1978) *Tenth Report from the Select Committee on Nationalised Industries, (SCNI Report)* Vols I & II, HMSO, Cmnd No. 637–I/II, 1978.

Siepmann, C.A. (1950) *Radio, Television and Society*, Oxford University Press, New York.

Smith, A. (1974) *British Broadcasting*, David & Charles.

Smith, A. (1980) *The Geopolitics of Information*, Faber & Faber.

Tunstall, J. (1986) *Communications Deregulation: The Unleashing of America's Communications Industry*, Blackwell.

Williams, R. (1974) *Television: Technology and Cultural Form*, Fontana.

Windlesham, Lord (1980) *Broadcasting in a Free Society*, Blackwell.

Winston, B. (1986) *Misunderstanding Media*, Routledge & Kegan Paul.

Wireless Workshop (1983) *New Radio Services in London*, Greater London Council.

Woods, C. & Anderson, P. (1986) *A Different Kind of Radio*, Public Broadcasting Foundation, Australia.

Wright, A. (1980) *Local Radio and Local Democracy: a study in Political Education*, Independent Broadcasting Authority.

Young, M., Peraton, H., Jenkins, J. & Dodds, T. (1980) *Distance Teaching for the Third World*, Routledge & Kegan Paul.

Young, M. & Wilmott, P. (1962) *Family and Kinship in East London*, Penguin.

Index

Institutions, etc., with abbreviations or acronyms are indexed under the full name. Such bodies are British unless otherwise indicated either by title or in brackets following.